*Adventures of a Church Historian*

# Adventures of a Church Historian

LEONARD J. ARRINGTON

UNIVERSITY OF ILLINOIS PRESS

URBANA AND CHICAGO

© 1998 by the Board of Trustees of the University of Illinois
Manufactured in the United States of America

C 5 4 3 2 1

*This book is printed on acid-free paper.*


Library of Congress Cataloging-in-Publication Data
Arrington, Leonard J.
Adventures of a church historian / Leonard J. Arrington.
p.   cm.
Includes bibliographical references and index.
ISBN 0-252-02381-1 (alk. paper)
1. Arrington, Leonard J.
2. Mormons—Biography.
3. Church of Jesus Christ of Latter-day Saints—History.
4. Mormon Church—History. I. Title.
BX8695.A77A3   1998
289.3'092—dc21   97-33895
CIP

*To my partners: James B. Allen, Davis Bitton, and Thomas G. Alexander; to my research assistant, Richard L. Jensen; to my secretaries: Chris Croft Waters, Nedra Yeates Pace, Kathy Gailey Stephens, Kathleen Hardy Anderson, and Marilyn Rish Parks; and to two outstanding research assistants and biographers: Rebecca Foster Cornwall Bartholomew and Lavina Fielding Anderson*

# Contents

*Illustrations follow page 138*

# Introduction

WHEN I WAS BORN in an isolated Idaho farmhouse on July 2, 1917, the third of eleven children, the United States had just declared war on Germany and would soon be declaring war against Austria-Hungary. Although my father was exempted from service because he was a farmer with a family of three children, rising farm prices improved our prospects. In the spring of 1918 my father purchased a twenty-acre farm immediately north of the rough wooden shack in which I was born, and we moved to our Old Home Place east of Twin Falls, Idaho, where we remained until 1939. Our home was on the road from the city of Twin Falls to Shoshone Falls, a natural wonder. For a year or two, because of favorable prices for potatoes, sugar beets, and other crops, my father earned a good income. After the war, when I was only two, my family suffered from the same deadly influenza epidemic that swept the world. Although all of us were near death, my mother, father, older brother, and I were saved, as my mother believed, by the efforts of a tenacious volunteer practical nurse and the fervent anointings and prayers by my mother and the nurse to a responsive Deity.

The depression that followed the end of World War I was catastrophic for Idaho farmers, including the Arringtons. Despite hard work, farmers received little income from crops and livestock to pay mortgages on home and lands and no cash to buy seed, farm implements, and school clothing. My father bought some of our clothes from the Salvation Army. The postwar depression dawdled on until 1930, when the Great Depression that struck the rest of the nation worsened things in Idaho as well. My father sold 100-pound sacks of potatoes for $.75 in 1929, and the price declined to $.10 per sack in 1932, hardly worth harvesting. Sugar beets dropped from $15.00 to $5.00 per ton. My father was unable to make payments on our farm, and we were able to hold on only because creditors generously reduced our debt and postponed interest. By the time I was sixteen, in 1933, recovery agencies of the New Deal began to provide some relief. These programs continued to expand as I enrolled at the University of Idaho in 1935.

Just three months after my graduation in 1939, Hitler's panzers crossed the border into Poland, launching World War II. I attended graduate school at the University of North Carolina in Chapel Hill until the United States entered the war. In 1942 I volunteered for a naval officer appointment and was turned down because I was too short, less than five foot six. I volunteered for the Air Force and likewise failed acceptance, so I left my position as instructor in economics at North Carolina State College in Raleigh to work as an economist for the North Carolina Office of Price Administration. Six months later, in March 1943, I was drafted by the army. I served for fourteen months as a prisoner-of-war processor in Morocco, Algeria, and Tunisia, followed by fifteen months with the Allied Commission in Italy. Although a private first class during the first half of my service and a Tech 5 corporal during the second half, my experiences as a serviceman overseas were singular. In Italy I served for nine months as the Allied *controllore* of the Italian Central Institute of Statistics and for another five months as Allied representative with the Committee for Price Control in Northern Italy.

The years that followed my discharge were largely devoted to teaching at Utah State University, with occasional interruptions for other assignments—a year in southern California researching and writing at the Henry E. Huntington Library and Art Gallery, a year at the University of North Carolina finishing my Ph.D. degree in economics, a year in Italy as a Fulbright professor of American economics, and a year at UCLA as a visiting professor in western American history. Having written several books on Mormon and western history, having drawn together Mormon historians to encourage historical scholarship, and having rendered worthy service as a local ecclesiastic, I was appointed in 1972 by the First Presidency to be church historian of the Church of Jesus Christ of Latter-day Saints. I was the first professional historian to fill that position. At the same time, as a way of matching my former professorial income, I was appointed Lemuel H. Redd Professor of Western History at Brigham Young University. I held the position of church historian for ten years. In 1982, at the age of sixty-five, I moved with most of my professional staff to Brigham Young University to become director of the newly created Joseph Fielding Smith Institute for Church History, a position I held for five years. Still retaining the Redd Chair, I continued my research and writing on the Mormon and western past until my retirement in 1987 at age seventy.

The last Mormon historian to leave a record of his dealings with Mormon thought and leadership was Andrew Jenson, who published an autobiography in 1938. Sixty years have passed since then, and so my personal recollections of LDS practices and personalities might have some interest, particularly to Latter-day Saints. General authorities of the church and general church officers, for reasons of policy or personal preference, have chosen not to leave autobiographical public records of their dealings and associations with each other, so that church members have no way of knowing what goes on inside church headquarters. Do general authorities ever disagree? What are they like as human beings when they shed their official status as prophets, seers, and revelators? Along with their significant strengths are there also weaknesses—or at least misunderstandings? This book seeks to give some glimpses of the spiritual and organizational aspects of Mormon history and historiography that may add another dimension to understanding LDS life and leadership.[1] The Apostle Paul gave sound advice: "Let us keep the feast [the writing of history], not with old leaven, neither with the leaven of malice and wickedness, but with the unleavened bread of sincerity and truth" (1 Cor. 5:8).

John A. Widtsoe, a Mormon scientist and educator who became a university president and then a member of the Quorum of Twelve Apostles, serving in the latter capacity for thirty-one years, illustrates the circumspection of most leaders. He introduced his autobiography, *In a Sunlit Land,* written in 1945, with the declaration, "After some reflection, personalities, hundreds of which have entered my life, have been almost entirely omitted. If mentioned, comments would probably follow. That might hurt the feelings of some. So the easier way was followed."[2] The "easier way" suggests a spirit of harmony that passes over the fallibility of human nature and the inevitable conflicts that creep into the relationships of the Quorum of the Twelve Apostles and the three members of the First Presidency who, in a spirit of revelation, govern the church. When he wrote the authorized biography of J. Reuben Clark Jr., Frank Fox was advised by Clark's literary executor, Marion G. Romney, as related in the book's foreword:

> Any biographer of President Clark must write the truth about him; to tell more than or less than the truth would violate a governing principle of his life. When I first met with those who are writing his biography, I explained that I did not want them to produce a mere collection of uplifting experiences about President Clark (although I knew that numerous such stories could be told), nor did I want a detailed defense of his beliefs. I wanted a biography of the man himself, as he was, written with the same kind of courage, honesty, and frankness that J. Reuben Clark himself would have

shown. An account of his life should tell of his decisions and indecisions, sorrows and joys, regrets and aspirations, reverses and accomplishments, and, above all, his constant striving to overcome any and all obstacles.[3]

I am confident that biographies of this type are not damaging to the prestige of our leaders nor will they undermine the mystique that rightly surrounds the headquarters of a dynamic religious organization. Biographies of Presidents Harold B. Lee and Spencer W. Kimball also exhibit splendid writing and scholarship, describe both the positive and negative aspects of their subject's personality, and are biographies of real persons, not pastiche leaders. We may not be edified by every move they made, but we are warmed by their humanity.[4]

Latter-day Saint prophets and other leaders, in past years and during my lifetime, were great men and women who were close to God, but they were also human beings. What Lorenzo Snow, president of the church from 1898 to 1901, said of Joseph Smith is worth repeating: "I saw Joseph Smith the Prophet do things which I did not approve of; and yet . . . I thanked God that He would put upon a man who had these imperfections the power and authority which He placed upon him . . . for I knew I myself had weakness and I thought there was a chance for me. These same weaknesses . . . I knew were in Heber C. Kimball, but my knowing this did not impair them in my estimation. I thanked God I saw these imperfections."[5]

Even Brigham Young, who loved Joseph Smith with a constancy that bordered on idolatry, admitted in a discourse on loving-kindness in the Salt Lake Bowery that he sometimes thought that the prophet was not always right in his management of affairs. "It gave me sorrow of heart [to see this]," he said, but "I clearly saw and understood, by the spirit of revelation manifested in me, that if I was to harbor a thought in my heart that Joseph could be wrong in anything, I would begin to lose confidence in him, and that feeling would grow . . . until at last I would have the same lack of confidence in his being the mouthpiece for the Almighty." So Young decided to let the Lord deal with Joseph's failings. "Though I admitted in my feelings and knew all the time that Joseph was a human being and subject to err, still it was none of my business to look after his faults. . . . He was called of God; God dictated [to] him, and if He had a mind to leave him to himself and let him commit an error, that was no business of mine. . . . Though he had his weaknesses," Young continued, "he was all that any people could require a true prophet to be."[6]

Joseph Smith's diaries show that he was fully aware of his weaknesses and found it a struggle to live worthily in every respect. He prayed often—

to be forgiven, for help in overcoming his weaknesses, for his personal salvation. He loved people, he was a warm and engaging personality, he was extremely generous with his time and means, he loved learning, he believed the world was a wonderful place—all healthy attitudes for an imperfect human striving to perfect himself.

Brigham Young also was human in many respects—he could be harsh in his censure; he occasionally showed contempt for intellectuality; he could be very stubborn; he sometimes stretched the truth in his use of hyperbole; and he sometimes called upon people to make unconscionable sacrifices. But partly because of his human qualities the Saints loved him, admired him, willingly followed him, and sought his advice. I have written lovingly of both Joseph Smith and Brigham Young and, steadfastly professing faith in the gospel, have written this memoir as a useful and positive telling of an important episode in church history.

In a church that continues to expand its membership and embrace new cultures and worldwide concerns, the tensions of writing religious history continue. In this memoir I have tried to recount my experiences and impressions at the time they occurred, without subsequent editorial intervention. I have relied heavily on my diaries and letters. I have been helped by a three-volume work, "Doves and Serpents: The Activities of Leonard Arrington as Church Historian, 1972–1982," prepared in 1982 by Lavina Fielding Anderson at my request for my children and associates but not intended for publication. *Adventures of a Church Historian* is the story of my professional activities. I have published privately a series of illustrated works that chronicle our family experiences.

This is not an autobiography, a personal life that begins with birth and proceeds to the date of writing without omitting significant events and influences. It is a memoir—a rehearsal of a portion of my life that was particularly intense and meaningful. In opening this window into one phase of my life, I do not pretend that my memory is completely reliable, or even that the diary entries on which it is based are a completely accurate reflection of what was really said and done. My remembered truth may not be the same as that of my associates and adversaries. But my children, my associates, and my friends will know that I am writing in a spirit of honesty and sincerity. I have not purposefully invented or embellished any thought or episode. I also want to acknowledge that those who were critical of me as an administrator and writer were well-intentioned and earnest in their efforts to keep the faith, as they understood it, pure and undefiled.

My children (James and Carl Arrington and Susan Madsen), my stepchildren (Annette Rogers, Rick Sorensen, Heidi Swinton, Stephen Moody), and my wife Harriet have encouraged me to prepare this memoir, and I have been urged by many colleagues to publish it as a contribution to Mormon historiography. I have written it in an honest and positive vein, a reflection of how I feel. I believe "the truth" can be both constructive and therapeutic. My fellow church members have a right to an understanding of the matters I discuss. I do not wish to do harm to anyone or any good cause. Above all, I believe that Latter-day Saint readers, as well as my children and close friends, have a right to this personal recital of their father's, friend's, and leader's experience in a key post in the kingdom of God. I hope that readers will be reassured by the words in 2 Nephi 9:40: "The words of truth [may be] hard . . . ; but the righteous fear them not, for they love the truth and are not shaken."

I do not descend from Latter-day Saint pioneers or leaders. As a believer, however, I have a reverence and respect for our LDS history and culture. My father, Noah W. Arrington, was born in the hills of eastern Tennessee; his ancestors had migrated from northern Ireland to Virginia in the seventeenth century and had settled in the mountains of western North Carolina about the time of the Revolutionary War. One hundred years later my grandfather, Lee Roy Madison Arrington, crossed the French Broad River and settled in eastern Tennessee. A self-sufficient farmer, he married Priscilla Brisendine and became the father of ten. Mormon missionaries wandered into the area in the 1890s and baptized first my grandmother, then an aunt. In 1905 my grandfather, father, and most of his brothers and sisters were baptized in Rossville, Georgia, just south of Chattanooga, Tennessee. The family had been staunch Free Will Baptists.

My mother, Edna Corn, was born in southern Indiana; her ancestors were Scots-Irish immigrants who settled northern Kentucky in the eighteenth century and moved across the Ohio River into southern Indiana.

In 1900 and 1905 the families of my mother and father moved to adjoining farms in Faxon, southern Oklahoma, and in that frontier settlement the two went to school, courted, married, farmed, and then migrated to Twin Falls County, Idaho, in 1913. My mother, who grew up as a Methodist, was baptized in Twin Falls, Idaho, in 1915. From that date both parents were loyal Latter-day Saints. My mother served as a Relief Society president and in many other leadership capacities; my father served a mission to the southern states when I was a boy, was a high councilor for seventeen years, and a ward bishop for another seventeen. I was reared as an active Latter-day Saint; my religious beliefs, however intellectual they were to become, were sincere and consistent.

In trying to be both circumspect and honest in this memoir, I draw comfort from the Bible and the Book of Mormon, texts I first read in full when I was thirteen and have continued to read. Biblical writers had an insistent tendency to avoid hiding or concealing the sins and misdeeds of the persons they wrote about, whether they were the chosen people of Israel or individual prophets, patriarchs, and apostles. Moses, the greatest character in the Old Testament, and Peter, the apostle of Jesus, are three-dimensional persons, capable of both error and wondrous uprightness. Even Jesus once lost his temper with a fig tree (Matt. 21:19); but he also remembered that a little girl, when she recovered from a fever, would be extremely hungry (Mark 5:38–43).

The same censure and encouragement were given early members and officers of the LDS Church in the Doctrine and Covenants. If Bible authors seem to go out of their way to show the weaknesses of religious and community leaders, their approach suggests that salvation comes from the Lord, not from divinely appointed leaders, and that the thousands of "little people" who have personal burdens have reason to be reassured. If the general authorities have struggled to overcome weaknesses, their triumphs may inspire the rest of us.

In similar fashion, Book of Mormon authors were candid in recognizing the good and less-than-good in the lives of all, whoever they were and whatever their position. Nor did Book of Mormon prophets hesitate to find fault with the church of their day. Nephi, for example, charged that those inclined to proclaim uncritically "all is well in Zion" (2 Nephi 28:21–29) were following the precepts of men. As we write we must "behold our weakness" (Ether 12:25) and write with integrity to ourselves and to God.[7] Or, as Will Rogers said, "It's great to be great, but it's greater to be human."[8] In any case, I have endeavored, as did the Apostle Paul, to "speak the truth in love" (Eph. 4:15).

Certain recurring themes carry this book forward. First, writers of religious history are obligated to inform readers of both naturalistic explanations and divine influences. Second, the church builds good will with both members and the media by policies of openness and candor. Third, administrative policies sometimes have unintended consequences, as when LDS officials decided to turn church history over to professionals, causing some controversy within their own ranks over the publication of some rediscovered materials and new interpretations. Fourth, in a church leadership usually regarded as monolithic—a product of the promptings of the Holy Ghost—assertive individuals sometimes may effect policies without prior approval.

Historians are encouraged by the plainspokenness of early church members who endured malicious neighbors, an inhospitable environment, and a government that warred against them. Humor and forthrightness helped early Latter-day Saints dispose of contradictions, conflicts, and frustrations in a socially healthy manner. There was, for them, no conflict between piety and moderate levity, reverence and straightforward candidness. The documents of church history are replete with missionary stories, occasional pranks, and the bestowal of nicknames as a means of deflating pretension, hypocrisy, vanity, and excessive pride. They also contain celebrations of the goodness of God, the complexity of the world he created, and the sublimity of the life he gives. The early Saints' sense of balance between candid humor and reverence did not undermine their faith, but instead gave them a strong sense of group identity and illustrated the strengths of their movement. Devotion to their cause allowed such balance. More generally, it helped them develop the evolving self-respect that one would expect of a community of God's chosen people.

I hope that this book and others like it will broaden our understanding of the crucible of the Latter-day Saint experience. My colleagues and others who have endeavored to chronicle the cause of Christ in the latter days have tried to see, acknowledge, and give significance to the progress, the plateaus, the periods of pain, and the times of jubilation that accompany ongoing church history.

Readers of Mormon historical literature should bear in mind that, to follow scholarly practice, I have deleted titles of people used throughout this book (e.g., Elder, President) and retained them only when first introducing these persons, when their absence might be confusing, or occasionally when reintroducing them. Similarly, in reference to Joseph Smith and Brigham Young, I have used their last names instead of their first names. No disrespect is intended.

### Notes

For their help in preparing this volume I am grateful to Rebecca Foster Cornwall Bartholomew, Lavina Fielding Anderson, F. Ross Peterson, Davis Bitton, James B. Allen, Armand Mauss, Edward L. Kimball, Heidi Swinton, Sheri Dew, Jan Shipps, and Marilyn Rish Parks. None of those named, however, is responsible for the shortcomings of the book. I take full responsibility for the tone and content of this memoir.

1. There have been many biographies of presidents of the church and apostles, but most of them have been laudatory—telling of spirituality and important accomplishments but failing to mention mistakes and weaknesses. A valuable general authority memoir is Edwin B. Firmage, ed., *An Abundant Life: The Memoirs of Hugh B. Brown* (Salt Lake City: Signature Books, 1988). Containing helpful discussions of the Mormon leadership from an insider's point of view, Brown's memoir gives "great men" their due without unfairly discounting for their shortcomings, some of which he mentions. "Although I have had some rather difficult experiences since I became a General Authority by reason of some misunderstand-

ings and disagreements," he summarized, "it has been a truly wonderful experience" (115). In the same tradition of objectivity and honesty is Bishop Victor L. Brown (a nephew of Hugh B. Brown), *Personal History/Compiled 1984* (Salt Lake City: privately published, 1984).

2. John A. Widtsoe, *In a Sunlit Land: The Autobiography of John A. Widtsoe* (Salt Lake City: Deseret News Press, 1952), viii.

3. Frank W. Fox, *J. Reuben Clark: The Public Years* (Provo, Utah: Brigham Young University Press, 1980), xi. All three members of the First Presidency are generally given the title *President*.

4. Biographies that give reasonably full accounts of First Presidency activities are D. Michael Quinn, *J. Reuben Clark: The Church Years* (Provo, Utah: Brigham Young University Press, 1983); L. Brent Goates, *Harold B. Lee, Prophet and Seer* (Salt Lake City: Bookcraft, 1985); and Edward L. Kimball and Andrew E. Kimball Jr., *Spencer W. Kimball: Twelfth President of the Church of Jesus Christ of Latter-day Saints* (Salt Lake City: Bookcraft, 1977). My appraisals of Joseph Smith, Brigham Young, and Harold B. Lee are in Leonard J. Arrington, ed., *The Presidents of the Church: Biographical Essays* (Salt Lake City: Deseret Book, 1986), 3–40, 43–72, and 343–71.

5. Lorenzo Snow as quoted in the diary of George Q. Cannon, Jan. 7, 1898, Archives Division, Historical Department of the Church of Jesus Christ of Latter-day Saints.

6. Brigham Young, sermon, Mar. 29, 1857, in *Journal of Discourses*, 26 vols. (Liverpool: F. D. and S. W. Richards, 1854–86), 4:297.

7. See Eric C. Olson, "The 'Perfect Pattern': The Book of Mormon as a Model for the Writing of Sacred History," *BYU Studies* 31 (Spring 1991): 7–18. Robert L. Millet is among those who argue that Latter-day Saint history is a "sacred saga" and should be presented in a manner that expressly bears witness of God's hand and does not dilute that witness by emphasizing human weaknesses. See "How Should Our Story Be Told," in *"To Be Learned Is Good If . . . ,"* ed. Millet (Salt Lake City: Bookcraft, 1987), 1–2.

8. Quoted in Stephen Hess, "Big Bill Taft," in *A Sense of History: The Best Writing from the Pages of American Heritage* (New York: American Heritage, 1985), 581.

# I

# Standing at the Gate

He shall stand at the entering of the gate of the city, and shall declare
his cause in the ears of the elders of that city.
  —Joshua 20:4

ON JULY 29, 1946, less than a month after arriving in Utah from North
Carolina, I was in the lean private office of Joseph Fielding Smith, member of the Quorum of Twelve Apostles and church historian of the Church
of Jesus Christ of Latter-day Saints, to obtain approval for conducting in-
depth research in the LDS Church Archives. Twenty-nine years old, I had
taken a position as an assistant professor of economics at Utah State Agricultural College (USAC) in Logan and intended to write my doctoral dissertation on the economic activities of the Latter-day Saints in Mormon
country in the last half of the nineteenth century. Virtually all the pertinent records were housed in the Church Historian's Library and Archives,
located on the third floor of the Church Administration Building. Smith's
office was in the southeast corner, and that of his senior assistant, A. William Lund, was in the northeast corner. Several cataloguers and the reference staff had small offices in the public section on the east, while the library and archives was on the west, with Alvin Smith, Joseph Fielding
Smith's grouchy brother, and young, eager, always-busy Earl Olson as library and archives clerks.

Two weeks earlier I had approached John A. Widtsoe in his office on
the second floor of the Administration Building. He was a Harvard University graduate in chemistry who had served in turn as president of USAC
and of the University of Utah before his calling as apostle and LDS Commissioner of Education. Widtsoe discussed the dissertation topic with me,
emphasized that virtually all of the necessary information was in the archives, and counseled me to proceed quietly to obtain approval from Joseph Fielding Smith to use the archives. Widtsoe acknowledged that Smith,
his senior in the Quorum of Twelve Apostles, took a proprietary attitude

toward the vast archival materials in his care and was seldom persuaded that they should be made available to visiting scholars.

At age seventy, a man of medium height with a rumpled suit and white hair, Joseph Fielding Smith was the son of Joseph F. Smith, president of the church from 1901 to 1918, and Julina Lambson Smith. In 1910, at age thirty-three, he had been sustained as an apostle and assistant church historian, becoming church historian in 1921. He wrote *Essentials in Church History,* a text for priesthood and seminary classes first published in 1922 and subsequently updated and reprinted in many editions. The book was widely used as the standard one-volume history of the church. Smith was not a trained historian, however, and placed his reliance and focus on official church scriptures—the Bible, Book of Mormon, Doctrine and Covenants, and Pearl of Great Price. Austere and plainspoken, he was the church's primary scripturist and expounder of doctrine. His sermons were replete with divine warnings and calls to repentance. Although he could be compassionate on a personal basis and, as I learned later, had a healthy sense of humor, Smith had a reputation as a stern and demanding preacher of hard doctrine. He had little faith in scholarly studies, particularly in history and the social sciences.

The Church Historian's Office had existed from the founding (or "restoration") of the church in 1830. An official, always a member of the Quorum of Twelve Apostles since 1842, had been designated to record the church's story and preserve its records. In addition to his efforts, each of the auxiliary organizations of the church kept minutes of its meetings and other pertinent documents, individuals kept diaries and journals, and newspapers and magazines published items of contemporary and earlier history, all of which were collected by the church. Thus, a surprisingly complete record of the church and its instrumentalities, from 1830 to 1946, was to be found in the archives. The archives consisted of about two thousand diaries and personal histories; almost every book, pamphlet, and magazine article published by or about the church throughout its history; and thousands of minute books, letters, and historical materials.

Smith's attitude, during the twenty-five years he had served as church historian, was as an appointed watchman to protect the image of the church from potential critics and enemies. Few scholars had been given access to the primary documents in the archives. His loyal assistant church historian, A. William Lund (son of Anthon H. Lund, counselor to two presidents and former church historian), interviewed each person who requested the use of material and told Scandinavian-American stories (locally called Sanpete jokes) in the process of gently persuading them to content themselves with examining materials that had been published. Persons could

not do in-depth research without Smith's approval, and Smith seldom as-
sented. Widtsoe told me not to be discouraged by Lund and to insist upon
seeing Smith. Widtsoe wished me success and instructed me to mention his
name to Smith as an aid in persuasion. Here is my diary entry for the day
I met Smith:

> When I went to Elder Smith's secretary, Ruby Egbert, she asked if I'd like
> to see him right now. I replied yes. I asked, "What do I do? Knock on his
> door?" She said, "No, just walk in." So I opened the door, walked in, and
> timidly asked, "Elder Smith, may I see you for a moment?"
>
> He did not look up, did not say anything, made no sound. He seemed to
> be copying some scriptures out of the Bible and continued to do so. I stood
> in front of his desk for what seemed to be an interminable period. He didn't
> acknowledge me in any way. After I had stood there stone silent for several
> minutes he finally looked up tentatively, still holding the pencil in his hand
> and the Bible open to a given place. He said—he was obviously irritated—
> "Well?" I said, "Elder Smith, I have been talking with Brother Lund about
> doing a doctoral dissertation on the economic activities of the Latter-day
> Saints. For this purpose I need your permission to do research in the Ar-
> chives. I have talked with Dr. Widtsoe who thinks it is an appropriate top-
> ic, and I feel sure there is material in the Archives that will be helpful. May
> I have your permission to use the materials here in the Library?"
>
> Elder Smith simply said, "Well, you may," and looked down again at the
> books and papers on his desk and resumed his copying of scriptures. He
> did not look up at me again; he did not dismiss me. I was not quite sure he
> was through with me. I waited another two or three minutes, and he con-
> tinued his work, so I said, "Thank you, Elder Smith," and walked out.

When I exited, Will Lund motioned me into his office. I told him Smith
had given me the go-ahead. Despite his skepticism about Smith's approval, Lund assigned me a desk in a corner of the anteroom of the library and
asked what materials I would like to see. Widtsoe had given me advice on
that: First I was to ask to see published books and read them a few days.
Then I should ask for theses and dissertations and read those a few days.
Then I should ask for the Journal History of the Church, which would
likely take me many months, even years. After that I should ask for specific
documents I needed. Over time, I would build up their confidence in me,
they would see me as a serious scholar, and they would give me about
everything I wanted to use. As Widtsoe put it, like the proverbial camel, I
would stick my head in the tent, gradually move farther in, and ultimately carry the whole tent away.

This was my procedure; it was long and thorough. I spent the first week
reading published works. The second week I reviewed theses and disser-

tations. The third week I called for the legal-size volumes of the Journal History, conscientiously studying each, page by page, at the rate of about one volume per day. There were a total of about two hundred scrapbooks for the period 1847 to 1905, and I finished the task in the summers of 1946, 1947, and 1948.

This massive multivolume scrapbook record of the day-to-day activities of the church, with excerpts from available sources, both published and unpublished, was prepared by Andrew Jenson, assistant church historian from 1897 to 1941. I later discovered that there was an index to this mammoth collection, but I preferred to follow the flow of events day-by-day, week-by-week, month-by-month, and year-by-year, making my own index as I went. Although I was looking particularly for economic events and data, I realized that every program, every company, every activity had a setting in time, place, and circumstance, and so my written register had to be broadly based. In essence I was reading recorded church history, 1847 to 1905.

During these summers, Monday to Friday, I stayed in a rented room in a private residence in downtown Salt Lake City and interspersed my daytime study, 8:00 in the morning until 5:00 each evening, with occasional interviews with Salt Lake City residents. Thus, I took occasion to interview William Wallace, Utah's "Mr. Water," who told me of sitting on Brigham Young's lap when he was a boy; Leroi C. Snow, son of Lorenzo Snow, who was his father's assistant when he was president, 1898–1901; Preston Nibley, son of Charles W. Nibley, a counselor to President Heber J. Grant, who later served as assistant church historian; Leland Creer, a professor of history at the University of Utah, who advised me to restrict myself to the period before 1857 because everything after that date was "controversial"; Arthur L. Thomas, president of the University of Utah, who spoke of the inside of the statehood struggles of the 1880s and 1890s; several grandchildren of Brigham Young, John Taylor, and Wilford Woodruff; Juanita Brooks, a historian of southern Utah; Dale Morgan, a historian of early Mormonism; E. E. Ericksen, a professor of philosophy at the University of Utah, who was an authority on Mormon intellectual history; Lowry Nelson, a noted Mormon sociologist; Feramorz Y. Fox, president of the LDS Business College and a noted Mormon economic historian; G. Homer Durham, a political scientist at the University of Utah and son-in-law of Widtsoe; and other "just plain" oldtimers. I also had the opportunity of making contact with three collectors of Mormoniana: Asael C. Lambert of Los Angeles State College; M. Wilford Poulson of Brigham Young University; and my uncle, J. Earl Arrington, of Hollis, New York. The wily Lambert and the crusty Poulson had long collected Mormon curiosa helpful in understanding the early church; Earl Arrington had an unbelievably large collection of nineteenth-century books, magazines, newspapers, and notes, most of which are now in the Brigham Young University Library. All of these persons encouraged me to pursue my topic.

During the fall, winter, and spring, I would organize all the notes I had made in the summer and begin to write. I included some of the material in talks to university and town groups and to church firesides and classes. And I must emphasize that as I used the Church Archives no one checked my notes, no additional clearance was required, and no one raised any questions. Xerography was not yet introduced, so I copied everything I needed on my portable manual typewriter. I have thousands of pages of material I copied at that time.

I was interested in the firsthand accounts copied into the Journal History, and I was also interested in the serious studies made by scholars who had written doctoral dissertations before 1946. All of these were in the archives, and I was able to acquire microfilm copies for the USAC library. Of particular help were those by Edgar B. Wilson at the University of Berlin, 1906; Ephraim Ericksen for the University of Chicago, 1918; Andrew Love Neff for the University of California at Berkeley, 1918; Joseph A. Geddes for Columbia University, 1924; Leland Creer for the University of California at Berkeley, 1926; Dean McBrien at George Washington University, 1929; Lowry Nelson for the University of Wisconsin, 1929; Joel E. Ricks for the University of Chicago in 1930; Thomas C. Romney for the University of California at Berkeley in 1930; Feramorz Y. Fox for Northwestern University in 1932; Arden B. Olsen for the University of California at Berkeley in 1935; Edward J. Allen for Columbia in 1936; and Milton R. Hunter for the University of California at Berkeley in 1936.[1]

I was not the only person working in the Church Archives, although I was the only one researching consistently for the summers of 1946, 1947, 1948, and 1949. Others I met there and compared notes with were Richard D. Poll, Gustive O. Larson, Eugene E. Campbell, A. Russell Mortensen, M. Hamlin Cannon, Philip A. M. Taylor, T. Edgar Lyon, and Merle E. Wells. Thus, I became acquainted with much of the literature of Mormon history, almost everyone working in the field of Mormon history, and many persons in Salt Lake City who had information valuable to a historian.

My presence in the archives was rarely noticed. Each day I silently pursued my studies, often the only customer at the table in the small anteroom next to the library entrance. A few unforgettable moments stand out. Once when I was taking the elevator at the south entrance to the Church Administration Building to the third floor, Joseph Fielding Smith entered. He chuckled and asked me if I knew that King David was constipated. I was shocked but mumbled that I had no idea. He explained that in the Book of Kings it says that King David sat on his throne for forty years and was not moved.

Another time Smith was in the elevator with a medical doctor who, I learned later, was being called to preside over one of the church's missions. Smith's eyes twinkled as he, with considerable relish, reminded the doctor of a humorous passage—one of the few in the Bible—in Second Chronicles (16:12–13). He had apparently taken special pains to memorize it: "And Asa in the thirty and ninth year of his reign was diseased in his feet, until his disease was exceeding great: yet in his disease he sought not to the Lord, but [went] to the physicians. And Asa slept with his fathers, and died in the one and fortieth year of his reign." Obviously, the inner man was playful and amusing.

On a third occasion, Hugh Nibley, famous biblical and Book of Mormon scholar at Brigham Young University, came to the library to see the diary of his grandfather, Alexander Neibaur—a diary that he had previously given to the Church Historian's Office. Lund refused to let him see it because it was restricted material. Despite Nibley protestations that he'd only just given the diary to Lund, he was refused. Later I saw Nibley at the table copying from the diary. He explained that he had gone to the president of the church, who instructed Lund to let him use it.

By the end of 1948 I had completed the Journal History to 1905. In the summer of 1949, I began inspecting ledgers, diaries, organizational records, and company files. In asking for these one at a time, I was never denied any desired item. Earl Olson was delighted that someone was interested in seeing these documents, most of which had never been available for scholarly analysis. I was even given the privilege of searching subject files in the interior of the archives. Among the records I found and studied were those of Brigham Young's dealings in gold dust, the Church Public Works Department, the General Tithing Office, the Deseret Currency Association, the Deseret Telegraph Company, the Brigham Young Express and Carrying Company, the United Order, Zion's Board of Trade, beet sugar companies, iron works, coal mines, church properties held by the federal government under the Edmunds-Tucker Act, and Relief Society enterprises as well as railroad contracts and tithing account books of donations for many causes and enterprises.

In one file was a document duly signed with the cross of Aropeen, leader of the Ute Indians, in which he gave to Brigham Young, Trustee-in-Trust for The Church of Jesus Christ of Latter-day Saints, his full claim to and ownership of the land and country known as Sanpete County (Utah), together with all timber and material on the same. Besides the land the document also conveyed 10 horses, 4 cows, 1 bull, 1 ox, 1 calf, 2 guns, and a few farming tools valued at $10. Indeed there was a regular interchange between Brigham Young and Chief Aropeen. On July 1, 1857, for example, Aropeen took into the tithing office in Salt Lake City 30 beaverskins, 3 buckskins, and 17 wolfskins and received in exchange 2 pounds of powder, 9 pounds of lead, 4 boxes of caps, 4 plugs of tobacco, 2 quarts of whiskey, 1 bed quilt, 1 brass kettle, and $30 in cash.

I studied records of the trustee-in-trust, of the Perpetual Emigration Fund, of the Indian Relief Societies, and of Brigham Young as a private entrepreneur. All of these had enormous interest to an economic historian, and I did not fail to take notes. The accounts were set up in double-entry bookkeeping style, with one side for debits and the other for credits. There were often cash books, day books or journals, and ledgers. I emphasize that these were available in 1949, but some were later closed. In short, the archives contained an essentially complete record of every important undertaking in which the Mormons were involved, and few had been previously examined by any scholar. From my standpoint, of course, I saw no reason why a scholar should not have access to this material. I could see no evidence of private abuse of public funds; on the contrary, the accounts seemed to be complete, honest, and evidence of the sincere and devoted service of church leaders and members.

From notes taken during the summer of 1949 and from task papers written during the school years 1946–47, 1947–48, and 1948–49, while I was teaching at USAC, I had many interesting, well-documented stories to tell, and I soon had more than a half-dozen articles ready to submit for publication in professional journals.

But I was still unsure of myself. Could I write well enough? Did I know how to present the material in a way satisfactory both to scholars and to "ordinary" readers like my parents, neighbors, and nonacademic friends?

In January 1947, shortly after I began my research, the University of Utah inaugurated a new regional quarterly, the *Utah Humanities Review*. The first issue carried articles by William Mulder, just returned to the English department of the University of Utah from service as a naval communications officer in Okinawa, who wrote on primitive artist C. C. A. Christensen; Albert Mitchell, just returned to the University of Utah after completing his Ph.D. in speech at the University of Wisconsin, who wrote on the pioneer players and plays of Parowan, Utah; Lester Hubbard, specialist in eighteenth-century English literature, who wrote on the songs and ballads of the Mormon pioneers; and Charles Dibble, an authority on the

Aztecs, who wrote on the Mormon mission to the Shoshone Indians. Succeeding issues carried articles on folk art, pioneer politics, minority peoples, plural marriage, folklore, recreation, history, and economics.

I was fascinated by their topics, their writing style, their tone, and their wording. I finally worked up the courage to visit Harold Bentley, the editor and a professor at the University of Utah, to explain my research and to ask if he would be interested in publishing one or two of my articles. He said he was interested but stressed that the articles had to be well-written. Knowing that I was an economist, he repeated that insistence several times in our hour-long conversation. I wanted very much to effectively tell the Mormon story, as it was revealed in the archives, well enough for publication in recognized journals like *Utah Humanities Review* (later, *Western Humanities Review*). I did, indeed, have the opportunity of publishing articles in the *Western Humanities Review,* the *Pacific Historical Review,* the *Journal of Economic History,* and a dozen other quality professional journals. Before that story is told, however, I should explain how I happened to walk through the gate that took me into the rich garden of Mormon history.

My first daunting interview with Joseph Fielding Smith in 1946 led to productive research that in turn opened many other doors. My study in the Church Archives, in turn, led to a deepening of my testimony of the gospel and to a resumption of full activity in the church.

### Note

1. See Leonard J. Arrington, "Scholarly Studies of Mormonism in the Twentieth Century," *Dialogue: A Journal of Mormon Thought* 1 (Spring 1966): 15–28.

# 2

# How I Got into Mormon History

[The Lord instructs us to obtain an understanding] of things both in
heaven and in the earth, and under the earth; things which have been,
things which are, things which must shortly come to pass; things which
are at home, things which are abroad; the wars and the perplexities of
the nations, and the judgments which are on the land; and a knowledge
also of countries and of kingdoms.
  —Doctrine and Covenants 88:79

HOW DID IT HAPPEN that an economics instructor at USAC, fresh from
three years in the military in North Africa and Italy, went to the Church
Archives to begin a systematic program of research in Mormon history?
Economists are usually pictured as dry-as-dust individuals who are especially interested in numbers, prices, statistics, and abstract theory. We were
always being reminded of the charge that economists would make marvelous lifeguards because they could go down deeper, stay down longer,
and come up dryer than anybody else. I did not intend that description to
apply to me. My broad reading and university training and my study of
Latter-day Saint pioneer diaries, letters, minutes of meetings, and speeches had impressed me with the human drama of Mormon country events. I
had many quotations that exhibited pioneer Mormon humor—jesting,
satire, parody, wordplay, hyperbole, and jokes. The narratives, I thought,
would read well if I was skillful in presenting them as they deserved.

The large family in which I grew up was of very modest means, but as
children we were molded by a good school system and by a caring LDS
ward. We had training in writing and public speaking, especially, in my
case, through the Future Farmers of America.

I did not expect writing to be easy, but, growing up on a farm, I learned
the habit and joy of work. Work did not seem onerous or burdensome,
but, as I remember it now anyway, a source of pleasure and accomplishment. "Blessed is he who has found his work," wrote Thomas Carlyle; "let
him ask no further blessedness."[1] Of course, doing historical research *was*

joy, especially in contrast to stacking hay, thinning sugar beets, and picking potatoes.

I grew up in an irrigated agriculture region in south-central Idaho that had been converted from a raw sagebrush desert by the construction of Milner Dam on the Snake River in 1905. The private development, supported by eastern capital, furnished irrigating water for 350,000 acres, providing a livelihood for approximately 15,000 farmers. My father and mother had settled in the tract, now called Magic Valley, in 1913, a few months after their marriage in Oklahoma. Raising sugar beets, potatoes, beans, wheat, and alfalfa in a crop rotation system, they reared nine children in addition to two that died as infants. The low prices during the agricultural depression that followed World War I meant years of struggle to hold on to our land. The depression of the 1930s was ruinous, and most farmers would have lost their land if local creditors, influenced by ministers and politicians, had not reduced payments. The recovery program of the New Deal helped us, but we were not finally out of the woods until the onset of World War II, when farm prices rose to satisfactory levels. The farmers in Magic Valley were hardworking, frugal, and fiercely loyal to American values, and they displayed a spirit of mutual helpfulness. Although farmers are often characterized as individualistic, those in our region joined together in haying, threshing, and helping those with temporary illnesses and disabilities.

We were part of a small minority of Latter-day Saints in a predominantly Protestant community. The Twin Falls Ward, organized in 1910, consisted of a few dozen families of farmers and shopkeepers who had moved to the area from Utah and other locations. My father, then only twenty-nine, was a member of the original high council when Twin Falls Stake was organized in 1919.

I had been introduced to Mormon history in 1929, when I was twelve years old. Our ward started a junior genealogical society in lieu of our regular Sunday school class, and I became fascinated with family history and genealogy. For this class I wrote an eleven-page autobiography and histories of both my father's and my mother's families. I completed pedigree charts and family group sheets, corresponded with my mother's oldest sister to get the history of their family, recorded a number of faith-promoting incidents, and gave several talks in Sunday school about our family history projects. Unfortunately, the program in our ward was dropped after one year because instructions from Salt Lake City discouraged wards from adopting any program that had not been initiated by church headquarters. All of the local leaders wept but dutifully discontinued the program. However, my interest in family and church history had been ignited.

Our struggling LDS ward formed a Boy Scout troop when I was thirteen, and our young men earned merit badges and exercised leadership in church and community. We took seriously our assignments in the Deacons' and Teachers' Quorums, where we alternated caring for the sacrament, teaching the Sunday morning class, and giving talks in Sunday school and sacrament meeting.

When I was fifteen, Bertha Mae Hansen, a neighbor woman I visited monthly as a home teacher, gave me a recently published book, *Joseph Smith, an American Prophet* by John Henry Evans. I read it, enjoyed it very much, and gained a new appreciation for the prophet and for church history.

As with other farm boys, I enrolled in vocational agriculture in high school, conducted a large poultry enterprise, and received training in public speaking, writing, and bookkeeping. I was active in the Twin Falls chapter of the Future Farmers of America, which won national honors for its leadership training activities. In successive years I became the chapter reporter, president, state president, and national vice president. In the latter capacity I took trips to Kansas City, Washington, D.C., and New York City, as well as chapter meetings in southern Idaho communities. I was a member of the Idaho State Grange, won state public speaking prizes, and sent letters of instruction and encouragement to chapter officers in Idaho and other western states. We learned parliamentary procedure and other organizational skills. I was judge of poultry at two county fairs and spoke on three national radio programs. Future Farmers of America has done much to develop business competence and leadership talents among rural youth, as well as giving us an understanding and appreciation for rural virtues and farm life. Generally speaking, there was widespread admiration for Mormons among farm leaders and rural youth.

My relationships with others, virtually all non-LDS, provoked a heightened interest in Mormonism, a distinct minority religion in our circles. My relatives in Oklahoma, who I visited during my trips to Kansas City and who were staunch Methodists, had a hundred questions about the Mormons and Mormonism. So did my fellow national officers in the Future Farmers of America and, for that matter, members and debaters in Idaho. My father, being a high councilor, had received books from President Heber J. Grant, and I studied them: *Brigham Young's Discourses* (1925), Talmage's *Articles of Faith* (1890, 1924), and Widtsoe's *In Search of Truth* (1930). I also reread Evans's *Joseph Smith, an American Prophet*. As a high school senior I attended the M Men-Gleaner class in our Twin Falls Ward Mutual Improvement Association. We used the new manual written by Lowell Bennion, *What About Religion?* (1934–35). These readings satisfied my desire to know more and helped me to realize that I was committed to the church. Religiously, I was attracted to the goals and standards set up for young people.

Looking back, the most important thing I learned from this and other reading was the importance of study in building faith. The gospel embraced all truth; we should continue to study and acquire knowledge: "Seek ye out of the best books words of wisdom, seek learning, even by study and also by faith" (Doctrine and Covenants 88:118). I suppose the pursuit of truth fit in with my natural proclivities: When I was a child, my father always referred to me as Honest Leonard.

My work with poultry and the Future Farmers of America enabled me to earn a Union Pacific Railroad scholarship to the University of Idaho, where I was able to support myself by working in the chemical laboratory, the university library, and as an assistant in the economics department. The work was funded by the National Youth Administration, a federal program of the 1930s to provide jobs for students unable to finance their educations otherwise. University attendance was a new experience for our family; we had no understanding of the function of a college. I intended to learn to be a good farmer, but after one year in the College of Agriculture, I decided the college was in the business of training persons to be agricultural scientists, not farmers, and I had no desire to become a chemist, biologist, horticulturist, agronomist, or livestock specialist. I switched to the College of Arts and Letters and majored in economics, with minors in political science, history, and English literature. I read widely to obtain what was proudly called "a liberal education." I came to understand that, in addition to teaching useful information and skills, the university's task was to discover and transmit the truth and cultivate the life of the mind. The university was a promulgator of reason and knowledge—a center for the rational, dispassionate search for truth, a disseminator of knowledge for the sake of knowledge. The commitment to truth and knowledge were worthy spiritual goals, as I confirmed in rereading Widtsoe's *In Search of Truth*, Lowell Bennion's *The Religion of the Latter-day Saints* (1930), and Brigham Young's statements about truth in *Discourses of Brigham Young*. The Latter-day Saint goal of eternal progression was consistent with a lifetime adventure of inquiry, learning, and understanding.

## The University of Idaho

At the University of Idaho I was active in student politics as a co-founder of the Independent (nonfraternity) party, was elected to the executive council, and wrote for the student newspaper. I also learned to appreciate classical music, being particularly moved by a performance of Tchaikovsky's

Fourth Symphony, conducted by an imported Hollywood director, Vladimir Bakalinikoff, and a performance of Liszt's Hungarian Concerto no. 2 by, according to my memory, Sergei Rachmaninoff. I also enjoyed the poetry of Wordsworth and the plays of Ibsen. We had a strong social as well as learning environment in the LDS Institute of Religion, and I was happy to have been able to live there. I graduated with high honors and was elected to Phi Beta Kappa.

At the LDS Institute, I took courses that proved to be particularly relevant for my future. We were fortunate to have as a teacher George Tanner, a graduate of the University of Utah and University of Chicago Divinity School, who was interested in Christian as well as LDS history and doctrine. Under his direction, our Sunday school class studied the *Comprehensive History of the Church* by B. H. Roberts. During the four years I was at the university, we studied all six volumes. Tanner also taught classes in church history, Old and New Testaments, Book of Mormon, and comparative religions, so I had splendid university-level training in LDS and Christian history and doctrine. He welcomed questions and helped me reconcile my science study with Mormon beliefs.[2]

In addition to church history, Tanner introduced me to biblical scholarship—biblical criticism, modern translations, and the leading works of biblical literature. I derived much inspiration from James Moffatt's *The New Testament: A New Translation* (1922) and J. M. Powis Smith and Edgar J. Goodspeed's *The Bible: An American Translation* (1935). Both works helped me to realize that God was real, not simply an article of faith. I used the Smith and Goodspeed translated Bible during my tenure as a graduate student at the University of North Carolina and carried it with me overseas during World War II. Reading it regularly with pleasure and benefit in North Carolina, I drew from it in talks and classes in Mutual Improvement Association meetings, Sunday school, and Priesthood Quorums and in private devotions each evening when I was in the army. I learned to appreciate the insights, images, and stories of ancient Israelites and the early Christian movement; the book also helped me to live in a more trusting relationship with God and my fellow human beings. My battered, underlined, annotated copy is still on my desk. I also learned to enjoy religious articles in such journals as *Saturday Review, Atlantic Monthly, Harper's,* and *American Scholar,* as well as the *Improvement Era* and *The Instructor,* published by the church.

George Tanner; my major professor, Erwin Graue; and my Mormon upbringing all taught me that while the life of the mind was exciting and virtuous, it also involved responsibilities—there were limits. Building on the example of my mentors, I came to believe that we ought to make and advance knowledge by research and writing; we ought to transmit knowledge and skills by teaching and lecturing; and we ought to help others lead ethical, fulfilling lives by talks, counseling, and good example. As we devote ourselves heart and soul to solving particular intellectual and social problems, we must also keep our sights open to the large (not always answerable) questions of human and divine meaning and purpose. We must be lucid *and* humane, honest *and* helpful, devoted to our scholarly callings *and* loyal to our faith and community. We must cultivate both social skills and spiritual virtues—humility, faith, courage, and good will. Humility would dispose us to learn from others, faith in the gospel to retain our moorings, courage to open our beliefs to critical examination and change, and good will to be fair and just in considering the people and practices that come before us—these virtues were taught by the scriptures, by Joseph Smith, by modern revelation, and by the great philosophers; they would help us in our spiritual quest for exaltation. Above all, we ought to eschew the rootless life not tied to divine instruction, healthy tradition, and robust piety.

## The University of North Carolina

In 1939, having been awarded a Kenan Teaching Fellowship at the University of North Carolina in Chapel Hill, I undertook graduate work in economics. The opportunity to study at Chapel Hill was a distinct blessing. The University of North Carolina was unquestionably the leading university in the South. Here was an opportunity to study a culture, different from our western culture, that had so much influence on American thought. This also gave me the opportunity to get acquainted with "the plain folk" of the Old South, the people from whom my family was descended.

As a student at UNC I was the only Latter-day Saint, faculty or student, and the only church member in Chapel Hill. But I was far from lonely. My mother supplied me with the *Improvement Era* and with books and articles that would keep me in touch with our local culture, including Mormonism. In addition to widespread reading in economics and regular reading from my Bible and Three-in-one (Book of Mormon, Doctrine and Covenants, and Pearl of Great Price), I read Talmage's *Jesus the Christ,* Robert Shafer's *Christianity and Naturalism,* Fosdick's *Understanding the Bible,* Somerset Maugham's *The Summing Up,* John Henry Newman's *Apologia Pro Vita Sua, The Philosophy of William James,* and Sholem Asch's *The Nazarene.* There were long walks to black neighborhoods where families were gathered on the porch Sunday afternoons reading from the Bible and singing hymns. I enjoyed the football games sparkled by the running of Charlie Choo-Choo Justice; lectures by prominent philosophers; plays by Bernard Shaw and Paul Green and performances of Beethoven's Ninth Symphony, his Emperor Piano Concerto, and his touching violin concerto. I was well prepared for an eventual sojourn in Utah, where there were strong athletic rivalries and unforgettable musical and theatrical productions in Logan, Salt Lake City, and Provo. There was, however, no counterpart of the Mormon Tabernacle Choir.

These readings and experiences, and the spirited conversations with colleagues, none of whom were Mormons, helped me to realize the importance of being widely read and well-prepared intellectually. A rational foundation may not always lead to belief, but it helped me feel confident that I was on the right path. In my experience, the buildup of intellectuality is consistent with the strengthening of faith and indeed helps produce a deeper, more enduring testimony. Philosophy, I found, provided a climate in which belief could flourish, and my attachment to Mormonism was reinforced. My reading of Talmage, Widtsoe, and Bennion had been enormously helpful.

I read southern history and literature, went to southern plays, listened to lectures and sermons, went to Sunday afternoon "singings," and spent the summer of 1941 in a southern countryside measuring cotton. I was fascinated with the irony, wit, stylistic versatility, and exaggeration in southern literature and found in southern thought an authentic American conservatism. Rooted in Judeo-Christian values, Southern thought, as I learned, was essentially religious and moral, condemning a system that made the market the arbiter of our moral, spiritual, and political life, and likewise denouncing a radical individualism that took us away from family, community, and civic responsibility.

Through the efforts of Howard W. Odum and Rupert B. Vance, Chapel Hill was leading a study of the southern region. My advisor, Milton S. Heath, was an investigator of the southern economy. He kept telling me I should learn how to conduct regional studies because it was my responsibility, after earning the Ph.D. degree, to do a similar study of the Mountain West. Through a fellow graduate student, James Waller, I became acquainted with the literature of the southern agrarians; I read the works of John Crowe Ransom, Allen Tate, Frank Owsley, Robert Penn Warren, Donald Davidson, and Andrew Lytle. Influenced by the theology of Thomas Aquinas, the philosophy of Spinoza and Hobbes, and the neo-Catholicism of Hilaire Belloc, G. K. Chesterton, and T. S. Eliot, they were revolted by the industrialism, commercialism, and scientism of the modern world, which they thought were destroying the South in particular and America in general. They championed a revival of moral values and religious faith.

They were particularly interested in the small landholding farmer. They deplored the growth of tenantry, sharecropping, absentee landlordism, and industrial proletarianism. They advocated restoring the South to health by widely distributing land among small holders. They joined Thomas Jefferson in saying that the cultivation of the soil was an occupation singularly blessed by God, providing direct contact with nature and furnishing inspiration for the works of God and for the humane arts. Their approach appealed to me, a former farm boy, partly because of their advocacy of rural values and partly because of the strong religious beliefs that underlay their writings.

In December 1939 I attended the annual convention of the American Economic Association in Philadelphia, my first major professional meeting. It was my great good fortune to meet there that grand old man of economics, then in his eighty-fifth year, Richard T. Ely. He had founded the American Economic Association in 1885. I had left one session a little earlier to get a good seat at another lecture. Also arriving early at that session was Ely, his young second wife, and two children, the youngest of whom was only five years old. I took advantage of the opportunity and sat next to him and felt it a gift of heaven that I could talk with this short, pink-cheeked, boyish-faced man, who had influenced two generations of economists and economic policy. Economics, he had written, should serve as an ethical guide to marketplace economies. People, not mechanical "laws of the market," should be the focus of the discipline.

When Ely learned I was from an Idaho farm, he talked about irrigation and the West. Guessing that I was a Mormon because I volunteered that we grew sugar beets, he said that the Mormons, because of their large families and willingness to work, had developed a successful sugar beet culture in the West. Coloradoans and Californians, he said, used Mexican labor. No other Nordics but the Mormons would practice the stoop labor that the thinning and weeding of sugar beets necessitated. He reminded me that he had written a complimentary essay on the Mormons that was published in *Harper's Monthly Magazine* in 1903—the first published treatment of Mormonism by an economist. Fortunately, I was acquainted with this essay, one of the finest ever published and still worth reading. In a sense, my dissertation was merely an extension of his pioneering work. Ely firmly believed that religion was and should continue to be a major force in economic development.

## North Carolina State College

In January 1941, because the regular economics professor had a heart attack, I went to North Carolina State College (now North Carolina State

University) in Raleigh to teach, take classes in agricultural economics and rural sociology, and earn additional credit toward my doctorate. In reading for a rural sociology seminar, I found references to works on the Mormon village by Lowry Nelson, T. Lynn Smith, and other scholars. Indeed, I was delighted to learn of a small but impressive professional literature on the Latter-day Saints and their social system. Fascinated, I read everything I could find on Mormon economics and sociology in the libraries at North Carolina State College and at the University of North Carolina. In the process, I discovered articles by Richard T. Ely, Bernard DeVoto, Ephraim Ericksen, Juanita Brooks, and Wallace Stegner, as well as by other academicians. These stimulated me to write some papers on Mormonism for my graduate seminars.

Meanwhile, I had directed a weekly Mutual Improvement Association study group and was sustained as president of the newly organized branch of the church in Raleigh. At that time I met Grace Fort, a native of Wake Forest, North Carolina, who worked in Raleigh. She was interested in religion, enjoyed our Mormon get-togethers, had a delightful North Carolina accent, and was fun to be around.

## In the U.S. Army

With the outbreak of World War II, I worked as an economist for the North Carolina Office of Price Administration, married lovely and gracious Grace Fort, and then was drafted into the army, where I served almost three years in North Africa and Italy. Grace and I corresponded every day. My experience in Italy was a building one. Although I was a simple soldier (private first class, then Tech 5 corporal), I was given responsibilities in the economic section of the Allied Commission for Italy. As an Allied coordinator with the Italian Central Institute of Statistics in Rome and with the Office of Price Control for Northern Italy, I had experiences in economic investigation and reporting and in personnel administration, management, and decision-making that proved to be invaluable in my subsequent career as a teacher and administrator. I learned much about Italy, Europe, and human nature.

## Utah State Agricultural College

During my last year in Italy (1945), I thought a great deal about my doctoral dissertation and decided to propose to my committee a topic related to the economics of Mormonism. My cross-disciplinary training would be especially helpful. To simplify access to materials, I applied for a position at a western college and was offered one at USAC. Charming Grace and I moved to Logan, Utah, in July 1946. As soon as we were settled, I began work in the Church Archives reviewing material for a satisfactory dissertation. Our first baby, James Wesley, was not born until December 1948. Carl Wayne was born in September 1951, and Susan Grace in August 1954. Our children were smart and always active in church and school.

Needing another year of course work toward the Ph.D. at the University of North Carolina, I took leave without pay from USAC in 1949–50 and left Grace and James in nearby Raleigh with Grace's mother. On weekdays I stayed in a graduate dormitory in Chapel Hill. I had taught courses at USAC that prepared me for my work at Chapel Hill, so I was able to spend time working up stories of Mormon economic enterprises and analyses of policies that would add new understanding to the Mormon experience.

During the winter of 1949–50, although I was enjoying a warm weekend with Grace and little Jamie but back at the university each weekday, my mind was filled with the research I had done in the Church Archives during the preceding summers. One afternoon, early in 1950, sitting in a quiet alcove of the university library, I had what might be called a "peak experience"—one that sealed my devotion to Latter-day Saint history. Going over my extended notes, recalling the letters, diaries, and personal histories of the hundreds of past church leaders and members, a feeling of ecstasy suddenly came over me—an exhilaration that transported me to a higher level of consciousness. The Apostle John wrote that to gain salvation a person must receive two baptisms—the baptism of water and the baptism of the Spirit (John 3:3–5). My water baptism and confirmation had occurred when I was eight, but now, in a university library, I was unexpectedly absorbed into the universe of the Holy Spirit. (Mormons would say that I was receiving the gift of the Holy Ghost.) A meaningful moment of insight and connectedness had come to me that helped me to see that my research efforts were compatible with the divine restoration of the church. It was something like, but more intense than, the feelings that welled up in me when I listened to the finale of Beethoven's Ninth Symphony or was moved by Raphael's painting of the Madonna in the Vatican Museum at the end of World War II. In an electrifying moment, the lines and beliefs of nineteenth-century Mormons had a special meaning; they were inspiring—part of the eternal plan—and it was my pleasure to understand and write about their story. Whatever my talents and abilities—and I had never pretended that they were extraordinary—an invisible higher power had now given me a commission and the experience remained, and continues to remain, with me. Regardless of frustrations and obstacles that came to me in the years that followed, I knew that God expected me to carry out a research program of his peoples' history and to make available that material to others. Whatever people might say about this mortal errand, I must persevere, and do so in an attitude of faithfulness. My experience was a holy, never-to-be-forgotten encounter—one that inspired me to live up to the promises held out for those who receive the gift of the Holy Ghost. This is the first time I have mentioned this event publicly.[3]

## Return to Logan

In September 1950, shortly after our return from North Carolina, I read in our Logan newspaper that William Mulder, assistant editor of the *Western Humanities Review*, was going to present a talk in Logan. I telephoned to invite him to spend the night with us. He agreed. We had a nice dinner, and before he went to bed I trotted out one of my essays—one on the building of a dam at Deseret, in Millard County, Utah. It was the dramatic story of the attempt of a little community to build a dam that would furnish irrigating water for their crops. The first dam washed out, so did a second, and eventually a whole succession of dams were built before the pioneers finally solved the problem. I asked Bill to tell me frankly whether I could write. Bill read the piece before he went to sleep and the next morning said it was interesting and well done and he would accept it provisionally for publication. He suggested ways it could be made more artistic—a new introduction, a new conclusion, and some literary allusions here and there in the text.

After fussing with it for a week or two I sent it off, and he published it in the August 1951 issue under the title "Taming the Turbulent Sevier: A Story of Mormon Desert Conquest." By then I had prepared another article, "Zion's Board of Trade, a Third United Order," which he published the same year, followed by an article in 1953 on the Law of Consecration and Stewardship in early Mormon history and another in 1955 on the economic role of Mormon women that was quite possibly the earliest attempt to introduce Mormon women into the scholarly study of Mormon history. At the same time in 1951 I published an account of the Deseret Telegraph Company in the *Journal of Economic History*, "Property among the Mormons" the same year in *Rural Sociology*, and "The Transcontinental Railroad and Mormon Economic Policy" and "The Settlement of Brigham Young's Estate" in the *Pacific Historical Review* in 1951–52. There were also two articles in 1952 on Mormon coin and currency in the newly founded *Utah Historical Quarterly*.

Other articles I published in the early 1950s dealt more strictly with business and economics, although in each case there was Mormon involvement. There were articles in the *Business History Review* on iron manufacturing in Utah, banking history, and the Mormon tithing system; in the *Utah Historical Quarterly* on woolen manufacturing and the impact of the Civil War income tax; in *Agricultural History* on agricultural price control in pioneer Utah; and in *Pacific Historical Review* on the cotton industry in southern Utah. One article on Utah's railroad history subjected me to intimidation. Written for the *Utah Historical Quarterly* on a railroad operated by the Union Pacific Corporation in the 1870s and 1880s, the article was not flattering to Union Pacific. I decided, to be fair, that I would allow company administrators to see it before publication. The president of the railroad replied with a nasty letter, full of vituperation and threats: he would seek to get me fired and embarrass me with my church. He offered no specific suggestions with new evidence—just a rhetorical criticism. I replied that I could see no reason to change the article and that I was planning to send it on for publication.

Within a few days Franklin S. Harris, president of Utah State University, wrote me about the letter he had received from the railroad threatening to embarrass the university in the legislature the next time it went for funds. The president was good enough to tell me that if I felt justified in my conclusions, he would stand behind me. Within another few days, I had a letter from the president of the church, David O. McKay. He said essentially the same thing. I felt my scholarly integrity was protected. The article was soon published in the *Utah Historical Quarterly* for January 1955 under the title "Utah's Coal Road in the Age of Unregulated Competition." The Union Pacific archivist in Omaha, not knowing of the angry letter, wrote me a letter thanking me for bringing to light an obscure chapter in early railroad history.

## My Doctoral Dissertation

All of these essays focused on particular episodes and practices. How to devise a theme to thread them all together? The virtuosity of Mormon leadership was evident, and their articulated goal of building a kingdom of God was also unmistakable. In seeking to identify a unifying factor, I felt like a pig trying to walk on ice. The necessary inspiration came in 1950–51. Bill Mulder and Sterling McMurrin had organized in 1950 the Mormon Seminar (sometimes irreverently referred to as the "Swearing Elders"), which met every Thursday afternoon on the University of Utah campus to explore in an analytical way different aspects of Mormon life and thought. Each week different authorities talked on such subjects as Mormonism and evolution, Mormonism and psychiatry, the Book of Mormon and the pre-Columbian Indians, polygamy, Mormonism and literature, and Mormonism and education.

In March 1951 seminar leaders invited me to discuss Mormon economic history. This request forced me to focus seriously on the meaning of all my research. Influenced by my readings in American history, I decided that Brigham Young, Heber C. Kimball, George A. Smith, Daniel H. Wells, and other Latter-day Saint leaders brought up in America in the decades before the Civil War had been imbued with American ideals prevalent during that period. They had remained in relative isolation in the Great Basin during the years the rest of the country struggled through the Civil War and Reconstruction, which featured an overweening emphasis on private property, individualism, and free enterprising capitalism.

Here was a theme for my dissertation: the consistent applications of antebellum policies in the Great Basin while the nation was adopting a more individualistic and freewheeling capitalism. The basic social and economic objectives of the Latter-day Saints had been determined during the three years following the founding of the church in 1830. These included the gathering of church members into one place, the village form of settlement, group economic independence, comprehensive resource development to prepare the earth for the millennium, unified action and solidarity, and equitable sharing of the product of cooperative endeavor. Church officials attempted the redistribution of wealth and income, were charged with the regulation of property rights, involved the church in many types of business ventures, and assumed the ultimate responsibility for the development of the Mormon economy. The institutions and devices established to implement basic church policies, in general, were flexible, pragmatic, and provisional. They were also consonant with many small-group economies of antebellum America.

While the mobilization of capital and the application of administrative controls on the Mormon frontier resembled the contemporary devices of large-scale corporations and holding companies, the continuity of organized cooperation and careful long-range group planning stood out in sharp contrast to the individualism and short-sighted exploitation that often characterized the mining, cattle, wheat, and lumber frontiers of the far West. As one western historian wrote, the reigning philosophy was every man for himself, comparable to what the elephant said while he was dancing among the chickens. Whereas dominant American thought after 1865 held that superior results were to be achieved by laissez-faire institutions and policies, the seemingly unique policies of Mormon leaders, emphasizing as they did the welfare of the group, were nevertheless consistent with those commonly advocated and applied by secular government in the antebellum America that cradled Mormonism.

Having developed this theme, I set out during the winter of 1951–52 to write the dissertation while on six months' leave, again without pay, from USAC. I finished the degree in 1952. At the defense Heath remarked that he and the other committee members respected my faith but were gratified that it had not affected my work. The dissertation, entitled "Mormon Economic Policies and Their Implementation on the Western Frontier, 1847–1900," included eleven more or less independent essays: the historical and philosophical roots of Mormonism, the economic mind of Mormonism, the principle of consecration and church finances, the principle of stewardship and property institutions, the principle of gathering and the Perpetual Emigrating Fund, church public works, the principle of solidarity and the frontier market, the principle of economic independence and the coming of the transcontinental railroad, religious sanction and Mormon entrepreneurship, and the role of the Mormon church in the economic development of the West.

Heath encouraged me to submit the dissertation for publication by the Committee on Research in Economic History, of which he was a member. I revised and expanded the manuscript and submitted it in 1954. The readers praised my work and made substantive suggestions. As I reworked it, however, I could see that instead of the focus on economic policies, a chronological narrative of the development and evolution of Mormon institutions, practices, and policies would be more appropriate. I was granted a sabbatical leave from USAC in 1956–57, receiving only 60 percent of my base salary, and arranged for a fellowship at the Henry E. Huntington Library and Art Gallery in San Marino, California, to supplement my reduced income. I spent the year writing what turned out to be an economic history of the Mormons, the first such work to describe the Mormon experience. Completing one chapter a month, I finished the rewriting in a year.

In leaving Logan, I took a leave from my position as senior president of the 368th Quorum of Seventies of East Cache Stake, Grace was released as counselor in the Tenth Ward Relief Society, and we took along James, eight; Carl Wayne, five; and Susan, two. The boys attended a nearby public elementary school. We lived in Altadena until the end of 1956 and on a nice street above the Rose Bowl in Pasadena from January to July. We attended Pasadena Ward, where we had friends and were members of Pasadena Stake, of which the beloved stake president was Howard W. Hunter, a southern California attorney. We sensed he was "special," and in 1959 he was appointed to the Quorum of Twelve Apostles, and in 1994 became president of the church. He was an inspiring leader. We took advantage of our location to go to Disneyland, Knott's Berry Farm, Griffiths Park, the San Diego Zoo, Marineland, and other attractions. We saw the Tournament of Roses Parade and enjoyed association with neighborhood and school groups, including some movie and television stars. At the Huntington Library, I became well acquainted with other fellows: Allan Nevins, Paul Gates, Merrill Jensen, and Ray Allen Billington. It was a good year professionally for me and a memorable one for the family.

## Great Basin Kingdom

The revised and recast work of my economic history of the Mormons was resubmitted in 1957 to the Committee on Research in Economic History, which arranged for its publication by Harvard University Press as *Great Basin Kingdom*. Because the committee was the book's sponsor, it received royalties on the book until the committee was disbanded, after which the royalties went to the Economic History Association. I did not receive royalties until 1993, when the second edition was published by the University of Utah Press. *Great Basin Kingdom* expanded on ideas introduced in Bill Mulder's study of Scandinavian Mormons, Tom O'Dea's on Mormon sociology, Sterling McMurrin's on Mormon theology, George Ellsworth's on early Mormon missions, and Feramorz Fox's on Mormon economic organization. I also profited from conversations with Lowry Nelson, Hal Bentley, Richard Poll, Dale Morgan, Gene Campbell, Juanita Brooks, Gus Larson, and Ed Lyon. Above all, the needed perspective was available because the book was built on the indescribably rich and complete western collection of the Huntington Library, materials not available in the entirely Mormon-related Church Archives.

This version of my study benefited from the astute editorial comments of my good friend S. George Ellsworth, a professor of history at USAC, who reviewed the document carefully and made many helpful suggestions, and the editor at Harvard University Press, who provided consistency and saved me from egregious errors.

An honest, youthful assessment of the published book was made by my nephew, a high school student who was induced to read the book by my brother. He pronounced me "a pretty good writer" for producing a book "no duller" than I had.

*Great Basin Kingdom* was praised by colleagues, American historians, American sociologists, and others. I will cite just two: first, the flattering judgment of a fellow economist, Jonathan R. T. Hughes, Distinguished Professor of Northwestern University, who as late as 1992 was still requiring his graduate students to read it as an example of good economic history. He called *Great Basin Kingdom* "a giant structure of deep and trustworthy scholarship and judgment . . . with an analysis that is thorough, carefully laid out, and free of theoretical error." The economic story, he wrote, "is a masterpiece that made the Mormon Zion live again for readers all over the world and for generations to come." Second, the amusing comment on style by Richard Etulain, a former Idahoan now a Western literary historian at the University of New Mexico: "Arrington's sentences march across his pages like the orderly field rows of the Arrington farmlands bordering the Snake River."[4]

The local reception of the book was especially interesting. A. William Lund and the Church Historian's Office viewed the book as a secular treatment with naturalistic explanations of the people and the times. It did not follow traditional Mormon history, which is typically sprinkled with supernatural explanations. Although I received complimentary letters from leaders such as John A. Widtsoe, G. Homer Durham, and even Ezra Taft Benson, Lund decided if it wasn't pro-Mormon it must be anti, so he put a little letter *a* on the index card for the book in the Church Historian's Office. That label remained until I was appointed church historian in 1972. At the request of Howard Hunter, a new card was inserted without the *a*. At that time President Harold B. Lee assured me that the book was the finest historical work since B. H. Roberts's *Comprehensive History*.

Colleagues used it in Utah history classes: at BYU, Jim Allen; at USAC (converted to Utah State University in 1957), George Ellsworth; at the University of Utah, David Miller. Each independently asked his students to read the book, write a report on it, and, among other things, speculate on whether I was a Mormon. Each of the three professors then reported the students' reactions. About half of the students at each institution thought I was a Mormon and the other half thought I was not because the book was written so dispassionately. I regarded this as a profound compliment. There is a school today that contends that Mormon historians, if they are real Mormons, should so declare their commitment and should engage in what my editor at Alfred Knopf called "cheerleading." I tried not to do that in *Great Basin Kingdom*.

In the fall of 1963, five years after the book was published, I received a telephone call from Edward C. Banfield, a distinguished professor of public administration at Harvard who had just moved to a chair at the University of Pennsylvania. He was in Salt Lake City and wanted to meet me. I was aware that Banfield had spent several months in southern Utah in the late 1930s studying rural life among the Mormons for the Rural Resettlement Administration and had used his book, *The Moral Basis of a Backward Society* (1958), in my class on economic development. When he arrived at our house for dinner it was clear that he wanted to talk about *Great Basin Kingdom*—the background behind the publication, the research, the impetus to write on this topic. He had learned of the book at Harvard and wondered how such an important contribution had come from an obscure professor in Logan. While we were sparring back and forth, me wondering what he really wanted to know but was afraid to ask, Grace called us in to supper. As we sat down, I asked a blessing on the food, expressing appreciation also for the presence of the Banfields. Suddenly, he relaxed, enjoyed the meal, and soon headed back for Salt Lake City. He had come to Logan just to find out if I was a Mormon—and the blessing on the food was a dead giveaway. One of his students, Bob Huefner, now a dean of medical administration at the University of Utah, told me that Banfield had talked with him several times about *Great Basin Kingdom* and had wondered if I was a Mormon. Banfield had spent several months in Italy and had made a detailed study of "Montegrano," a mountain village in southern Italy. He argued that its extreme poverty resulted from the villagers' lack of collaboration to better their circumstances. He reported that he had been struck with the contrast between "Montegrano" and the equally large community of St. George, Utah, where, with far scantier natural resources at their disposal, the Mormon settlers had achieved, through mutual aid and self-government, one of the most highly organized societies in the West.

The same year of the Banfields' visit I received two stirring notices. The first was word that *Great Basin Kingdom* had been placed in the president's library in the White House, the only book dealing with the history of the Mountain West and one of only four books on the history of the American West. The second was an invitation from the University of Texas to give two lectures on the Mormons in its television series of addresses on the history of American civilization. The Ford Foundation had agreed to finance the series; Walter Prescott Webb, that grand old man of American history, was the director and had invited such people as Arnold Toynbee, Richard Hofstadter, Arthur Schlesinger, Samuel Eliot Morrison, Dumas Malone, C. Vann Woodward, Allan Nevins, Arthur Link, Henry Steel Commager, and Samuel Flagg Bemis to participate. I chose to speak on the significant place of Mormons in American history and on cooperation in Mormon communities. The series was widely used in university classes. Many young historians, in seeing my nametag at historical conventions, have said they saw me in this series. A follow-up to these lectures was the invitation to give the annual luncheon address to the Pacific Coast Branch of the American Historical Association, held at UCLA in 1964.

All copies of *Great Basin Kingdom* were sold by 1965. The University of Nebraska Press then reprinted the book eight times in its Bison paperback series. When those books were sold, the University of Utah Press issued a second edition in 1993.

## Fulbright Professorship in Italy

While I was at the Huntington Library working on *Great Basin Kingdom* (and other pieces subsequently published in the *Huntington Library Quarterly*), I met Andrew Rolle, a young professor at Occidental College, who had enjoyed a Fulbright Professorship in Italy. When he learned of my experiences in Italy during World War II and my knowledge of Italian, he encouraged me to apply for a Fulbright. I had known nothing of the program, but after talking it over with Grace I applied and was awarded a Fulbright Professorship of American Economics at the University of Genova for the academic year 1958–59. In Italy I wrote out in English the lectures for my economic history class and had the help of my graduate assistant, Giuseppe Felloni, in putting them into suitable Italian. The lectures were then published by a local bookstore under the title *Introduzione alla Storia Economica degli Stati Uniti* (Introduction to the economic history of the United States). Upon learning that I could handle Italian well, the local United States Information Service arranged for me to deliver lectures throughout the nation, at universities, for Italian-American groups, at town meetings, and at business fairs. Some of these addresses were published in local newspapers and in university and business periodicals.

Although they knew no Italian at the outset, our boys went to the Giano Grillo public school; James was in the fourth grade, Carl in the second. Both of them did well with the language and made good friends. Susan, only four, stayed home with Grace and her mother, Nina Fort, who spent the year with us. We had one month in Perugia, one month in Rome, two weeks in Germany and Switzerland, and the remainder of the year in Genova and traveling. One nice result of the year was that Grace learned to prepare several tasty Italian dishes, which she served often. The boys enjoyed a certain notoriety when they returned to their Logan school.

During our Fulbright year abroad, *Great Basin Kingdom* was published, and so I was not on hand when the book came out in the United States. There were no autograph parties. Upon our return from Italy in the summer of 1959, Grace and I received many invitations to speak before groups on Mormon history and our experiences in Italy.

In the summer of 1961 my colleagues in the USU Faculty Association asked me to give the annual faculty honor lecture in the spring of 1962.

Shortly before, I had read a line in Brigham Madsen's article on Utah for the *Encyclopedia Britannica* that mentioned the World War II War Relocation Camp for Japanese Americans at Topaz. I had never heard of it and wanted to know more, so when I received news of the lecture, I determined to make the Topaz camp its topic. I arranged to spend two weeks at the University of California Library in Berkeley, where the War Relocation Authority papers were deposited; I also read everything in the USU library on the subject. In the lecture, entitled "The Price of Prejudice: The Japanese-American Relocation Center at Topaz, Utah, during World War II," I discussed why the nine thousand Japanese Americans, mostly from the Bay Area of San Francisco, were incarcerated, the management of the center, the gradual resettlement of many of the residents in interior communities, and the eventual liquidation of the center after V-J Day. The lecture was published and distributed widely by the Faculty Association and later reprinted by the Japanese-American Citizens League of Salt Lake City and still later translated into Japanese and published in Japan. This study brought enormous personal pleasure and much community recognition.

Grace had some money she had saved from her earnings and the supplement the government sent her out of my small salary during World War II. Together with a bank loan under the G.I. Bill, we had purchased a home in Logan when we moved there in 1946, and we had modernized it. By 1962 we had saved enough to purchase a nearby lot and build a new home. Our well-planned home included an ample dining room, a living room, a kitchen, three bedrooms, and a study upstairs, and a full basement with two apartments downstairs. The building was completed and we moved in January 1963. All our spare time was devoted to working on the yard. Our old home was eventually sold to the Tenth Ward for parking space. With a large new lot, James, Carl, and Susan often had friends over to play.

The publication of *Great Basin Kingdom, The Price of Prejudice,* and of many essays, articles, and monographs in the late 1950s and early 1960s placed me, as my friends would say, among the leaders in the field of western American history. I was a charter member of the Western History Association, which was organized in Santa Fe in 1963. I attended each annual convention and read papers at most of them. In the summer of 1965 Keith Wallentine, public relations officer for Utah-Idaho Sugar Company, asked me to write a jubilee history of the company for publication in 1966. The book was published by the University of Washington Press under the title *Beet Sugar in the West*. In addition I wrote separate narratives of some of the company plants, which were published in *Pacific Northwest Quarterly, Idaho Yesterdays,* and *Utah Historical Quarterly.*

In the spring of 1966, while finishing *Beet Sugar,* I was planning a study of the federal government's role in the economic development of the West. USU had granted me six months' sabbatical and the American Council of Learned Societies had offered another six months' salary. I planned to visit each of the eight mountain states for several weeks to conduct research in its historical and government archives. The study never fully materialized, although I eventually published many articles on the topic.

In the late spring of 1966, just as my sabbatical was about to begin, John Walton Caughey, a professor of history at the University of California at Los Angeles, telephoned. Because he was taking a one-year leave, Caughey wished me to substitute for him at my USU salary plus 10 percent. Caughey, who edited the *Pacific Historical Review,* was the most respected and one of the most productive professors of western American history in the nation. To be asked to stand in for him was a great honor, real recognition in my discipline. I was appointed visiting professor of western history at UCLA, and we lived in Pacific Palisades during the 1966–67 school year. UCLA officials discussed with me the possibility of a permanent appointment, but I decided to return to Logan.

My son James spent his senior year at Palisades High and graduated with a fine scholarship in acting; Carl was active in sports and in academics; Susan did well at Paul Revere Junior High. Both James and Carl attended seminary conducted by Palisades Ward. Grace directed the publication of a cookbook for the Relief Society, and I was the gospel doctrine teacher in Sunday school.

At the October 1967 convention of the Western History Association (WHA) in Tucson, Arizona, I was elected vice president and president-elect, and in the December 1967 convention of the Agricultural History Society in New York City, I was elected vice president and president-elect of that association as well. My presidential address to WHA, meeting in Omaha on October 10, 1969, was entitled "Blessed Damozels: Women in Mormon History," which was subsequently published in *Dialogue: A Journal of Mormon Thought* in 1970. My presidential address to the Agricultural History Society, meeting in Los Angeles on April 17, 1970, was entitled "Western Agriculture and the New Deal," which was subsequently published in *Agricultural History.*

My year as president of WHA was concluded in typical fashion. At the annual banquet, in the Fontenelle Hotel ballroom in Omaha, Sam Arnold, who runs a western shop in Denver, presented to me, the outgoing "head ha'r lifter" of WHA, with the Green River knife used by western trappers and explorers. Sam asked all those attending, perhaps four hundred persons, to stand, lift their glasses, and repeat the "Mountain Man's Toast":

*Here's to the childs what's come afore.*
*An' here's to the pilgrims what comes arter.*
*May yer trails be free of Grizzlies,*
*Yer packs filled with plews,*
*And fat buffler in yer pot! WAUGH!*

The members of the Western History Association wished to develop a scholarly journal, but had been unsuccessful in finding a sponsor among many schools. In the spring of 1969 George Ellsworth, a professor of history, and I approached our USU administration and received tentative approval. We made a formal recommendation, and WHA agreed to the proposal. We estimated that the journal would cost about $50,000 per year, with USU contributing $30,000 and WHA $20,000. In essence, USU would furnish office space and pay the salaries of the editors and editorial staff. WHA would pay for printing and distribution to the three thousand or so members of the association. We felt that, as the incoming WHA president, I would almost certainly be approved as editor; George was not as well-known but would be confirmed as associate editor on my recommendation. Financial arrangements and our editorships were approved by the WHA council and ratified by the general membership in 1969. The first issue of *Western Historical Quarterly* was published in January 1970.

George and I both worked half-time with the *Quarterly* in 1969–70, and I worked one-third time in 1970–71 and 1971–72. The periodical was well received by the association and by the scholarly world. I resigned in 1972 and George Ellsworth, then better known, became editor. *Western Historical Quarterly* is still supported by USU and is well regarded as one of the finest historical journals in America.

Those were busy years for me. The Utah Commission for Higher Education for the year 1969–70 appointed me Distinguished Lecturer for Utah, and I was required to deliver at least one lecture at the University of Utah, Dixie College, the College of Southern Utah, and Weber State College, for which they paid me an honorarium and covered travel expenses. James left on an LDS mission to Brazil in December 1968 and returned in 1970 to become a student at Utah State University. After hitchhiking across southern Canada in the summer of 1970, Carl went on an LDS mission to Bolivia, where he was appointed assistant to the mission president. Susan was editor of *The Grizzly* during her senior year at Logan High, graduating in the spring of 1972. Grace was diagnosed with heart disease and trimmed down some of her activities, but she continued her engagements in the Relief Society and in civic affairs. She directed a successful drive to build a municipal swimming pool.

Other projects also got underway in 1970. Roland Rich Woolley, a prominent Hollywood attorney, asked me to coauthor a biography of his wife's father, Utah Governor William Spry. Woolley had previously asked William Roper, a California writer, to undertake the job but was dissatisfied and wanted me to do some research in Utah and put some substance into the projected volume. He would cover my expenses and pay me for my time. I agreed, employed Tom Alexander to write one of the chapters, and wrote some myself on the basis of research in the Church Archives and in the Utah State Historical Society Archives and Library. Published by the historical society, the book appeared in 1971 under the title *William Spry: Man of Firmness, Governor of Utah*.

Later in the summer of 1970 George Eccles, president of First Security Corporation, and Mason Smith, vice president, asked me to write a history of the corporation, which was approaching its seventy-fifth anniversary. They made a generous grant to USU, and I began direction of the research. I recruited some of my USU students, principally George Daines, to help, and we ultimately completed the 450-page manuscript in 1973. I undertook this as part of my USU position and was not paid separately. In the meantime, however, Marriner Eccles, chairman of the board of First Security, unaware of what George Eccles had done, commissioned Sidney Hyman of the University of Chicago to write a history. Because of Marriner's seniority, Hyman's project was published as the official history. My manuscript was never published, although copies are available in the University of Utah, Brigham Young University, and USU libraries.

The most important of my other assignments during this period were the American West Lecture at the University of Utah in April 1971 entitled "Manipulators of the Mormon Past"; a lecture to the Mormon History Symposium at BYU in May entitled "Centrifugal Tendencies in Mormon History"; and a lecture at the Salt Lake Symposium sponsored by the Junior League on the economic development of the Salt Lake Valley.

Let me add that during these years I was an active and loyal member of Logan Tenth Ward, East Cache Stake, and later an officer of Utah State University Stake. The church had always been precious to me, and I tried to serve in a spirit of obedience, loyalty, integrity, and wisdom. Grace was a counselor in the ward Relief Society and a teacher. Our three children were all active in ward, stake, and school affairs as well as in LDS seminary, and our sons participated in Boy Scouts of America.

Religious growth was an integral part of my intellectual and social development. I enjoyed speaking assignments and seldom declined an opportunity. I prepared and delivered sermons in ward sacrament meetings, at stake conferences, at ward and stake firesides, for chapters of the Daughters of Utah Pioneers and Sons of Utah Pioneers, and for various study groups. There were sermons on special days—religious and patriotic holidays—and at funerals, family reunions, the departure of a missionary, and the release of an official. Many of them dealt with the importance of a proper balance between faith and learning, which provided for some spiritualizing of the intellectual as well as intellectualizing of the spiritual.

Although my experiences in the church were fulfilling, I enjoyed also the quirks among members and leaders. Once a Logan Stake president invited me to speak in his stake priesthood leadership meeting on the Church Welfare Plan. He then proceeded, during the next half hour, to tell me what I should say. Certain that he did not want me to deviate one iota from his instruction, I finally excused myself: "Sorry that I cannot make the appointment; why don't *you* give the talk?"

Further, some Latter-day Saints were less than enthusiastic about my writings and speeches. Ernest Wilkinson, president of Brigham Young University, was respectful of my scholarship and wished to employ me. He made overtures to me frequently after 1956, when I was a visiting professor for the summer school. In 1968 he indicated his desire to appoint me as director of the Institute for Mormon Studies. When he presented the matter to the religion faculty members, they dissented. I was "too much of a humanist." My stake president spoke favorably of me, as did the director of the LDS Institute of Religion in Logan. But the spokesman for the religion faculty insisted that I was "a little left of center," gave undue emphasis to naturalistic explanations, and had a more flexible interpretation of "revelation" than the orthodox one. My "tone" was clearly too "liberal" for a person who would serve as director of the institute.[5] Not wishing to be labeled as a secular humanist or something akin to it, I might have responded, if invited to do so, that I was currently reading Russell Kirk's book *The Conservative Mind* (1960), which suggested that the spiritually stifling doctrines of secular humanism were not the only way of understanding our human potential. One could be intellectually objective without trimming faith to match the dominant thought of the times.

## President David O. McKay

During nearly all of these years the president of the church was David O. McKay. A native of Huntsville, Utah, a lover of horses and fast-driving cars, McKay had been sustained to the Quorum of Twelve Apostles in 1906 and served until 1934 when he became a member of the First Presidency. He remained as a counselor in that body until 1951, when he was sustained as president. Tall, dignified, with wavy white hair and penetrating, smiling, brown eyes, he looked and acted like a prophet. I very much admired him. He was an effective speaker, and I heard him in stake conferences, at college commencements, and at other special occasions. When McKay was of advanced age, the church leased a spacious apartment on the southeast corner of the eighth floor of the Hotel Utah as a home for the McKays. One morning McKay, returning from a meeting in the temple, stepped into the elevator, and just after him went a man with his young son. Delighted to see the president, the man said, "James, this is President David O. McKay, our beloved prophet. This may be your last chance to meet him; he's a very old man." (The president was 94.) President McKay grinned and said, "Don't be alarmed at my future, son. Very few men die at age 94."[6]

McKay, a strong believer in education, refused to sanction Joseph Fielding Smith's extreme anti-evolution views, expressed admiration for liberal-thinking Mormon philosophers William H. Chamberlain and Sterling McMurrin, thought science blended beautifully with Mormonism, and encouraged freedom of opinion and speech. Although, as one of his sons told me, he was sometimes "arrogant" and subject to "toadyism," we always saw him with a big smile and a saving sense of humor; he had a benevolent spirit and a tolerant attitude toward creative Mormon intellectuals. Some of his sermons and personal declarations acknowledged and affirmed intellectual diversity. A good friend related an experience with McKay at a reception. In a moment of courage, the hostess served rum cake. All the guests hesitated, watching to see what McKay would do. He smacked his lips and began to eat. One guest gushed, "But President McKay, don't you know that is rum cake?" McKay smiled and reminded the guest that the Word of Wisdom forbade drinking alcohol, not eating it.

I listened carefully to his sermons and believed him to be an excellent role model—a splendid exemplar of the teaching that "the glory of God is intelligence" (Doctrine and Covenants 93:36), a motto especially popular during his presidency. Above all, his talks were well organized, impressively delivered, full of substance, and resonant with sound advice and gems of inspiration. McKay represented, for me, the "voice of gladness" spoken of in the Doctrine and Covenants—a "voice of mercy from heaven; and a voice of truth out of the earth" (128:19). He was a true prophet. When he talked, as Laurel Thatcher Ulrich has written, there was "an infusion of the Spirit, a kind of Pentecost that for a moment dissolved the boundaries between heaven and earth and between present and past . . . a re-experiencing of the events [that happened to] the early Saints."[7]

## Notes

1. Thomas Carlyle, *Past and Present,* book 3, chap. 11, as given in *The Oxford Dictionary of Quotations* (London: Oxford University Press, 1941), 81.

2. See Leonard J. Arrington, "George S. Tanner: A Teaching Pioneer," in *Teachers Who Touch Lives,* ed. Philip L. Barlow (Bountiful, Utah: Horizon Publishers, 1988), 78–91.

3. Latter-day Saints believe that the Holy Ghost is a third person in the godhead. Having been overcome by this special awe-inspiring manifestation, I was quick to remember the blessings that came to those who had received the gift of the Holy Ghost. As a member of the Quorum of Twelve Apostles Parley P. Pratt had written in 1855: "The gift of the Holy Ghost . . . quickens all the intellectual faculties, increases, enlarges, expands, and purifies all the natural passions and affections, and adapts them, by the gift of wisdom, to their lawful use. It inspires, develops, cultivates, and matures all the fine-toned sympathies, joys, tastes, kindred feelings, and affections of our nature. It inspires virtue, kindness, goodness, tenderness, gentleness, and charity. It develops beauty of person, form, and features. It tends to health, vigor, animation, and social feeling. It invigorates all the faculties of the physical and intellectual man. It strengthens and gives tone to the nerves. In short, it is, as it were, marrow to the bone, joy to the heart, light to the eyes, music to the ears, and life to the whole being." Parley P. Pratt, *Key to the Science of Theology* (Liverpool, 1855), 61.

4. Jonathan Hughes, "*Great Basin Kingdom* after Thirty Years," in *Great Basin Kingdom Revisited: Contemporary Perspectives,* ed. Thomas G. Alexander (Logan: Utah State University Press, 1991), 104–5, 107; Richard W. Etulain, "Re-Visioning the Mormons: *Great Basin Kingdom* as Historical Literature," in *Great Basin Kingdom Revisited,* 48.

5. Ernest Wilkinson to Daniel Ludlow, Feb. 19, 1968, and LaMar Berrett, "Statement," no date, both in Manuscripts Division, Harold B. Lee Library, Brigham Young University, Provo.

6. Leonard J. Arrington and Heidi S. Swinton, *The Hotel: Salt Lake's Classy Lady: The Hotel Utah, 1911–1986* (Salt Lake City: Westin Hotel Utah, 1986), 56.

7. Laurel Thatcher Ulrich, "Lusterware," in *A Thoughtful Faith: Essays on Belief by Mormon Scholars,* ed. Philip L. Barlow (Centerville, Utah: Canon Press, 1986), 203.

# 3

# Counselor in the Utah State University Stake

The duty of the elders . . . [is] to teach, expound, exhort, baptize, and
watch over the church; and take the lead of all meetings.
  —Doctrine and Covenants 20:38–44

WHEN I WENT TO the University of North Carolina to pursue a graduate
course in economics in 1939, there were no Latter-day Saints in Chapel
Hill, so I attended the local Presbyterian church—the church in which my
graduate advisor, Milton Heath, was an elder. After appropriate inquiries, I found that a Mormon branch, with about fifty members, held services in Durham, thirty-five miles away. I later learned that my father had
organized that branch in 1925 when he was a missionary there. I did not
have a car, so I took a bus each Sunday, attended Sunday school, usually
ate lunch with a member family, went to sacrament meeting, and then returned to Chapel Hill. When I moved to Raleigh in January 1941 to serve
as a substitute instructor at North Carolina State for an ill professor, I
learned that missionaries had just organized a Sunday school in Raleigh,
which met in the third story of the Independent Order of Odd Fellows Hall.
Two missionaries and two families of members were in attendance. We met
regularly and added a Sunday sacrament service as well. In the fall of 1941
three Latter-day Saint graduates of Brigham Young University, each married with small children, arrived to complete their doctorates. They not
only added to our Sunday school and sacrament meetings but their presence allowed us to hold Mutual Improvement Association meetings each
Tuesday evening as well. Because they were heavily involved in course
work, the students asked me to give the lessons, which I was glad to do.
We did not have any manuals from Salt Lake City, so we prepared our own
lesson outlines. By the spring of 1942 a missionary with authority organized the Raleigh Branch, with me as the president, and I served as branch
president until I was inducted into the army in March 1943. There were

perhaps thirty members and perhaps a dozen interested friends. Some of the members were connected with the university; others were business people from town or from neighboring villages.

My duties as branch president required me, with my two counselors, to arrange for and supervise baptisms of new members, hold funerals, arrange programs and preside at sacrament meetings, appoint teachers for Sunday school and Mutual, report tithing, conduct home teaching, and in other ways represent the church. Although there is now a significant Mormon presence in Raleigh, it seemed a hotbed of anti-Mormonism at the time. I and another LDS professor at the university were told by our deans to be as innocuous as possible. And the women's club where we met told us to rent elsewhere. But our little group was happy, loyal, and faithful.

I was never aware of any Latter-day Saint meeting held overseas during the time I was with the army. Upon my discharge in January 1946, I attended the Raleigh LDS Branch briefly before joining the economics department of USAC in the summer of 1946.

As a new member of the Logan Tenth Ward, East Cache Stake, I was sustained as president of the Young Men's Mutual Improvement Association, an assignment that I very much enjoyed for three years. The Young Women's president and I sponsored dances, parties, classes, musicals, talent shows, and speech contests. Grace was a popular counselor in the Tenth Ward Relief Society presidency. Grace and I were released when we went to North Carolina for the 1949–50 school year. Upon our return to Logan in the summer of 1950, the East Cache Stake presidency and First Council of the Seventy in Salt Lake City appointed me to serve as one of the seven presidents of the 368th Quorum of the Seventy. Because of the release of some of the presidents to hold other positions, I became senior president in 1952 and held that position until I went to Italy in 1958. As Seventies, we conducted missionary work, held dinners and parties, taught classes, and held Sunday afternoon quorum meetings once a month. It was a pleasure to work closely with some splendid local residents and students. Grace continued to be active in the Tenth Ward Relief Society.

After our return to Logan in 1959, I was set apart to be a member of the Utah State University Stake High Council. The stake included both married and single students. At the end of World War II, American college campuses, including USAC, were flooded with young veterans. Their presence at the university was to a large extent the result of the passage of the G.I. Bill, which guaranteed military personnel a year of education for ninety days service, plus one month for each month of active duty, for a maximum of forty-eight months. Tuition, fees, books, and supplies up to $500 a year were paid directly to the college or university. Single veterans were given

$50 a month subsistence pay; married veterans, $75 a month. Enrollment at Utah State doubled. There were not enough beds, teachers, classrooms, and laboratories. The college brought in Quonset huts and surplus barracks for single students and set up a trailer camp on the north side of the campus for married students. The East Cache Stake also secured a Quonset hut and organized the Canyon Heights Married Student Branch, which soon became a ward, then two wards. The large influx of single students, both veterans and nonveterans, with a different pattern of life than members of the residential wards, caused local wards and stakes to organize student wards to accommodate them. Student wards had their own rhythm—suspended during the summer and university holidays. With students often away on weekends to visit families and friends, some on missions and some returning, there was heavy turnover in student leadership.

Following a pattern initiated at Brigham Young University in 1956, the church organized Utah State University Stake on April 13, 1958, with Reed Bullen, a Logan radio station owner and state senator, as stake president, with Reynold K. Watkins, a professor of mechanical engineering, and Wendell O. Rich, director of the Logan LDS Institute of Religion, as counselors. After being informed that our family was going to Italy for the year, the new officers asked me to attend the organizational meeting and said they would hold for me one of the twelve positions on the high council until we returned. On September 9, 1959, I was ordained a high priest by Alma Sonne, an assistant to the Quorum of Twelve Apostles, and sustained as a member of the University Stake High Council. In 1961, with the appointment of Reynold K. Watkins to the General Priesthood Committee of the church, Wendell Rich became first counselor and I was called as the second counselor in the presidency, with Reed Bullen continuing as president.

After the organization of the stake in 1958, Bullen had arranged with the university to exchange land east of the campus that was ideal for a student stake center. The site was dedicated in August 1959 by David O. McKay. On that dry-as-dust day, the eighty-six-year-old president was assisted up a plank to an observation platform by Bullen and the president of the university, Daryl Chase. When McKay began his talk he said he was "fit as a fiddle" but had experienced some difficulty getting on the platform because he had to drag two others up with him. Construction began immediately, and the completed Student Stake Center was dedicated on June 3, 1962, by McKay. Designed by Gene Haycock, a brilliantly imaginative Logan architect, the building was strikingly beautiful and has become a community landmark. The gold aluminum roof is thought to be the only one in the church. Bullen had sufficient stature that he was able to clear the design with the Church Building Committee. The center provided two chapels, classrooms, offices, and recreational facilities for the students and their leaders. The two chapels, seating 360 and 400 persons, served four wards. There was a junior Sunday school auditorium with appropriate classrooms. The cultural hall, one of the largest in the church, was designed to accommodate basketball and other indoor sports, dancing, and drama. The hall seated 2,700 persons for large meetings. A kitchen had facilities for serving 600.

In 1960, while the stake center was being constructed, Bullen acquired for the stake ten acres of property on the northeastern edge of the campus. The church then constructed seven dormitories to house LDS students. At the time, these were the only dormitories built by the church on a state university campus except the LDS Institute dormitory built at the University of Idaho in 1930. Completed in 1962, these and the Delta Phi fraternity house on the same property were dedicated as the David O. McKay Student Living Center. Housing was provided for 576 students—72 in each dorm. The dorms, impishly referred to as "Morm Dorms," were named for prominent Latter-day Saint men and women—Snow Hall, for Eliza R. Snow, poet and longtime president of the Relief Society; Wells Hall, for Emmeline B. Wells, longtime editor of the *Woman's Exponent* and later president of the Relief Society; Maughan Hall, for Peter Maughan, pioneer colonizer and presiding bishop in Cache Valley; Rich Hall, for Charles C. Rich, a member of the Quorum of Twelve Apostles and founder of sixteen LDS communities in Bear Lake Valley; Card Hall, for Charles O. Card, who supervised the construction of the Logan Temple, served as president of Cache Valley Stake, and founded Mormon communities in southern Alberta, Canada; Ivins Hall, for Anthony W. Ivins, a member of the church's First Presidency and strong supporter of USAC; and Moyle Hall, for Henry D. Moyle, a member of the First Presidency who had been instrumental in arranging for the recent organization of USU Stake, the construction of the stake center, and construction of the student living center.

Appointed director of housing for the Student Living Center was Jack Nixon, a Logan native who had previously worked in student housing at Brigham Young University. The center was operated by the stake until 1977, when, as part of a divestiture decision, the church turned the facility over to Utah State University. Now called the USU Student Living Center, the names of the halls have been changed to reflect areas in Utah: Wasatch, Davis, Summit, Jones, Morgan, San Juan, and Uintah.

The LDS population grew proportionally with campus growth, and a second stake center with two ward chapels was built immediately south of the student living center. Designed by Sterling Lyon, this was dedicated in 1967 and the Utah State University Second Stake was organized, with

Reynold K. Watkins as president. With the large increases in enrollment at USU in the 1970s and 1980s, a third university stake was organized in 1976, with LaGrande Larsen as president, and a fourth university stake formed in 1989, with Russell Warren as president.

The student stake was a new phenomenon in church government. One had been organized at BYU in 1956, but ours was the first at a state university. Many questions arose. When the Canyon Heights wards were organized in 1946, the first branch presidencies and Relief Society presidencies consisted of advanced graduate students and wives. As they left, we were faced with the prospect of replacing them with younger students. At first, the University Ward bishoprics consisted of a professor or local resident as bishop and two student counselors; in the single wards, with mostly very young men and women, we asked the bishops to choose professors or local residents as counselors. Although half the original stake high council members were students, these were gradually replaced with professors and local residents. When young men were ordained high priests, as had to be done for them to serve on the high council and in bishoprics, they were out of place in the communities where they settled after leaving the university. Since most High Priest Quorums consisted of older men, usually ages forty to eighty-five, this group of men was being confronted with new members who were only twenty-three. Although we faced that problem with members of bishoprics and high councils, we did not have a similar problem in the Relief Society. Those presidencies continued to be students and wives of students. When they moved away, they easily made the transition into a new Relief Society, since everywhere the group consisted of women eighteen and over. The young Relief Society presidencies were wonderful—intelligent, efficient, enthusiastic, devout, and imaginative.

We chose men from wards around Cache Valley to recommend to church headquarters to be bishops. Bullen was well acquainted with Cache Valley people; having been president of the Faculty Association I knew most of the LDS faculty. The proposed bishops needed the approval of the stake president and Salt Lake City officials. Once we had clearance we talked with them and their wives about service in our stake. By and large they enjoyed their work with our student members. They usually chose as their counselors persons they knew who were young professors or administrators at the university or, less often, downtown businessmen or professionals. Most stake presidents were glad to release persons to work in our stakes, but in one case we were turned down by a stake president who said he couldn't approve the man because he was an active Democrat. In only one case did a person we approached turn down the call; he was leaving the next quarter to complete his doctoral degree. Our ward and stake officials were wonderful—faithful, hardworking, loyal, and loved by the students over whom they presided. The wives and children of our bishops and counselors stayed in the local residential wards, and the men paid their tithing and obtained their temple recommends in their local wards. In essence, they served a mission in the university stake. Students were called on church missions by their local bishops, not the university ward bishops.

Single university students who had grown up in Cache Valley and who continued to live at home during college posed a new concern—should they remain in their local wards or should they affiliate with a university ward where they would form new friendships and enter into fellowship with persons of the same age who had similar goals and aspirations? Local wards, of course, did not want to lose their bright young people to the university wards, but we were eventually allowed to encourage students living at home to affiliate with the university wards and stake.

Our stake presidency and high council met each Monday evening, when we discussed relationships with the university, relationships with the town and valley wards and stakes, the appointment of ward and stake officers, appropriate themes for talks we would give, the management of chapels and meetinghouses, the challenges of a growing student population, the unique religious needs of our membership, and the division of responsibilities for various church programs. Because he was a state senator, Bullen was absent for approximately three months of each year, and Wendell Rich and I took care of various assignments he left with us. We interviewed hundreds of young men who were ready to be ordained elders, many couples who were to be married in the temple (93 percent of our student members were married in the temple), and persons being called to ward and stake positions. In these interviews I became close to many students and their spouses; some of them are still friends. We visited ward meetings each Sunday, usually with a speaking opportunity, whether in Sunday school, Relief Society meeting, Elders' Quorum, or sacrament service. We went to the Logan Temple monthly, held occasional dinners for the leadership and spouses, and had stake family meetings and stake priesthood meetings once a month, and, of course, stake conferences every three months. We were always blessed with a visiting general authority for each of our conferences, and they gave us good instruction. Among those who visited were Joseph Fielding Smith, Henry D. Moyle, and N. Eldon Tanner of the First Presidency; Boyd K. Packer of the Quorum of Twelve Apostles; S. Dilworth Young, Bruce R. McConkie, Marion D. Hanks, and Paul H. Dunn of the Seventy; and John Longden, Thorpe B. Isaacson, Theodore M. Burton, and Alvin R. Dyer, assistants to the Twelve.

Sometimes we entertained general authorities in the university cafeteria and sometimes in a downtown restaurant, but usually with meals in one of our homes. I remember a breakfast for Joseph Fielding Smith and Jessie Evans Smith. As we sat around the table, Bullen's teenage daughter came around to get our orders for drinks—did we want postum, hot chocolate, milk, or water? Jessie responded that she would like coffee. This threw the girl into a tailspin; she went out and reported to her mother, who promptly sent her back. When the girl asked for clarification Jessie acknowledged that although she'd like to have coffee, she also knew she wasn't allowed to drink it. She opted for postum instead.

Jessie injected her personality into our conference, endearing her (and her husband) to our student congregation. Jessie was a famed operatic contralto and member of the Mormon Tabernacle Choir. She was not only a lovely singer but also a vivacious and jovial personality. Knowing that her husband was viewed as a solemn and stern scripturian at the pulpit, Jessie wanted the students to see his human side. During our conference session, Joseph Fielding leaned over to Bullen and instructed him to inform the session that that Jessie would speak for a few minutes. Jessie made as if to glower at him, then smiled, and went to the pulpit to tell about her experiences—of her early desire to be a singer and how she decided to come home to be with the Saints in Salt Lake City. Among other things, she became Salt Lake County Democratic executive secretary. After a whisper from Joseph Fielding Smith, Bullen then announced that Jessie would sing a couple of songs; Jessie accused Joseph Fielding of pulling rank on her and now she was going to pull rank on him. She went over, pretended that she was grabbing him by the ear, and pressed him into singing with her. So they sang a couple of duets, and she remarked to the students between the numbers, "You see how I get even with him!" The students loved them.

We did not have a Mutual Improvement Association program—we felt the dormitories, sororities, and fraternities and the LDS Institute of Religion maintained programs that would take its place. We strongly encouraged students to take classes at the institute and participate in its social programs and were pleased with the high proportion who followed this advice. Even before the family home evening program was launched by the church, the LDS students, encouraged by the stake, met as groups once a week, often with an invited speaker, to discuss the gospel. The Sunday school, priesthood, and Relief Society classes in university wards were wonderful, and the sacrament meeting talks were surely among the best in the church. Home teaching was willingly done, as elders met with men and women students in their rooms or other agreed-upon locations. By and large our wards and stake and their activities were well respected on campus. There was no significant anti-Mormon feeling at USU.

As a member of the stake presidency, I was required to interview each young man recommended to be ordained an elder—a position in the Melchizedek priesthood. The church had a set number of questions I should ask: Are you honest? Are you moral? Do you obey the Word of Wisdom? Do you pay tithing? Do you support the leaders of the church? In one interview, the young man answered all these questions affirmatively and I was about to sign an approval. Then I paused to ask if he had problems with any doctrine or procedure in the church. The young man suddenly became very earnest: "There is just one thing that bothers me," he said. "I am not really sure there is a God."

At Bullen's suggestion, my talks were "spiritual" and at the same time analytical treatments of issues vital to questioning college students. Bullen's talks usually focused on personal behavior and Rich's on doctrine. Some of my sermons were written out; others consisted of notes and outlines and scriptural references. To avoid duplication I kept nearly all of them. There were sermons for weddings, missionary farewells and missionary returns, installations of bishops and Relief Society presidents, and organization of new wards. There were sermons given on special days: New Year's Day, Valentine's Day, Easter, Mother's Day, Father's Day, Independence Day, Pioneer Day, Columbus Day, Thanksgiving Day, and Christmas. At Bullen's suggestion there were sermons on the Church Welfare Program, the history of Sunday school and Relief Society, the importance of priesthood and home teaching, how to teach a lesson effectively, and the blessings of temple marriage. Finally, there were messages delivered at each of the stake conferences—three per year. Some of the talks represent, as Bullen intended they should, a kind of intellectualization of the gospel. They were redeemed from tedious intellectualism by generous amounts of human drama—stories about Joseph Smith and Brigham Young, David O. McKay and Belle Spafford, George Washington and Abraham Lincoln, Clara Barton and Helen Keller, Winston Churchill and Christian X of Denmark, and my own experiences as a boy, soldier overseas, and graduate student in North Carolina. My talks often included poetry, scriptural quotations, historical incidents, and stories of personal experience, and I encouraged students to make religion, morality, and church activity a part of their college experience. I gave one memorable sermon at the end of a long afternoon session of stake conference when each designated speaker had taken more time than allotted. For some reason that I do not now remember, the general authority had spoken first, not last. The time was up but Bullen, out of loyalty, called on me for concluding remarks. I had a prepared talk but I left it in my coat pocket. "The gospel is true," I said, "and we will all be blessed by living as we should. Amen." There was a short prayer, and the conference was over. Few dared tell me they liked my sermon best.

Using scripture and quotations from church leaders; logic and writings of philosophers, novelists, and poets; and personal experiences I usually emphasized one or more of the following points:

1. The gospel expects us to study and learn.
2. Depth in learning will increase your attachment to the church and will build your testimony.
3. The gospel embraces true principles, whether they come from science, philosophy, literature, or revelation.
4. The gospel includes both intellectual and spiritual truths—truths of the mind, body, and heart.
5. Because modern university instruction does not include much about religion and morality, we must make up for that lack by individual study, by learning together in Sunday school classes, by participation in worship services, and by frequenting the LDS Institute of Religion.
6. We must strive for balance in our lives—balancing intellectual, social, physical, and spiritual attainments.
7. We are all part of a great family and we must treat each other as brothers and sisters. We must share our talents, our knowledge, our time, and our hearts with our brothers and sisters.

One natural catastrophe early in the life of our stake brought disaster to some of our married students. On Sunday evening, October 8, 1961, a strong wind began to blow west over the campus from Logan Canyon. The trailers in our Tenth Ward were threatened. Charles L. Kleinman, the young bishop of the ward, and Sid Smith, the trailer park manager, mobilized teams to move the occupants' car against each trailer and point it away from the wind, so that the car would be a buffer. They worked all night in darkness because the wind had blown down electric poles and lines. By dawn the wind had escalated to hurricane force with gusts of 125 to 140 miles an hour. The wind tore down the tower on the gold-domed stake center, toppled two trailers, and completely blew apart one trailer. The occupants, a young married couple and their new baby, were in bed, and suddenly the walls and roof were gone. They found the baby underneath a mattress, which had protected it from flying debris. The remainder of the trailers were saved but about a dozen were blown off their foundations. Some food supplies were lost and furniture damaged. Two men had slight injuries, but everyone had survived.

A constant danger during the heaviest wind was being struck by flying debris, especially garbage cans and garbage can lids. Early Monday morning, when I heard of the disaster, I drove up to the trailer park. As I headed east, I saw two large garbage cans flying west in the other lane of traffic. If either can had veered into our lane and hit the car, it would surely have totaled it. One trailer park resident told me that a flying garbage can lid had just missed his neck; a few inches closer and it would surely have severed his head from his body.

Early Monday morning Kleinman and Bullen took a pickup truck to the bishop's storehouse in downtown Logan to get food. The caretaker was hesitant—this was an unusual request from a nonresidential ward. Bullen placed a call to a representative at General Welfare headquarters in Salt Lake City, who instructed the man to give Bullen all that he wanted, so they headed back to the park with the load. Under the direction of Gwen Miner, the stake Relief Society president, and Berniece Smith, the Tenth Ward Relief Society president, the women were quickly mobilized and there was breakfast, lunch, and dinner on Monday, and then breakfast and lunch the next day for those who required it. By Tuesday, every student was back in class and every family cared for. Observers were impressed with the effectiveness of church organization in turning a disaster into something other than ruination.

Of the many questions that came up in our stake, one deserves mention, partly because it originated in the same ward. Bishop Kleinman, ever wishing to strengthen spirituality, thought it would help the members to be more aware of the meaning of the Lord's sacrament if he served grape juice instead of water. He thought the symbolism was better. After all, Jesus had served grape juice or wine (scholars are not sure which), and the bishop could find no prohibition against it in church history or scripture. He asked our advice about doing so and we suggested he write the church's scriptural authority, Joseph Fielding Smith. Smith replied by letter saying there were no scriptural objections; he was free to do so if the stake presidency agreed. Our stake presidency deliberated and prayed and told him to go ahead for one sacrament meeting, but we cautioned that the meeting might be attended by visiting parents and others who might think wine was being served and recoil in horror. This, indeed, is what happened and the bishop stopped the practice.

In ordaining me a high priest and setting me apart as a high councilor, and later as a member of the stake presidency, Alma Sonne, a very large man with a very large heart, blessed me that my professional labors as a university teacher, researcher, and writer would not suffer as the result of my stake call, and that, indeed, I would get more professional recognition as I entered into and magnified my church calling. This proved to be true. I say this not to boast but to acknowledge gratitude for Sonne's priesthood power and the blessing he gave us to do greater things in helping to forward the Lord's kingdom on the USU campus.

It is a curious coincidence that the year I was released from the stake presidency to become a visiting professor of western history at the University of California at Los Angeles (1966) was a year of student revolt on many campuses. In Logan I was replaced as second counselor by Reynold K. Watkins, who had previously served as a member of the General Priesthood Committee of the church. In their letter of release, the new stake presidency thanked me for "your willingness to put aside personal interests for the benefit of these students, your acceptance of responsibility, and your pleasant attitude toward students and their spiritual well being." N. Eldon Tanner also sent me a letter in which he took note that I would be conducting an extensive program of research and writing along with my teaching. Because the heart of my studies was concerned with the history of the Latter-day Saints, President Tanner felt inspired to call me on a mission to be a Latter-day Saint historian. "You should consider your LDS history research," he wrote, "equivalent in importance with your assignment the past few years in Utah State University Stake. We commend you for your studies and for your faithfulness."[1]

We rented the home of a professor on leave in Pacific Palisades, and our family soon became active in the school and ward of that community, so near to Malibu and the Pacific Ocean. Grace published a cookbook for the Relief Society, and I served as the gospel doctrine teacher. Although my lectures at UCLA were well received and I was offered permanent employment there, we returned to Logan in the fall of 1967. Bullen placed me on the University Stake High Council again and I worked closely with the Relief Society, Elders' Quorum, and in other programs. I did not see that the USU campus had been affected much by the national youth revolt. LDS influence had not diminished, and USU remained a splendid example of faith and learning.

### Note

1.  Reed Bullen, Wendell O. Rich, and Reynold K. Watkins to Leonard Arrington, Aug. 8, 1966; N. Eldon Tanner to Leonard Arrington, June 15, 1966; copies of both in the Leonard J. Arrington Collection, Special Collections and Archives, Utah State University Libraries, Logan.

# 4

# The Fraternity of Mormon Scholars

Seek ye diligently and teach one another words of wisdom, . . . seek ye
out of the best books words of wisdom, seek learning even by study
and by faith.
    —Doctrine and Covenants 109:7

AT THE ANNUAL CHRISTMAS SOCIAL of the faculty of USAC in 1950
Grace and I met George and Maria Ellsworth. Tall, slender, and friendly,
George had just completed work for the Ph.D. at the University of California at Berkeley and had returned to his alma mater to join the history
department as an assistant professor. Born in 1916, George had graduated in 1941 from USAC, enrolled at Berkeley, joined the Army Air Force,
and eventually became a chaplain in the Philippines. After the war he completed work at Berkeley with a brilliant study of Mormon missionary activity to 1860. It was with enormous pleasure and excitement that I met
for the first time this person with whom I would share so many interests.
Above all, here was a person who knew the sources and literature of
Mormon history and had studied early Mormon history in depth. He also
had perfected the historian's craft and could tell me about footnotes, quotations, paragraphing, and all the paraphernalia of scholarship. He was a
great teacher and a warm friend.

We learned that Eugene Campbell would soon join us. A former army
chaplain in Europe, Campbell was completing a Ph.D. at the University
of Southern California with a dissertation on the history of the LDS Church
in California and would serve on the staff of the LDS Institute in Logan.
Another kindred soul at the Logan Institute was Wendell Rich, who had
completed an Ed.D. at USAC in educational philosophy and was a descendant of member of the Twelve Charles C. Rich. The four of us and our spouses
formed a church history circle, meeting once a month at each other's
homes and presenting papers on LDS history and culture. These were stimulating events both intellectually and spiritually. I still have copies of papers that were delivered at these sessions, some of which were published

later. Soon we broadened our associations to include persons interested in Mormon history and culture at other universities, some of whom belonged to separate study groups and invited us to make presentations. In this way we became acquainted with the studies of scholars at BYU, the University of Utah, and special visitors from other universities.

As a part of my training I took two graduate seminars in historical method from Ellsworth, who gave us instruction in the proper use of sources and the need for substantiating any conflicting evidence. He taught us to be acutely aware of the limitations of historical research: the paucity of and incompleteness of records, the selectivity inherent in the writing of history, the fallibility and subjectivity of the writer, and thus the imperfect, tentative, and partial nature of every historical study. But he also praised historians for their strenuous efforts to curb and control these deficiencies and try to be as objective as possible—to strive for accuracy, veracity, and impartiality. There was a commitment to truth, knowledge, and objectivity. In writing my dissertation and in preparing articles for submission to professional journals I drew upon this instruction.

There were other occasions when I met and exchanged findings and interpretations with other scholars working on Mormon topics: the semi-annual meetings of the Utah Academy of Sciences, Arts, and Letters; the annual conventions of the American Historical Association, the Organization of American Historians, and the Pacific Coast Branch of the American Historical Association; and the monthly meetings of the Cache Valley Historical Society and the annual meetings of the Utah State Historical Society. All of us in the field occasionally wrote historical articles for outside or national professional journals, for the church's *Improvement Era,* and for the *Utah Historical Quarterly,* which was resumed in 1952 after a lapse of many years. At the national meetings I even became acquainted with Robert Flanders, leading historian of the Reorganized Church of Jesus Christ of Latter Day Saints in Independence, Missouri. He was a professor at Graceland College—the RLDS equivalent of BYU. Through him I met other RLDS historians and church officers.

A challenging assignment came in 1955 when a group of us at USAC were asked to prepare chapters for a centennial history of Cache Valley, to be completed the following year. From the church historian's collection of ward and stake records, Works Progress Administration surveys and papers, and the extensive collection in the USAC library, nine of us contributed seventeen chapters on the development of the valley. I covered economic development from the pioneer era to 1956 in four chapters entitled "Life and Labor among the Pioneers," "Railroad Building and Cooperatives 1869–1879," "Transition to the Modern Era 1890–1910," and

"Economy in the Modern Era," which included developments during the depression of the 1930s. My colleagues and I had made an exhaustive search for sources, and the Cache Valley story was told without prejudice or partiality, with a wealth of colorful detail about the early settlements. The book won an Award of Merit from the American Association for State and Local History and was praised in critical reviews. This was a labor of love—there was no compensation.

The recognition that had followed the publication of *Great Basin Kingdom* induced the University Research Council at USU to grant me an annual appropriation to support my continuing research. This would pay for secretarial help, supplies, research assistants, research travel, and conventions. The move was somewhat precedent shattering: the university, in addition to its federally supported agricultural research, had previously supported research in the physical and biological sciences but not in economics or history. My university research project was one of the first created after the research council was formally instituted. In the next few years I undertook the following projects:

1. Studies in Utah economic history: mining, railroads, banks, colonization, and irrigation.
2. Studies of Utah's defense industry: missiles and air force, naval supply, and Defense Department installations.
3. Studies of Utah reclamation projects.
4. Studies of World War II defense-related industries: Geneva Steel, Small Arms Ammunition Plant in Salt Lake City, and other enterprises.
5. Studies of the sugar beet industry.
6. Studies of the changing economic structure of the Mountain West based on census and other data.
7. Studies of the Japanese-American Relocation Center at Topaz during World War II.
8. Studies of the history of USAC during its first seventy-five years.

All of these resulted in thirty or forty books, monographs, pamphlets, and articles in professional journals. When I made substantial use of material researched by a graduate assistant, I listed his or her name as coauthor; in this way I became acquainted with many young scholars, including Thomas G. Alexander, F. Ross Peterson, James B. Allen, D. Michael Quinn, Jon Haupt, Wayne K. Hinton, Richard L. Jensen, Gene A. Sessions, George Jensen, and Richard E. Bennett.

Some of us in the field of Mormon studies discussed the founding of a journal of Mormon history, even toying with possible names for the journal such as "Latter-day Saint Quarterly," "LDS Historical Review," or "Journal of Mormon History." These discussions were temporarily ended by the creation of *BYU Studies* in 1959. Although the first editors of *BYU Studies* were anxious to print sound historical essays, we were startled when an interpretive article I wrote for the first issue, as I learned from BYU president Ernest L. Wilkinson, created such opposition from Elder Mark Petersen of the Twelve that the journal was suspended for a year.

The offending article was entitled "An Economic Interpretation of the 'Word of Wisdom.'" In reviewing the history of the revelation, I suggested that many Latter-day Saint pioneers regarded the revelation as a piece of good advice but not prohibitory. Some officers and members felt free to drink an occasional glass of wine, chew tobacco when teeth were aching, and sip a cup of tea. I quoted from Brigham Young's kindly but disapproving remarks about tobacco in the Old Tabernacle on March 10, 1861:

> Many of the brethren chew tobacco, and I have advised them to be modest about it. Do not take out a whole plug of tobacco in meeting before the eyes of the congregation, and cut off a long slice and put it in your mouth, to the annoyance of everybody around. Do not glory in this disgraceful practice. If you must use tobacco, put a small portion in your mouth when no person sees you, and be careful that no one sees you chew it. I do not charge you with sin. You have the "Word of Wisdom." Read it. Some say, "Oh, as I do in private, so I do in public, and I am not ashamed of it." It is, at least, disgraceful. . . . Some men will go into a clean and beautifully-furnished parlour with tobacco in their mouths, and feel, "I ask no odds." I would advise such men to be more modest, and not spit upon the carpets and furniture, but step to the door, and be careful not to let any person see you spit; or, what is better, omit chewing until you have an opportunity to do so without offending. . . . We request all addicted to this practice, to omit it while in this house [the tabernacle]. Elders of Israel, if you must chew tobacco, omit it while in meeting, and when you leave, you can take a double portion, if you wish to.[1]

Apparently, the reference was correct, but the quote was better forgotten. I should have learned a lesson from this.

The dullest meetings facing Utah educators were the annual September sessions of the Utah Conference on Higher Education. At these sessions administrators from Brigham Young University, the University of Utah, Utah State University, and the various junior colleges in the state harangued us on administrative problems and policies. In anticipation of the conference to be held on September 9, 1965, at Logan, a group of us decided to hold our own "rump session" to discuss the formation of a Mormon history association. Ellsworth, Campbell, Rich, and I arranged the meeting. We had strong letters of support from Davis Bitton and John Sorenson, both then in Santa Barbara, California. We also had verbal support from several scholars at prestigious national universities, as well as from many at BYU and elsewhere in Utah. We had acquired helpful information about the American Catholic Historical Association and the Jewish Historical Society.

The fourteen persons at the meeting decided to organize. After some discussion of alternative names—Organization of Mormon Historians, LDS History Association, and Mormon History Association—we voted for the latter. We appointed Eugene Campbell to draft a constitution, asked Thomas Alexander to arrange a time and place for us to meet in connection with the annual meeting of the American Historical Association in San Francisco that year, and appointed a nominating committee chairman. The group asked that I serve as a focus for communications and that all who were interested in joining send one dollar for costs of mailing newsletters. Richard Bushman and James Allen were asked to arrange for a program, and Stanford Cazier agreed to coordinate transportation to take advantage of group rates for ourselves and spouses to and from San Francisco.

Approximately eighty persons attended our first meeting, held December 28 in the Monterey Room of the Sir Francis Drake Hotel in San Francisco, including five or six from other disciplines as well as history. As temporary chairman I conducted the meeting and asked each of the committees to report. The proposed name of the association was accepted, a constitution was adopted, and the following officers were unanimously elected:
President: Leonard J. Arrington, Utah State University
First Vice President: Eugene E. Campbell, Brigham Young University
Second Vice President: James L. Clayton, University of Utah
Secretary Treasurer: Dello G. Dayton, Weber State College
Council Members: Alfred Bush, Princeton University
　　　　　　　　　Robert Flanders, Graceland College
　　　　　　　　　Davis Bitton, University of California at Santa Barbara
　　　　　　　　　Merle Wells, Idaho State Historical Society
Our association agreed to support *Dialogue: A Journal of Mormon Thought* that was being launched by an LDS group at Stanford. Richard Bushman led a discussion of projects and programs for the association, including the preparation of a history of the church for the sesquicentennial. We also listened to a panel, consisting of James B. Allen, Ralph Hansen, and Klaus Hansen, discuss writing Mormon history. A major goal of the association, agreed upon by all, was to include Reorganized LDS members, non-Mormons, lapsed Mormons, and persons who were not professional historians.

We agreed to meet at each annual meeting of the Pacific Coast Branch of AHA and to hold smaller sessions at meetings of the Western History Association and the Organization of American Historians.

Subsequent newsletters invited the submission of articles to be published in the Mormon History Association (MHA) issue of *Dialogue* (Autumn 1966); informed members of get-togethers at professional meetings; and announced that eighty charter members had paid their dues by February 1, 1966, of which two were Reorganized Church historians (Richard Howard and Robert Flanders) and three were non-Mormons (Merle Wells, Jan Shipps, and Philip A. M. Taylor). The memberships included a liberal sprinkling of professors outside of Utah, LDS Institute instructors, and persons not affiliated with academic or archival institutions (e.g., Juanita Brooks, David L. Wilkinson, and Ward Forman). Indicative of the important role women would play in the organization, five women were charter members. The roster of members included persons living in all sections of the United States and at least two in foreign countries. Some were professors or students specializing in western American history. Others were in ancient, medieval, modern European, Latin American, and American history and in such other fields as literature, economics, sociology, and anthropology. Amateurs who wished to deepen their understanding of Mormon history and to support the various undertakings of the association also joined.

In the three years that followed, MHA held its annual meeting in August in association with conventions of the Pacific Coast Branch. In 1970 the official meeting was in Los Angeles during the April meetings of the Organization of American Historians. In 1971 the business meeting was held in October in Santa Fe, in connection with the convention of the Western History Association. During these years meetings were also held in association with the Organization of American Historians in April, Pacific Coast Branch in August, Western History Association in October, and American Historical Association in December.

Finally, in 1972, with a membership of three hundred, the officers decided to hold three-day conventions in the spring in chosen settings separate from other historical organizations. The flowering of scholarship was such that there were dozens of persons to present papers and hundreds of interested nonprofessional historians to hear them. This move also coincided with the creation of the LDS Historical Department and the appointment of a group of professional historians to do sponsored research, writing, and publication in the field of Mormon history.

Since 1972 the custom has been for MHA to hold meetings one year in a historic Mormon setting (Palmyra, Kirtland, Nauvoo, Lamoni, Independence, and Winter Quarters) and the next year in the Far West (Logan, St. George, Rexburg, Ogden, Provo, Salt Lake City). Officers have conscientiously sent out newsletters, arranged programs, and conducted other business appropriate for the association. In 1974 the organization, with almost one thousand members, confidently announced the beginning of the annual publication of the *Journal of Mormon History*. In addition to MHA business and announcements, the journal has contained papers presented in the annual meeting and other submitted articles. Beginning in 1992, two issues have been published each year.

If one of the purposes of MHA was to stimulate research and the exchange of ideas among historians, the organization has been remarkably successful. The number of papers presented at our meetings now runs into the hundreds, and many of these have been published in refereed journals. The number of persons who attend the annual MHA conventions now exceeds five hundred.

In addition to the contributions that went to *Dialogue,* professional historical journals, and other outlets, we Mormon historians sought to use our influence in opening up materials on Mormon history in the Church Archives. We also attempted to use our influence in getting good scholarly articles submitted to and published in the *Improvement Era* and, later, *The Ensign.* We held a series of meetings with Jay Todd, managing editor, toward this goal, and these were to some extent successful. We attempted to stimulate good research and writing by awarding prizes to persons who wrote the best books and articles on Mormon history.

In 1977, I think, the year we met in Ogden, the dean of BYU's College of Religious Instruction presented a paper that was subjected to the usual ritual of a commentator making suggestions for improvement. The dean did not like the commentator's tone. Nor did he like a paper he heard presented in another session by a historian the dean regarded as "lacking testimony." The dean made up his mind to take action. BYU's College of Religious Instruction would no longer support any member of its faculty in attending future meetings of the Mormon History Association. The rule still holds. If any faculty member wishes to attend the MHA convention, and some do, the individual must pay and use vacation time. I wondered whether someone who heard a talk in sacrament meeting he didn't like would discontinue taking his children to meetings in that ward. Or, whether one who had seen an article in *The Ensign* she didn't like would cancel her subscription. I believe it is shortsighted to discourage the attendance of College of Religious Instruction faculty at MHA conventions, because they teach many courses in church history and they, of all people, need to know of new developments in the field.

Contemporaneous with the development of MHA was the initiation of *Dialogue: A Journal of Mormon Thought.* I had been to Washington, D.C., in the spring of 1965 to attend a convention and to conduct research in the National Archives, Franklin Institute, and the Library of Congress. Traveling back by air, I happened to sit next to Eugene England, a young Latter-day Saint poet and teacher, who was returning to Stanford. He told me a group of young Latter-day Saint "intellectuals" were planning to publish a journal, and he asked if I would agree to join Lowell Bennion as an advisory editor. The journal would be an independent publication to deal with Mormon thought and culture and the general relation of religious and secular life by means of articles, essays, reviews, and the presentation of poetry and the visual arts. The journal would be published by the Dialogue Foundation, a nonprofit entity incorporated in Utah. All editorial and staff efforts would be voluntary contributions, as would be the manuscripts and art work. A six-dollar annual subscription fee would cover the costs of printing and mailing. The editorial staff would include Eugene England and Wesley Johnson as managing editors; Paul Salisbury as publication editor; and a score of prominent educators, professionals, and businessmen as directors. Although *Dialogue* was not an official publication of the LDS Church, the editors and associates were committed to the church and its ideals. The aim was to reinforce the sense of community among thinking Mormons, to help Mormon students as they met the challenges of university life, and to demonstrate that scholars need not relinquish their faith to be intellectually respectable, nor relinquish their intelligence to be faithful. Our historical community needed an outlet for our serious historical articles because most historical journals would run articles on Mormon historical topics only rarely.

The first issue of *Dialogue,* which appeared in the spring of 1966, carried as its lead article the paper I gave to the Western History Association in October 1965, "Scholarly Studies of Mormonism in the Twentieth Century." I contributed other articles in subsequent issues and remained an advisory editor for the next five years. As other historians contributed to its pages, it became a major and welcome outlet for Mormon historical scholarship. Partly because of the competition offered by *Dialogue, Brigham Young University Studies,* usually referred to simply as *BYU Studies,* was reinvigorated and began to feature historical articles. An enlarged summer issue, composed primarily of historical articles built around a common theme, has appeared annually since 1969, and "The Historian's Corner," with short articles, notes, and documents of interest to historians, was inaugurated as a regular feature in 1970. In 1974 LDS women in the Boston area founded *Exponent II,* stimulating some scholarship with respect to the role of women in the LDS experience. Two years later a group of young Mormon intellectuals founded *Sunstone,* which also featured Mormon history.

As a counter to the development of these publications, overwhelmingly positive toward the church, other publications stemmed from "career apostates" Jerald Tanner and Sandra Tanner, a couple who have devoted their lives to "exposing" and trying to destroy Mormonism.[2] Reared in a Mormon home of stress, Jerald began questioning the historical consistency of Mormonism as a teenager, was attracted to fundamentalist Protestantism, and began holding evening religious meetings while training in 1958 to be a machinist in Salt Lake City. Sandra McGee, a descendant of Brigham Young who had grown up in the Los Angeles area, attended one of these meetings. After a short courtship, they married. In 1959 they began a lifetime of publishing anti-Mormon tracts, pamphlets, and books, with the intention of embarrassing the church by showing the inconsistencies and changes in Mormonism since its early days. In 1964 Jerald quit his machinist job to devote his full time to anti-Mormon publishing under the name Modern Microfilm Company, renamed the Utah Lighthouse Ministry in 1983. The Tanners also published a flier, the *Salt Lake City Messenger.* The character of the Tanners' writing is suggested by the obtrusive underlining, large capitals, and large capitals with underlining. There are consistent sharp attacks on Joseph Smith and other church leaders.

The Tanners' work—and that of a few others—sometimes created doubts in the minds of church members and provided ammunition for anti-Mormons generally. Tanner publications assumed the worst possible motives of church leaders and judged Mormon beliefs not within the church's framework but in contrast to the normative Christianity that early Mormons rejected. They took quotations and actions out of context, made unwarranted conclusions about activities of leaders faced with complex problems, and were simply not fair as they omitted or twisted evidence to prove that Mormon claims were false and indefensible. Their caustic interpretation of Mormon history was both beguiling and deceptive. Misled by their out-of-context quotations, some Mormon readers saw all unapproved church history as an enemy. This made the independent historian's work suspect. To defend against the distorted depiction of Mormonism, constructive historians had to develop a fuller picture that also showed that the historical understanding of such conservative Mormon works as Joseph Fielding Smith's *Essentials in Church History* was incomplete and out of date. This in turn led some officials to charge historians with disloyalty and irreverence. Fearful of impious and damaging research, Mormon conservatives used the work of the Tanners as a reason to restrict

access to vital Mormon records, leaving responsible historians with limited access. Few indeed were the historians who were given permission to
use records that had previously been open. The solution to the publication of one-sided views by the Tanners, it seems to me, is not to deny that
their view has *any* basis, but to show the whole picture, to provide context, to show that their view is misleading. The church's history may not
have been unblemished, but it has survived and flourished because its
members understand that any "error" is a minor brush stroke in a very
large painting.

If Mormonism had no redeeming features, as the Tanners have seemed
to think, the faith would not have had the appeal that has made it an as-
tounding success. By means of continuous revelation, new ways have been
defined whereby principles that are eternally valid can be better understood
and expressed in the face of ever-changing circumstances. The Tanners and
others like them have forced the church to face up to "problems" in our
history, acknowledging the inadequacy of a simple, protected view, but they
have also created myths that historians and truth-seekers may never be able
to destroy. There is a danger in being open-minded to error; there is also a
danger in being so zealous in protecting the Saints from new views that
free inquiry is stifled.

## Writing Religious History

The challenge of writing religious history is an old one. The ancient He-
brews incorporated history into their scriptures, the Book of Mormon
prophet Nephi kept a historical as well as a spiritual record, and Luke the
physician is but one historian whose writings were canonized in the Christian New Testament. That the same facts could look quite different when
viewed through various religious glasses was made clear, if it had not been
so before, by the writing of St. Augustine in *City of God*. The monastic
and ecclesiastical histories of the Middle Ages tended to set forth the drama of salvation, while secular histories, when they finally began to appear,
were little more than chronicles or annals of rulers and battles. Histories
of families, guilds, towns, and nations gave emphasis to the political and
economic realities of life but did so with little analysis. Indeed, history was
more a branch of literature than of science. To worshipful and believing
Christians, history was a vast pool from which could be drawn moral lessons, faith-promoting stories, and examples of dedication.

The problem is that facts never speak for themselves. Chronicles and
testimonies and stories mean different things to different people. The inevitability of diverse opinions on the meaning of historical events became

clear in the long path of Christian history. Could the real bearers of the Christian message be, not the successors to the bishop of Rome, but those persecuted by the established church—the Waldensians, for example? This version of "a saving remnant" was picked up by the Reformers in the sixteenth century, and the Reformation brought about a great confrontation of different versions of church history: Catholics vied with Protestants, and Protestants with Protestants. The writers in all camps faced questions about assumptions, about interpreting events, about the metahistorical meaning behind the events. And there were practical, immediate questions. Could the historian really establish without question the dealings of God in the affairs of people? And what did one do with documents that turned out to be spurious, as the techniques of textual criticism were brought to bear? Most early historians felt justified in leaving out anything that did not fit their purposes. Confident of their right to decide the content of their works, historians were positive that God had affirmed the great teaching function of history and that their primary task was to conform to what was consistent with his will.

Long before the restoration of the gospel by Joseph Smith in 1830, therefore, a series of questions about the relationship of history to religion had been raised. Was the primary purpose of such history to be faith-promoting? Should it ignore or leave out items that did not fit the purpose? Should the less than admirable activities of religious leaders be mentioned? What reliance should be placed on interested testimony? Should the archives of churches be open to research? What does one do when anecdotes purveyed by earlier historians, especially if they filled a moral and faith-promoting purpose, lack credence in the light of later examination or contradictory evidence? Are historians well-advised to abandon what they can document only in part and with the greatest difficulty, namely, the spiritual and supernatural, to chronicle mundane topics like changing administrations, the construction of chapels, and the establishment of new congregations? Is it possible for nonbelievers to write accurate and reliable history about a religion? For that matter, is it possible for believers to write accurate and reliable history about their church? And should the denomination paying the piper—employing the historian—call the tune? Every one of these questions had been raised and wrestled with before the founding of the church in 1830.

When the church was organized on April 6, 1830, the Lord commanded, by revelation, that "a record . . . shall be kept among you." In a subsequent revelation the responsibility of the historian was made more explicit: to "write and keep a regular history" (Doctrine and Covenants 21:1, 41:1). At first, Oliver Cowdery was appointed to supervise history-gathering efforts. Because his ecclesiastical responsibilities as second elder and, later, as counselor in the First Presidency, were quite demanding, he was soon replaced by John Whitmer. Although he did compile a short chronicle of early activities, Whitmer was excommunicated for "un-Christianlike conduct," and George W. Robinson was appointed in his stead. When Willard Richards was appointed church historian in 1842, it became an established practice that a member of the Twelve serve as church historian; that tradition continued with few variations as George A. Smith, Wilford Woodruff, Albert Carrington, Orson Pratt, Franklin D. Richards, Anthon H. Lund, Joseph Fielding Smith, and Howard W. Hunter served.

Thus, from the very day of the organization of the church, a church historian was charged with the responsibility of keeping records and writing history. At the same time, at every stage in the history of the church, others—private individuals independent of church headquarters—made contributions to the writing and understanding of LDS history.

The first systematic attempt to prepare an official history of the growing church began in 1839 when Joseph Smith and his clerks and associates began the preparation of a multivolume documentary record called the "History of Joseph Smith." When Joseph Smith was murdered on June 27, 1844, the history was complete only through August 5, 1838. The scribes and clerks continued to assemble material and write in the years that followed.[3]

In the meantime, however, the manuscript was published serially in *Times and Seasons* (1842–46, covering the years 1805–34); *Latter-day Saints' Millennial Star* (1842–45, covering 1805–44); and the *Deseret News* (1851–58, covering 1834–44). The process of preparing the manuscript for publication in a multivolume bound work began in 1900, when George Q. Cannon was assigned by the First Presidency to begin the compilation. After his death in 1901 the task was reassigned to Brigham H. Roberts, who worked from 1906 to 1912. Unfortunately, Roberts entitled the publication *History of the Church of Jesus Christ of Latter-day Saints, Period I: History of Joseph Smith, the Prophet, by Himself,* thus creating a misunderstanding that exists to this day. The entire work was written by church-employed scribes and clerks, using diaries of Joseph Smith and his clerks and associates as well as other documents. Having been instructed to use the pronoun *I* because it was Joseph Smith's history, the clerks continued that practice even after the prophet's death. The history to 1838 presumably benefited from the perusal of the prophet, but the remainder was completed after his death. Roberts' edition even included his own corrections, deletions, and emendations, sometimes without explanation.

After the history was complete through August 8, 1844, the clerks in the office of the president of the church continued it as the "History of Brigham Young." As in the case of the Joseph Smith history, this was an "annals" approach to church history, and documents from a wide variety of sources were used to tell not only the history of Brigham Young but also the history of the church over which he presided. To this date, the only portion of this history, which consists of forty-eight volumes of about one thousand pages each, that has been published is that from 1844 to 1847, issued under the editorship of B. H. Roberts in 1932 as volume 7 of *History of the Church*.[4] Historians hope that additional volumes of the massive Brigham Young history will eventually be edited for publication. The volumes are good historical accounts up to about the year 1858, after which they are more of a scrapbook of information.

The most systematic and professional attempt to collect, preserve, and write LDS history was launched in 1891 with the appointment of Andrew Jenson as assistant church historian. Jenson collected and wrote biographies of the founders and subsequent officers of the church, published as *Latter-day Saint Biographical Encyclopedia*, 4 vols., 1901–36; prepared a highly useful encyclopedia of church history, published in 1941 as *Encyclopedic History of the Church;* directed the preparation of a 700-volume scrapbook record of the day-to-day activities of the church, with excerpts from available sources, both published and unpublished, called the Journal History of the Church; and published numerous articles in professional and church-sponsored periodicals as varied as "Danes on the Isle of Man," "History of the Las Vegas Mission," "Orderville: An Experiment in a Communistic System, Called the 'United Order,'" and "Day by Day with the Utah Pioneers." He also wrote a full history of the Scandinavian Mission, which has stood well the test of time. Jenson's work established the Church Historian's Office as the major preserver and producer of Latter-day Saint history.

During Jenson's lifetime of labor in the Church Historian's Office, other historians, not with church sponsorship but with church cooperation, began to write narratives that were, to some extent, analytical and interpretive. The two principal contributors to Mormon historiography in the nineteenth century were Edward W. Tullidge and Hubert Howe Bancroft. With limited access to documents in the Church Archives, Tullidge wrote *The Life of Brigham Young; or, Utah and Her Founders* (1876); *The Women of Mormondom* (1877); *Life of Joseph the Prophet* (1878); *History of Salt Lake City* (1886); and *History of Northern Utah and Southern Idaho* (1889). These tended to be adulatory and heavily documentary, but they were nevertheless valuable sources for early Utah history and, to a lesser extent, for early Mormon history.

The prominent Western historian and publisher Hubert Howe Bancroft, in his *History of Utah, 1540 to 1886* (1889), told the story of the Mormons during the pre-Utah period as well as the history of Utah after the Mormon settlement. Much of the volume was written by Alfred Bates, one of Bancroft's employees. Bancroft was supplied with a great deal of material by the church and its members, and his interpretation was regarded as generally favorable to the church, with the anti-Mormon allegations carefully couched in the footnotes.

Orson F. Whitney, a member of the Twelve and the assistant church historian, followed in this tradition. His four-volume *History of Utah* (1898–1904), written in sesquipedalian prose, is a compelling narrative of Utah's history, from a Mormon point of view.

During the same years that Whitney served as assistant church historian (1902–6), a colleague of equal rank was Brigham H. Roberts. An old fashioned orator (as was Whitney) with a searching mind and a majestic style, Roberts entered upon the writing of a comprehensive history that would counteract the unfavorable image of Mormonism resulting from the long antipolygamy crusade of the 1880s, the 1899 controversy over his election to the House of Representatives, and the testimony given in the trial of Senator Reed Smoot for seating in the Senate in the early years of this century. Courageous and indefatigable, Roberts wrote a full history that appeared in serial form in the *Americana* magazine from 1909 to 1915. With some updating and additional material, this was published as a six-volume set in connection with the church's centennial observance in 1930 under the title *A Comprehensive History of the Church of Jesus Christ of Latter-day Saints: Century One*. Roberts's work, while still worth reading, is not definitive. Documents since uncovered have rendered some of his interpretations inaccurate, and his preoccupation with the conflict between the church and the federal government along with other personal biases are evident in his reconstruction of a number of critical episodes in Mormon history. Moreover, the volume fails to say much about cultural, social, and economic history and covers incompletely the years after 1915. It is an epic work, appropriate for its time, but hardly satisfactory for modern readers.

While no historian would wish to denigrate or detract from the enormous significance of these histories, it is nevertheless essentially true that "objective," "scholarly," and "systematic" treatises on the Mormons and their culture began in the twentieth century as a product of students' work toward the Ph.D. in history and the social sciences. One notes, in particular, the sociological dissertations of Ephraim Ericksen, Joseph A. Geddes, Lowry Nelson, and Thomas F. O'Dea; the economic history of Feramorz Y. Fox, as well as my own; and the history dissertations of Andrew Love Neff, Leland H. Creer, Joel Ricks, Thomas C. Romney, Milton R. Hunter, Richard D. Poll, S. George Ellsworth, Philip A. M. Taylor, Merle E. Wells, Eugene E. Campbell, Kent Fielding, Warren Jennings, Klaus Hansen, Carmon Hardy, Robert Flanders, and Jan Shipps. In addition are a few other works, such as those of Juanita Brooks, which are as scholarly as these dissertations. Less defensive than the earlier writers, these authors have been fully professional in identifying and using sources, more persistent in seeking additional information, and more willing to advance honest answers to hard questions.

During the 1960s Joseph Fielding Smith, church historian and recorder, recognized the need for a professionalization of the Church Library and Archives and instructed his assistant church historian, Earl Olson, to join and "be active in" professional library and archival societies. Thus began, particularly after 1963, the employment of professional librarians and archivists, the systematic cataloguing of record books and manuscripts, and the planning for adequate facilities in the new Church Office Building, the construction of which was first announced in 1960. When Smith became president of the church in 1970, he appointed Howard Hunter, of the Twelve, as church historian and recorder, with the understanding that Hunter would further these efforts toward professionalization and greater openness. As Hunter's assistant historian, Earl Olson continued to upgrade the Church Historian's Office. Hunter appreciated the growing desire of members and nonmembers for more information about LDS and Mormon history. In the years after World War II public interest in religion had grown considerably. In the United States membership in a church soared to an all-time high of 69 percent of the population in 1960, and 96 percent of Americans identified themselves with a particular denomination. The rise in LDS membership was even more startling, climbing from less than 1 million in 1946 to 1.7 million in 1960 and 3.1 million in 1971. Historians of religion were serving a growing readership. And Latter-day Saints, at least as interested as others, eagerly followed the articles and books about Mormon history.

Before the transformation of the Church Historian's Office in 1972, the attitude of Mormon historians, if I may speak for one of them, was that the aim of history is to tell what happened—names, occurrences, places, dates, and causes.[5] One must have respect for the past as it really was, and one must be impartial and objective in telling the story. As professional historians with an understanding of the balance of faith and detachment, we (or at least I) did not pretend that we could be fully disinterested and objective historians. Every historian's judgments were inescapably influenced by their interests, values, and private beliefs. We did not suppose that we were writing with bloodless detachment. We had our own perspectives and acknowledged that they may have filtered into our writing projects. The will-to-truth that impelled some of us (those who were active Latter-day Saints) was, we believed, fully compatible with our Latter-day Saint faith. True historical understanding did not rule out the supernatural intervention of God. What we tried to do was not just reconstruct a chronicle based on the facts we could uncover but also relive and recreate sympathetically the basic intentions and purposes of the prophets, their men and women associates, and their fellow members.

Although a fully objective history was impossible as a general proposition,[6] we tried to make judgments about people and events that were appropriate, relevant, cogent, well-founded, and entitled to scholarly credence. Accepting Joseph Smith's own story in the Pearl of Great Price and in missionary tracts, we sought to know its true significance. We could see that many records of the early church were not objective historical sources but highly interpretative documents that reflected the culture and beliefs of the people and the times. If many historians conceived of history in terms of an objective, dispassionate reconstruction of "facts," our view was grounded in an awareness that history did not consist so much in facts as in the purposes and meanings of the actions and directives of early leaders and followers. We had to be open for underlying intentions, willing to question sources, and ready to suspend judgment and question the answers and understandings that we had at the outset. Our historical objectivity, in other words, was manifested in the capacity to withhold judgment until we had sound reasons for making it. As Van Harvey expressed it in *The Historian and the Believer,* "The question is not whether historians can be objective, but whether some selective judgments about a course of past events are more entitled to credence than others. . . . The issue is whether human beings possess sufficient possibilities of self-transcendence to arrive at unpleasant truths, that is, at judgments which run counter to their treasured hopes and desires."[7] At least some of us prayed for the blessings of the Holy Spirit as we encountered new information and entered imaginatively into claims and understandings that were unexpected.

In my addresses to the Mormon History Association and in articles for *Dialogue* and *BYU Studies,* I summarized what I thought we should do in terms of four guiding principles. First, we should rise as far as humanly possible above all parochialism of time and place that might narrow or distort our historical vision. In making judgments of people we should acknowledge their standards as well as those of our day.

Second, granting the inevitability of judging men, women, organizations, policy decisions, and programs, we should obtain and weigh all the relevant data first. Those of us who have been in the field for many years recognize that the result of a long and honest attempt to research all the historical evidence about any disputed event or personality is an overwhelming sense of the complexity of the issues. In trying to be fair, we tend to show mercy. To take a concrete case, historians who write about the Prophet Joseph Smith are sooner or later forced to form an attitude toward him. We struggle to see him in his weaknesses and his strengths, his compromises and his triumphs, his creative decisions and his forced compliances with circumstances beyond his control. In the resulting judgment justice is tempered with mercy.

Third, we should deal realistically with the competition of individuals and groups for wealth and power, the game of power politics, the cruelties that poverty forces on people, and the awful destruction of natural forces and events such as earthquakes and wars. At the same time, however, we will see instances of unexpected and unexplainable triumphs in human nature. Although we must be realistic, our realism should be balanced by a certain wonder and appreciation of the potentials for goodness and greatness in human beings.

Fourth, we should understand that most policies and procedures, standards and expectations are subject to change. But while men and women are immersed in history, they may also, with God's help, transcend history. In giving economic, political, and intellectual factors their due, we must also give faith and religion theirs.

In a way, the Latter-day Saint historians mentioned in this chapter had certain advantages in writing the history of their people. We were under an obligation to apply in our professional work the doctrine of consecration and stewardship. The work of historical inquiry was a way of sanctifying ourselves—a way of exercising our stewardship. This meant that we had an added incentive to be diligent, hardworking, and honest, even when fidelity to the documents forced us to speak contrary to the "accepted" ideas on the subject or disputed previous presumptions. Historical research conducted with the usual rigor was for us not only a professional requisite but also a spiritual journey. Research into the history of the church was both a vocation and at times a religious experience.

If we did our work properly, we hoped to become associated in the minds of our fellow members and nonmember colleagues with a certain attitude toward history, with the quality of our genuine concern, with the sense of reverence and responsibility with which we approached our assignments. To say this another way, our self-image and our public image would be influenced by the quality of our individual religious faith and life. There would be a certain reverence and respect for the documents we worked with, a feeling for human tragedy and triumph in history. As with dedicated historians generally, we would try to understand before we condemned, and if we condemned we would do it with the sense that we, too, being human, were involved in any judgment we made of others. We would not use history as a storehouse from which deceptively simple moral lessons might be drawn at random. In not knowing it all we submitted our analyses as tentative and subject to refinement. We wanted neither to sell our fellow human beings short nor to overrate them. Behind the personal decisions and the vast impersonal forces of history, we also saw divine purposes at work. We looked for the working of God both in the whirlwinds and in the still small voices.

One of the things that excited us about our work was the way in which it enabled us to have an encounter with our fellow Saints of former years. LDS history was more than the establishment of certain objective facts; it was a history of Saints, their mutual relationships, their conflicts and contacts, their social intercourse and their solitude and estrangement, their high aspirations and their errors and corruptions. In fulfilling our obligations as scholars we wanted to be responsible to the whole amplitude of human concerns—to human life in all its rich variety and diversity, in all its misery and grandeur, in all its ambiguity and contradictions.

We historians were resolved that our histories would be marked by thorough research, superior writing, and the display of the true spirit of Latter-day Saintism so that our history would give us and our readers new understandings of Mormon experiences in the past and present.

### Notes

1. Brigham Young, sermon, Mar. 10, 1861, in *Journal of Discourses,* 26 vols. (Liverpool: F. D. and S. W. Richards, 1854–86), 8:361–62; Brigham Young, sermon of May 5, 1870, *Deseret News Weekly,* May 11, 1870.

2. The best treatment is Lawrence Foster, "Career Apostates: Reflections on the Works of Jerald and Sandra Tanner," *Dialogue* 17 (Summer 1984): 34–60.

3. See especially Davis Bitton and Leonard J. Arrington, *Mormons and Their Historians* (Salt Lake City: University of Utah Press, 1988).

4. See also Elden J. Watson, ed., *Manuscript History of Brigham Young, 1801–1844* (Salt Lake City: privately published, 1967); Elden J. Watson, ed., *Manuscript History of Brigham Young, 1846–1847* (Salt Lake City: privately published, 1971). What Roberts published in *History of the Church of Jesus Christ of Latter-day*

*Saints, Period II: From the Manuscript History of Brigham Young and Other Original Documents* (Salt Lake City: Desert News, 1932), 7:247–603, was the manuscript history for August 9, 1844, to February 1846.

5. In preparing this section, I benefited from reading Van A. Harvey, *The Historian and the Believer* (New York: Macmillan, 1966); C. T. McIntire, ed., *God, History, and Historians: An Anthology of Modern Christian Views of History* (New York: Oxford University Press, 1977); Robert N. Bellah, *Beyond Belief: Essays on Religion in a Post-Traditional World* (New York: Harper and Row, 1970); George Santayana, *The Life of Reason: Reason in Religion* (New York: Charles Scribner's Sons, 1936); Herbert Butterfield, *Christianity and History* (New York: Scribner's, 1950); E. Harris Harbison, *Christianity and History* (Princeton: Princeton University Press, 1964); and Arnold Toynbee, *An Historian's Approach to Religion* (New York: Oxford University Press, 1956).

6. Considerable debate has arisen in the historical literature about the impossibility of pure objectivity. Bernard Bailyn, a distinguished historian who digs hard, writes well, and maintains strict respect for the otherness of the past, quotes a trenchant reply of Robert Solow to the fashionable relativisms of "the modern era": "The fact that there is no such thing as perfect antisepsis does not mean that one might as well do brain surgery in a sewer." Bernard Bailyn, *On the Teaching and Writing of History,* ed. Edward Connery Lathem (Hanover, N.H.: Montgomery Endowment, Dartmouth College, 1994), 73.

7. Harvey, *The Historian and the Believer,* 213–14.

# 5

# The Founding of the LDS Church
# Historical Department

He shall continue in writing and making a history of all the important
things which he shall observe and know concerning my church.
—Doctrine and Covenants 69:3

THE FOUNDING OF THE Historical Department of the church in 1972 may
be traced to preparatory actions taken by N. Eldon Tanner and Howard
W. Hunter. In 1963 Tanner, having served with the Twelve for one year,
was sustained as second counselor to President David O. McKay. Sixty-
five years old, a native of Alberta, Canada, Tanner had been a schoolteach-
er, provincial legislator, speaker of the assembly, minister of lands and
mines, and president of Trans-Canada Pipe Lines Company before he was
called to be an assistant to the Twelve in 1960. Tanner was well-educat-
ed, an experienced politician, and an efficient administrator. He was also
a devout and loyal Latter-day Saint, having served as a bishop, stake president, and mission president. He often stated that his success in politics
and business came from finding the very best person for a job and then
giving him or her a free hand in managing the affairs. He was willing to
pay whatever was necessary to secure the services of that "best" person.

As a counselor in the First Presidency, Tanner sought to acquaint himself with the current research in the field of church history. He met several
times with the historian Lyman Tyler, director of libraries at Brigham Young
University, to discuss historical literature, to learn more of LDS scholarship,
to obtain suggestions on the proper management of archives, and to explore
how to encourage research. Lyman was a friend of mine; we had known each
other as boys in Twin Falls, Idaho. In 1966, at Lyman's invitation, I drove
from Logan to Salt Lake City to attend one of these meetings.

Tanner was friendly, asked me many questions, and seemed interested
in my answers. I sensed that he had understood the historians' frustrations
about obtaining access to the abundant manuscript materials in the Church

Historian's Library and Archives and that he sympathized with my arguments for more openness. But he was a diplomat, reserved in expressing his opinions. It was clear that he admired Mormon scholars who remained loyal and active Latter-day Saints.

To my surprise and delight, about six months later I received a letter from the First Presidency signed by Tanner. It was a thank you for the honesty and helpfulness of the earlier interview but went beyond courtesies to create what amounted to a virtual calling. On June 15, 1966, he wrote that members of the First Presidency appreciated my role in promoting scholarship, especially considering the intensive labor involved, and "would suggest that you consider your participating in this program equivalent in importance to other major assignments you have held in the Church."[1]

Three months later we left for Pacific Palisades. During the winter of that year I received several letters from Alfred A. Knopf in New York, the "dean" of western publishers, and Rodman Paul, a distinguished western historian at the California Institute of Technology in Pasadena, urging me to prepare a volume on the Mormons' role in the settlement and development of the West. Such a work, wrote Knopf, agreeing with a similar pronouncement by Paul, would "fill the biggest gap in Western American history." I was interested in such a project—a natural companion volume to *Great Basin Kingdom*—but knew the book could not be written without access to primary materials in the Church Archives. On January 11, 1967, I wrote Tanner, explaining the request and pointing out that this was the first time a leading national publisher had asked an active Latter-day Saint to write a major work on the history of the Mormons. I asked if the First Presidency would grant permission to use the necessary primary materials, including correspondence, the diaries of certain leaders, minutes of specific meetings, pertinent financial records, and other documents. "I regard this opportunity as a splendid chance to demonstrate that Mormon scholars can write responsibly and professionally about their faith, their Church, and their people," I wrote.

Within a week I had a reply from the First Presidency. The members enclosed a copy of a record from their meeting of January 17, which said that Hugh B. Brown and Tanner "both felt it was an opportunity for us to have a professional writer who is a devoted Church member prepare such a history. It was agreed that authorization may be given to use the materials in the Historian's Office, with the understanding that he could not take any of these materials out of the office."[2] Tanner's accompanying letter of January 18 stated: "With President Joseph Fielding Smith's approval I am authorized to tell you that it will be quite in order for you to arrange with Earl Olson of the Historian's Office to use material available in that office and library."[3]

I immediately wrote to Earl Olson, who quickly confirmed the approval and promised full cooperation. Knowing the importance of this permission, I turned down an offer to remain permanently at UCLA and, on July 1, 1967, resumed my position at Utah State University, where I would be able to commute to the Church Archives. That summer I spent many days examining materials in the archives and continued this effort, when possible, in the years that followed. During these visits I became well acquainted with that devoted and intelligent archivist, Dean Jessee, a cataloguer of manuscripts, who introduced me to many documents that had not previously been studied by historians. I also enjoyed association with Edyth Romney, who worked in the archives with her husband, Thomas Cottam Romney, and after his death she continued to make typescript copies of original manuscripts. In the years that followed, unsolicited invitations were sent from the historian's office to several Latter-day Saint scholars (and a few others) to conduct research in the archives. These included James B. Allen, Davis Bitton, Truman Madsen, Kenneth Godfrey, Richard Anderson, Charles S. Peterson, T. Edgar Lyon, Robert Athearn, and Donald Moorman—the latter two not church members. President Tanner had taken a major step in opening the archives to earnest and established historians.

The completion of my book, however, had competition for my attention. The archive holdings were so vast, so unbelievably complete and rich, that I could not possibly compass them in a few months. I taught a full load of economics classes at USU during this period and, at the request of the research council of the university, directed several projects that brought in grants and awards. With the council's encouragement and support, I continued to produce articles on western economic history, and with the help of USU students, wrote monographs on federally financed industrial plants and reclamation projects in Utah, coauthored a biography of Governor William Spry, compiled a history of the First Security Corporation, and began biographies of David Eccles and Charles C. Rich.

Upon the death of McKay in January 1970, Joseph Fielding Smith, then president of the Twelve, became president of the church. The church historian position was vacant. Since 1842 the church historian had always been one of the Twelve. Even if tradition had not been a consideration, internal promotion seemed unlikely. A. William Lund, in his eighties, was not a candidate; and Earl Olson, although a grandson of Andrew Jenson, had no college training in history. Smith and his counselors chose Howard W. Hunter as the new church historian.

Hunter, a native of Idaho and a corporate attorney from southern California who had been our stake president when I was at the Huntington Library, took his appointment seriously. With the approval of Tanner, he held several conversations with prominent LDS historians. I was a member of the Committee of Historians called to his office on August 24, 1970, to discuss the organization and function of the Church Historian's Office. Also present were Davis Bitton, professor of history at the University of Utah; James B. Allen, professor of history at BYU and vice president of the Mormon History Association; LaMar Berrett, chairman of church history and doctrine at BYU; and Reed Durham, director of the Institute of Religion at the University of Utah. I think Earl Olson may also have been present for at least part of the meeting. At the request of Hunter, I later sent him a letter summarizing this committee meeting. As outlined in the letter, we historians made six suggestions, all important in the later establishment of the Historical Department of the church:

1. That an advisory council of LDS historians be appointed to meet quarterly with Hunter. The council would include representatives from the departments of history and church history at BYU, departments of history at the University of Utah and USU, the Institutes of Religion of the church, the Utah State Historical Society, and LDS historians outside the mountain states area.

2. That the church appoint a professionally trained person as assistant church historian who would be a coordinator and supervisor of historical research and publications. A budget should be established for a staff of five persons—a secretary, an editor, a director of research, an investigator who would serve the needs of general authorities and other church officials and agencies, and a traveling historian-librarian who would uncover documents, letters, journals, and diaries in the homes of members and conduct oral history interviews.

3. That the Church Historian's Office make available fellowship grants to established historians to do work in the archives—summer fellowships to Mormon and non-Mormon historians and internships to promising graduate students.

4. That the assistant church historian maintain close relationships with professional historical associations related to LDS history: the American Historical Association, the Organization of American Historians, the American Society of Church History, the Western History Association, and the various historical associations of the states with substantial numbers of Latter-day Saints.

5. That sequels to the seven-volume documentary *History of the Church* and Andrew Jenson's *Biographical Encyclopedia* be prepared.

6. That a multivolume sesquicentennial history of the church be prepared for publication in 1980.

Hunter probably included many of these concepts on his agenda as he met with the First Presidency and others in the months that followed.

Less than six months later, on February 8, 1971, A. William Lund died at age eighty-four. Earl Olson remained the sole assistant church historian, and many LDS historians fervently hoped that Hunter would appoint a professionally trained historian to assist Olson. When Hunter again convened the Committee of Historians in Salt Lake City on November 19, 1971, he confessed that those in the Church Historian's Office had done almost nothing to compile church history since 1930, although earlier revelations had clearly required them to do so. They had not published important documents, had not compiled biographies, and had not written narrative or interpretive history. Put simply, little had been done to compile material on church history in the twentieth century. Discussing the possible appointment of a professional historian as assistant historian in charge of research and publications, Hunter pointed out the limited budget for the Church Historian's Office. Our committee then suggested a dual appointment by BYU and the Church Historian's Office, with the appointee spending half-time at BYU and half-time at the Church Historian's Office. Presumably this director of research would be furnished with funds to employ a staff of historians to work on important projects. Even a part-time appointment would make possible documentary histories that would satisfy the canons of scholarship and open the way for writing interpretive histories that would be simultaneously friendly and intellectually respectable.

Hunter seemed excited with this suggestion. During November and December he had private conversations with various historians, especially Richard Bushman, who was then serving as the Boston stake president, in whom he had great confidence. I was informed, much later, that Davis Bitton, as president of the Mormon History Association, had sent a rather detailed letter to Hunter nominating me and explaining why I would be an excellent choice. On January 5, 1972, Tanner telephoned me in Logan to set up an appointment at my earliest convenience. I taught my 8:00 class at Utah State the next morning and then drove with Grace to Salt Lake City. I suspected that Tanner might ask for my recommendation for an assistant church historian. I had someone in mind and organized my arguments to promote my candidate.

When I entered his office, tall, slender Tanner smiled warmly and motioned me into the big leather easy chair next to his own. Tanner immediately informed me that leaders had devised a general reorganization of the church and wished to restructure the Church Historian's Office. Tanner told me that the First Presidency wanted Alvin Dyer to be managing director of the Historian's Office, Earl Olson to be church archivist, and me to be church historian. I was astonished but tried not to show it.

We spent most of the next hour talking about the new post. Tanner acknowledged that despite specific revelations to record church history for succeeding generations, no one had done so for forty years. He expressed confidence in my ability to take on this task. An endowed chair at BYU would cover half my salary, and the church would pay the other half. He asked me to share the news of my appointment with just Grace and President Glenn Taggart at USU until the church and BYU could make a joint announcement. Tanner then telephoned President Dallin H. Oaks of BYU, who suggested they make the announcement on January 14. Tanner said he would announce this departmental change at a meeting of the Historian's Office staff, which he hoped I would attend. He wanted me to start immediately, but I pointed out that I had classes at USU and would not be able to leave until the end of the winter quarter, about the middle of March. He urged me to come to Salt Lake City as often as possible in the interim to get things started. He said that Hunter was not a historian and would be delighted to have me take his place.

As I left the office about noon, I saw Grace waiting for me in the antechamber. Tanner asked me to bring her in, shook hands with her, and gave her the news. She was as surprised as I had been and was both delighted and chagrined. While she was pleased for me and for the cause of church history, she loved Logan, thoroughly enjoyed the home we had built, and was visibly dismayed at the thought of leaving her many friends and pleasures in a move to Salt Lake City. However, her instinctive supportiveness caused her to say yes when Tanner asked if she approved.

Tanner set another meeting for the afternoon, after he had talked with Dyer and Olson, neither of whom had previously been approached. In that session, again just with me, Tanner said that Dyer had agreed to serve as my liaison during the organizational phase to ensure that I received the cooperation and help of the Twelve and the First Presidency. Dyer, a former counselor in the First Presidency and at that time an assistant to the Twelve, was in a good position to arrange coordinating meetings for Olson and me with key personnel and to obtain clearances for appointments and programs.

I have the highest praise for Dyer's support. From our first meeting a few days later until his service was curtailed by a stroke on April 21, 1972, Dyer firmly reiterated his desire to give the new historical team "the wheels to run on." And he did so with enthusiasm and eagerness. He arranged for Earl and me to attend a meeting with the Twelve in the upper room of the Salt Lake Temple and for us to meet several times with the First Presidency. He presented me to church magazine editors for interviews that were later published. Over and over Dyer asked what he could do for us that would move the work along.

Born in Salt Lake City into a family of thirteen children in 1903, Dyer was sixty-nine at the time of his appointment as managing director. A hardworking, successful businessman, he was sustained as assistant to the Twelve in 1958 and ordained an apostle (but not a member of the Twelve) in 1967. The next year he was sustained as a counselor in the First Presidency of David O. McKay. Upon McKay's death in 1970, he resumed his position as assistant to the Twelve, which position he held while he was our managing director.

Dyer had been a bishop, high councilor, president of the Central States and European missions. Active in the Missouri Historical Society, he had written a book about the history of the church in Missouri. A sheet metal journeyman as a young man, he became manager of a heating and air conditioning firm and eventually established his own distributing business in Salt Lake City. He was known far and wide as a baseball pitcher. Dyer seemed to us to be forthright, energetic, well-organized, highly spiritual, and anxious to be of service. He regarded his assignment as that of a general authority expediter. He secured the approval of the First Presidency and the Twelve for programs, arranged for a budget to employ necessary personnel, and encouraged us to go "full steam ahead." He did not look over our shoulders at what we wrote; he did not tell us what programs we should follow. He held regular meetings with Earl and me to learn what he could do to help, and he always took us with him to meetings of the First Presidency and the Twelve so they could, as the Mormon expression goes, "feel our spirits" and give us counsel.

At the January 14 announcement meeting Tanner quoted from various revelations with commandments that we must keep and write our history, and he concluded with a verse from the book of Joel in the Old Testament: "Tell ye your children of it, and let your children tell their children, and their children another generation" (1:3).

The weeks until the end of the quarter at USU were crammed. I was teaching history of economic thought and government regulation of business and supervising several research projects. With the approval of my department head, B. Delworth Gardner, I was able to travel to Salt Lake City two days a week. We put our Logan house up for sale and purchased a Salt Lake home. I stayed in it part of the week and returned to Logan to administer research projects the rest of the days. We moved the family to

Salt Lake City when school was out in June. A lot of media attention was given to my appointment, and my children and colleagues felt that a great honor had come to me. There were many calls and letters of congratulation from the East, Pacific Coast states, and Canada as well as locally.

Dyer, Olson, and I in our first meeting on January 20, 1972, discussed a possible change in the name and organization of the Church Historian's Office to reflect that it now included more than a church historian. In a follow-up meeting on January 25, we agreed to change the name to Historical Department of the Church of Jesus Christ of Latter-day Saints, with the Archives Division headed by Earl Olson, the Library Division directed by a trained librarian (Donald T. Schmidt, librarian at BYU, was appointed to this post on March 10), and the History Division that I supervised. Later, in 1974, the department created the Arts and Sites Division, with Florence S. Jacobsen as church curator. Florence had previously served as a consultant to Mark Petersen's committee on museums and visitors' centers. Under her leadership, Arts and Sites collected art and artifacts and planned the magnificent Museum of Church History and Art that was opened in 1980. Florence, the gracious and lovely granddaughter of two prophets, Joseph F. Smith and Heber J. Grant, had served as general president of the Young Women's Mutual Improvement Association, 1961–72, and was a member of the governor's committee for cultural and historic sites, vice president of the National Council of Women, and treasurer of the International Council of Women.

During the week between Tanner's appointment and the official announcement, I considered possible assistant historians. There was a precedent for two. Since I was from Utah State University, it was logical that I should ask for one from the University of Utah and one from Brigham Young University. For budgetary reasons I should also ask for them on a half-time basis, just as I would be. On the day my appointment was made public, I telephoned James B. Allen and Davis Bitton, both close personal friends for many years, and asked if they would agree to serve with me. Both replied in the affirmative. I explained that an official call would have to follow official clearance. In the January 25 meeting I requested the appointment of Jim and Davis, each to remain at his university and serve half-time with me. Dyer said he would interview them as soon as possible.

I also requested that Dean Jessee be shifted from his work in the Church Archives to work with me in what came to be called the History Division. A native of Springville, Utah, Dean fulfilled a proselytizing mission to Germany, earned a master's degree in church history from BYU, taught seminary at West High School in Salt Lake City for four years, and then, in 1964, began to work in the Church Historian's Office as an archivist.

Intelligent, well-informed, hardworking, and modest, he knew more about the documents of LDS history than any other person.

I first became acquainted with Jim Allen, a native of Logan, in 1953–54, when he was a senior at Utah State University. We both took a graduate seminar from George Ellsworth on historical methods and literature. In that seminar Jim wrote a paper on the creation of Utah's counties that was published in the *Utah Historical Quarterly*. He went on to teach seminary at Kaysville, Utah, and Cowley, Wyoming, and to do graduate work in history at BYU. In the summer of 1956, when he was completing his graduate courses and George Ellsworth and I were teaching summer school at Brigham Young University, we drove each weekend from Logan to Provo; we established a firm friendship. Jim went on to southern California, where he was an institute director and worked on a Ph.D. in history from the University of Southern California. He completed that degree in 1963, with a dissertation later published by the University of Oklahoma Press as *The Company Town in the American West*. He then moved to BYU as a professor of history, where he remained until his retirement in 1992. Jim was a many-sided man—superb classroom teacher, student advisor, university citizen, bishop, high councilor, and district Republican committeeman. With Marvin Hill he had prepared *Mormonism and American Culture*, which was published by Harper and Row in 1972, and he had published sixteen articles, some of them prizewinners, on Mormon, Utah, and western American history in the *Improvement Era, Arizona and the West, Dialogue, Utah Historical Quarterly, BYU Studies,* and *Pacific Historical Review*. President of the Mormon History Association in 1971–72, Jim was an outstanding candidate for the position of assistant church historian.

I met Davis Bitton in the spring of 1956 when he was a senior in history at Brigham Young University. President of the BYU chapter of Phi Alpha Theta, the history honorary, he had invited me to give the address at the spring banquet. I had been impressed with his senior honor's paper published in the *Utah Historical Quarterly,* "The B. H. Roberts Case, 1898–1900," and had written him a letter of commendation. From BYU Davis went to Princeton University, where he received an M.A. in 1958 and a Ph.D. in modern European history in 1961. I stayed with Davis, professor of European history at the University of Texas, when I delivered the History of American Civilization lectures in 1964. Davis moved to the University of California at Santa Barbara in 1964, then to the University of Utah in 1966, where he remains. Although his fields were early modern French history and European intellectual history, about which he had published books and professional papers, he made significant contributions to Mormon history as well, including articles in *Dialogue, Utah Histori-*

*cal Quarterly, Arizona and the West,* and *BYU Studies.* He had nearly completed work on the *Guide to Mormon Diaries and Autobiographies,* which was published by BYU Press in 1977. He had served as the president of Mormon History Association, 1970–71, the year before Jim Allen. Like Jim, he was an excellent teacher and active in the church. Born in Blackfoot, Idaho, he attended Blackfoot High, where he was active in sports, debate, scouting, and music. After two years at BYU, he served a mission in France, where he was editor of *L'Etoile,* and then served in the U.S. Army during the Korean conflict. He had been a ward organist, ward chorister, Elders' Quorum president, gospel doctrine teacher, and LDS Institute instructor. In my opinion he was the finest Latter-day Saint intellectual in critiquing professional papers. We depended heavily on him to review material we wrote for publication. Jim, Davis, and I made up a unified and imaginative "troika" in administering the History Division of the Historical Department. Each of us produced books, many articles, and gave dozens of speeches in sacrament meetings, study groups, civic clubs, and professional societies. We also built our faith as we engaged in this honorable calling.

In presenting the names of Jim and Davis for official approval, I prepared a page outlining their qualifications, and Elder Dyer held conversations with his advisors from the Twelve, Howard Hunter and Spencer Kimball, and the First Presidency. The chief problem, as it turned out, was the arrangement to have them work half-time. At this point budgetary constraints had been overlooked. Why shouldn't they work full-time as other church employees did? The church had a deliberate policy of paying below competitive salaries; there were no employees, or none that we could discover, who received salaries equal to those of a full university professor. The paltry church pay would have to be supplemented by a university stipend. Both wished to keep their university affiliations and may not have accepted the appointments if they had been forced to give up their university connections. There was also an enormous advantage in having a connection with each university and its history department. Considering the industry and productivity of Jim and Davis, I was sure we would get essentially full-time work out of each.

After further discussion the Twelve endorsed the appointments at a meeting in the temple on February 24, to which Dyer, Earl Olson, and I were invited. In this meeting the First Presidency and the Twelve approved the new name for the department and heard oral reports from Earl and me. It was a solemn, even sacred, moment as we watched them raise their hands to sustain us and our plans.

Because this was the first time that the church historian had not been a member of the Twelve, the council named Spencer Kimball and Howard Hunter to serve as our advisors from the Twelve and as advisors to the Twelve on historical matters. As assignments of the Twelve were shifted, these advisors were replaced. Thus, when Kimball became president of the Twelve in July 1972, he was replaced by Delbert Stapley, who was later replaced by Bruce McConkie, and still later by Gordon B. Hinckley.

After the meeting in the temple Hunter invited me to his office, where he candidly discussed the condition and function of the Church Historian's Office during the two years he had been church historian. He was very relaxed and friendly. He said that my appointment was prompted by the strong feelings of some of the brethren that the church needed a professionally trained historian. The professionally trained historians they had consulted recommended me. He further said that he felt the church was mature enough that our history should be honest. Our faith should not overpower our collective memories and documented experiences. He did not believe in suppressing information, hiding documents, or concealing or withholding minutes for "screening." He thought we should publish the documents of our history. Why should we withhold things that are a part of our history? He thought it in our best interest to encourage scholars—to help and cooperate with them in doing honest research. Nevertheless, Hunter counseled me to keep in mind that church members reverenced leaders and their policies. To investigate too closely the private lives of leaders and the circumstances that led to their decisions might remove some of the aura that sanctified church policies and procedures. If the daylight of historical research should shine too brightly upon prophets and their policies, he cautioned, it might devitalize the charisma that dedicated leadership inspires. I accepted Hunter's counsel as a mandate for free and honest scholarly pursuit, with a warning that we must be discreet.

Shortly after these meetings Dyer left for conference appointments in Central America, which postponed his formal calls to Jim and Davis until March 10. On that Friday I drove from Logan to Salt Lake City to be present for this important event. Upon learning that the appointments had been made and accepted, something for which I had fasted and prayed, I called Dean Jessee into the office and Dean, Jim, Davis, and I knelt in prayer to express our thanks and to ask blessings upon our endeavors as we entered into our work.

During this earnest and solemn prayer session, each of us participating, I felt an exhilaration that transported me to a higher level of consciousness, similar to that which came to me at the University of North Carolina in 1950. The challenges of my appointment as church historian, the confidence I felt in these colleagues, and the warm support that had been extended to me by Elders Tanner, Hunter, and Dyer had lifted me to a similar higher sphere. I arose from the prayer with a certainty that the Lord was cognizant of and approved our appointments and would bless us in our endeavors. I have always felt that my assignment to direct and participate in the writing of church history, imperfect as my work may have been, was a special endowment from on high. And I have always believed that my "counselors," Jim and Davis, were the best persons in the church to help direct the work we were expected to do.

In the weeks that followed I asked for additional historians to do research and writing of benefit to the church. Among the first of these associates whom Dyer interviewed and cleared were Dean Jessee, D. Michael Quinn, Richard L. Jensen, William G. Hartley, Gordon Irving, Maureen Ursenbach Beecher, and Ronald K. Esplin. Except for Dean Jessee, these were all younger, well-trained, and eager scholars. Richard Jensen, a history graduate from Utah State University and one of my assistants on the Charles Rich biography, was completing a master's degree at Ohio State University. D. Michael Quinn was finishing a master's degree at the University of Utah. He worked only a year and one-half before going to Yale to earn a Ph.D. under Howard Lamar and then accepting an appointment at BYU as a professor of history. Bill Hartley, a history graduate of BYU, was working on an advanced degree at Washington State University. Gordon Irving was a superior history graduate at the University of Utah, while Maureen Ursenbach Beecher, a native of Alberta, Canada, had been assistant manager of the *Western Humanities Review* and was in the final stages of completing a doctoral dissertation in English at the University of Utah. Ron Esplin had graduated from the University of Virginia and was completing a master's at BYU. All of these active Latter-day Saints had a high standard of integrity, and all proved to be highly productive historians.

In the next few years we added temporary and permanent staff, including Bruce Blumell, Glen Leonard, Jill Mulvay Derr, Dean May, Rebecca Foster Cornwall Bartholomew, Gene Allred Sessions, Ronald Walker, and Carol Madsen. A native of Canada, Bruce Blumell had completed a Ph.D. under Vernon Carstensen of the University of Washington, and we hoped he would write a history of the LDS welfare system. He was also a star basketball player. With a Ph.D. in history from the University of Utah, Glen Leonard became editor of the *Utah Historical Quarterly* and was added to the History Division staff in September 1973 to help write the *Story of the Latter-day Saints*. The next addition was Jill Mulvay Derr, a native of Salt Lake City, who had graduated from Harvard with a teaching M.A. and taught a year in Massachusetts before returning to the West. She worked on LDS women's history. I met Dean May at the Cambridge, Massachusetts, education week in 1972 and urged him to join our staff as soon as he completed his Ph.D. at Brown. He joined us in January 1974, remained until he completed a draft of *Building the City of God: Community and Cooperation among the Mormons* (1976), and then moved to the University of Utah. Rebecca Foster Cornwall Bartholomew worked for me primarily on projects financed by special outside grants or by myself personally. Although not a permanent employee, she helped me enormously on the biographies of Edwin Woolley and Brigham Young, the personal history of my wife Grace, and my biography. A writer of fiction and intelligent and loyal, she was an extremely helpful assistant. As a student in Washington, D.C., Gene Sessions had done work for me in the National Archives under a grant I had had from Utah State University. When he finished his Ph.D. at Florida State University, he began work with us and remained until 1976, when he joined the history staff at Weber State University. He wrote books from the papers of James H. Moyle and Jedediah M. Grant and published *Latter-day Saint Patriots,* with chapters on seven prominent Latter-day Saints who had fathers and grandfathers in the Revolutionary Army.

Ron Walker filled Gene's vacancy in 1976. Ron was a graduate of Stanford and one of the church's most sophisticated writers. After several years as an Institute of Religion director in southern California, Ron was assigned to the University of Utah Institute, where he was able to complete his Ph.D. Ron has since served as a president of the Mormon History Association and as acting director of the Charles Redd Center at BYU and has done substantial work on a biography of Heber J. Grant, Mormons and the Indians, the Godbeites, and other topics of Mormon history. The final full-time employee of our history staff was Carol Cornwall Madsen, who was hired in 1977 to finish the centennial history of the Primary Association of the church. After a career as wife and mother, which included part-time work in English, and a graduate degree in history at the University of Utah, she contributed substantially to our studies of LDS women. In addition to serving as a president of the Mormon History Association, she has demonstrated outstanding scholarship.

No one can doubt that, with the approval of the First Presidency, the Church Appropriations Committee, managing directors, and special advisors, we were able to accumulate an impressive pool of talent to carry out our given assignment of writing the history of the church and its officers and members. Each of these scholars has continued to make important contributions to Mormon history. Their output has been, to use the words of one of my grandchildren, "awesome."

While mentioning the names of our professional staff, I should also mention our secretaries, whose contributions should not be underestimated. My secretaries have included Chris Croft Waters, who remained from 1972 until 1975 and then earned an M.A. in history at the University of Utah and became a teacher and mother; Nedra Yeates Pace, 1975–76, a splendid entertainer who also became a teacher and mother in Box Elder County; Kathy Gailey Stephens, 1976–79, a member of our Logan Tenth Ward who was a mother and bass violist and now is executive secretary of the Mormon Youth Chorus and Symphony; Kathleen Hardy Anderson, 1979–84, who had been the president's secretary at Ricks College and is now a mother of four in Layton; and Marilyn Rish Parks, from 1985 to the present. Marilyn continues as administrative secretary of the Joseph Fielding Smith Institute for Church History. Each woman has been intelligent, efficient, loyal, and helpful. My having a personal secretary for these ten years was an enormous advantage and pleasure. Each took dictation for the many letters I wrote, typed everything my collaborators and I produced, helped me keep a full diary of my work, did all my photocopying, received the many persons who came to visit me, and otherwise kept the office environment a happy and productive one.

The principal staff secretaries and typists were Edyth Romney, a long-time historical office employee, who typed thousands of pages of hard-to-read handwritten letters, diaries, minutes of meetings, and other manuscripts; Pat Jarvis, who later joined Macmillan Company in New York City as a copy editor; Debbie Liljenquist Biggs; Kathy Robison; Val Christensen Searle; Kathy Gilmore; and perhaps others I do not now recall. We also had the assistance of Flore Chappuis, particularly on foreign mission history; several volunteer assistants, including Shirley Schwartz, Pearl Ghormley, and Jean Sorensen; and those receiving short fellowships, including Glenn Humpherys, Henry Wolfinger, Betty Barton, Kathryn Hanson Shirts, Melodie Moensch Charles, and Jessie Embry.

A special moment for our department was April 6, 1972, when the names of Jim Allen, Davis Bitton, and myself were read for a sustaining vote in the general conference. I attended the conference with Jim and Davis and we sat on the second row of the middle section, just in front of the general authorities on the stand. We were particularly gratified when Dyer mentioned in his general conference address his pleasure in working with us. After the session many friends and former associates came up to congratulate us and shake our hands, including former students, political leaders, and of course many general authorities.

The three-day conference from April 6 through April 9 was held in the historic Mormon Tabernacle on Temple Square in Salt Lake City. Approximately 8,000 persons were in attendance, including bishops and stake presidents from all over the world. Sitting so near to the front, we had an unparalleled location to watch the general authorities and hear the world-famous Mormon Tabernacle Choir. The effect was far more electric and stirring than when we had watched the sessions on television. The music was magnificent and moving, as were many of the addresses. We were particularly impressed with Spencer Kimball's sermon "Keeping the Lines of Communication Strong"; Tanner, who admonished priesthood bearers to overcome temptation; and Boyd Packer's sermon on moral cleanliness. Each was important, well prepared, and well delivered. Their talks and the singing of the choir, with its unbelievable precision in timing, rhythm, and tone color, touched our hearts with uplifting and deep inspiration. The choir was led by director Richard Condie, assisted by Jay Welch.

After the session where we were sustained, many friends and former associates came up to congratulate us and shake our hands. Included in the felicitations were many of my former students, now serving in bishoprics and stake presidencies around the world; several political leaders; and, of course, many general authorities, including Hunter, Dyer, and Packer. They all wished us well.

It had been a busy week for me. I spoke at a devotional at Ricks College in Rexburg, Idaho, on Tuesday; had dinner with the *BYU Studies* editorial board after conference on Thursday, where I talked on the relationship between *BYU Studies* and the Historical Department; spoke to the University of Utah LDS Institute at noon on Friday on the importance of history; and the following Wednesday left with Earl Olson for Independence, Missouri, to attend the annual meetings of the Mormon History Association. We took advantage of the opportunity to attend the World Conference of the Reorganized Church of Jesus Christ of Latter Day Saints and visit historic Mormon sites in Missouri.

Grace and I moved to Parley's First Ward in June 1972. At the time our oldest son, James, had returned from his LDS mission to Porto Alegre, Brazil, had attended BYU where he earned a Master of Fine Arts degree, and was in San Francisco as a member of Actors Conservatory Theater. Our son Carl was an assistant to the LDS mission president in Bolivia. He returned to Salt Lake City in 1973 and attended the University of Utah for two quarters before enrolling at Utah State University. Our daughter, Susan, was completing her first year at Utah State University and living in the Eliza R. Snow Hall of the Morm Dorms. She began courting Dean Madsen, a Utah native, who had completed a Ph.D. in music at the University of Oregon and was an assistant professor of music at USU. They married in 1974. Grace's mother, Nina Fort, moved with us to Salt Lake City. All three of our children were married in the temple after our move. Grace was a teacher in Parley's Ward Relief Society, James acted in several church plays and was an officer in a regional youth council, Carl was an intern with the *New Era,* and Susan was an intern with *The Friend.*

Although we had enjoyed our friends and neighbors and life in Logan, we found pleasure in the splendid cultural offerings of Salt Lake City: the Utah Symphony, Utah Opera, Ballet West, Pioneer Memorial Theater, Promised Valley Playhouse, Friday evenings in the Assembly Hall on Temple Square, and events in Parley's First Ward and Parley's Stake. Through the intercession of David Evans, a prominent Salt Lake advertiser and publisher with whom I had worked on several publishing projects, I was invited to join Salt Lake Rotary, Club 24; Grace and I also joined the Cannon-Hinckley Church History Group that met monthly in the Lion House; and we were occasionally invited to the homes of prominent church officials: Franklin D. and Helen Richards, Sterling and Doris Sill, Theodore and Minnie Burton, and in many other homes where study groups met. Grace, who was much admired by Boyd K. Packer, made him a southern pecan pie each Christmas that I was delighted to deliver. On one of those visits I learned that Packer spent some of his spare time carving replicas of birds and ducks. He later carved a beautiful meadowlark to place in a cage in the Historical Department suite where the managing director and assistant managing director and secretary have their offices.

A special pleasure for me was working with the Church Hospitality Committee as a guide and translator for Italian government officials, businessmen, and educators who visited Salt Lake City. I learned from a friend among the general authorities that I had been approved as president of the Italian mission when it was opened in 1967, but just prior to my call an article written by J. D. Williams that was regarded as critical of Ezra Taft Benson had appeared in *Dialogue.* Because of my connection with *Dialogue,* my name was withdrawn. Although I had nothing to do with the approval of the article, I lost this opportunity of preaching the gospel in Italy in Italian.

Until November 1972 we were housed on the third floor of the Church Administration Building. I was placed in the office previously occupied by A. William Lund, the same one occupied for many years by Susa Young Gates, sometimes called the Thirteenth Apostle because she was the only woman with an office in that building. Our staff was located along the east end of the third floor in a series of desks that faced my office. The library and archives occupied the west end of the third floor and much of the basement.

The setting of the columnal, five-story neo-classic Church Administration Building was remarkable. Built of Utah granite in 1917, the building housed the offices of the First Presidency, the Twelve, and other general authorities of the church. Situated on the what was known as the Tithing Block (the General Tithing Office had been located there in pioneer days), it was just east of the Hotel Utah, an impressive ten-story building built by Mormon and non-Mormon leaders in 1911 to lodge important visitors to Salt Lake City. The flower gardens around the buildings were magnificent. Immediately to the east of the Church Administration Building was the gabled three-story Lion House, historic mansion of Brigham Young's plural household, that had been restored and converted into a social hall for wedding receptions, club luncheons and dinners, and the serving of meals to workers and visitors in downtown Salt Lake City. Just to the north on the south side of North Temple Street, construction companies were completing the twenty-eight-story Church Office Building which, when completed in November 1972, housed the Historical Department, including our offices, research rooms, library, and archives. We occupied all four stories of the east wing. To the south, between the Church Office Building and the Church Administration Building, Mormon philanthropist-jeweler O. C. Tanner had built a lovely fountain in the center of landscaped gardens, statues, flower beds, and decorative shrubs, providing a splendid festoon of color and texture for the entire complex. Just west of the Church Office Building on the corner of North Temple and Main Streets was the three-story classic Relief Society Building, completed in 1952, that housed offices and committee rooms, a women's library, and various exhibits and displays.

My birthday celebration that year was a happy affair. There were wonderfully supportive letters from Smith's counselors, N. Eldon Tanner and Harold B. Lee. Lee was gratified to see how, with the help of our advisors, the staff and I had infused the department "into the competency I have so much desired in the years that have gone by."[4]

To our dismay Joseph Fielding Smith died the same day, July 2, at ninety-five. His funeral, the first of a general authority I had attended, affected me deeply. Bruce McConkie's tribute was masterful. Harold B. Lee, president of the Twelve who would succeed Smith as prophet, described in his address a special manifestation giving confirmation of the office he knew he would hold and of his counselors: N. Eldon Tanner and Marion G. Romney.

When I was asked to speak at the sunrise service of the Sons of Utah Pioneers in the Salt Lake Tabernacle on July 24, I was invited to focus on Smith, using him as an exemplar to illustrate pioneer traditions, strengths, contributions and achievements, and their qualities of industry, stability, dogged determination, humor, and compassion. Along with others, I published a tribute to Smith as a historian in the next issue of *Dialogue*.

As president, the ninety-five-year-old prophet was reasonably alert, understood the general events that transpired, but did not have the physical or emotional energy to initiate and supervise the execution of programs. My impression was that the programs initiated under his presidency were planned and administered under the direction of his two counselors, Harold B. Lee and N. Eldon Tanner. Smith made no attempt to impose on the church his rigidly orthodox doctrinal position nor did he object to our opening the archives for scholarly research. His image as president was one of a kindly patriarch who smiled benignly in approval as the councils of the church called competent persons to positions and inaugurated programs.

### Notes

1. N. Eldon Tanner to Leonard J. Arrington, June 15, 1966, copy in Leonard J. Arrington Collection, Special Collections and Archives, Utah State University Libraries, Logan.

2. Record of the meeting of the First Presidency on Jan. 17, 1967, copy in Arrington Collection.

3. N. Eldon Tanner to Leonard J. Arrington, Jan. 18, 1967, copy in Arrington Collection.

4. N. Eldon Tanner and Harold B. Lee to Leonard J. Arrington, July 17, 1972, copy in Arrington Collection.

# 6

## Conferences with New Leaders

For unto you, the Twelve and . . . the First Presidency are
appointed . . . to be your counselors and your leaders.
   —Doctrine and Covenants 112:30

THE NEW PRESIDENT OF the church, sustained on July 7, 1972, was seventy-three-year-old Harold B. Lee. Born in 1899 at Clifton, Idaho, on the northern edge of Cache Valley, Lee had been educated at Albion State Normal School, had served as a teacher, and was a missionary in the Western States Mission, where he met his wife, Fern Tanner, who was also a missionary. They married after her release and moved to Salt Lake City, where he was a grade school principal. In 1932 he was appointed Salt Lake City commissioner for streets and public property. He also served as president of Pioneer Stake, a serious responsibility in those days of the Great Depression. Because the needs of his stake members cried out for solution, he inaugurated a welfare program that attracted wide attention. In 1935 President Heber J. Grant called him to his office to discuss welfare and asked him to direct a welfare program for the entire church. Five years later, in 1941, at age forty-two, Lee was ordained an apostle. He was a fine speaker, a firm administrator, and performed many responsibilities as a member of the Twelve, including being chairman of the Servicemen's Committee during World War II. He was the architect and first executive director of the Correlation Committee, created in 1960, that had the responsibility of developing a curriculum to teach the gospel in its every phase to church members.

Although he had a sharp tongue and was occasionally intensely critical in his judgments, Lee had been cordial to me when he was a counselor of President Smith and continued to be so until his unexpected death in December 1973 after only a year and a half as prophet of the church.

In February 1972 our Historical Department executives were charged with mapping out a detailed program of action for presentation to the First Presidency. Dyer made several attempts to hold such a meeting, but it was repeatedly postponed. The first opportunity to present our proposal was on August 8, after Lee and his counselors had served approximately a month.

The principal parts of the program we presented may be summarized as follows:

1. The inauguration of a program of oral history.

2. The preparation of a series of articles for *The Ensign* and *New Era*.

3. The commencement of the Mormon Heritage Series of books to be published by Deseret Book. These would be edited documents like the diaries of Joseph Smith, letters of Brigham Young to his sons, letters of Brigham Young to Native American leaders, selections from the letters and diaries of women, and so on.

4. The preparation of a sixteen-volume sesquicentennial history of the church—some of the volumes to be written by historians who were not members of our staff.

5. The preparation of two one-volume histories of the church—one, to be published by Deseret Book, intended primarily for members of the church, the other, to be published by Alfred Knopf, intended to reach non-members.

6. The preparation of biographies of Brigham Young, Eliza R. Snow, and other church leaders.

7. The publication of a *Guide to Mormon Diaries and Autobiographies*, prepared by Davis Bitton with the assistance of staff and others.

8. The creation of the Mormon History Trust Fund, a private fund administered by my colleagues and I, designed to hold the royalties and honoraria we received by virtue of our appointments. The fund would assist in historical research by paying for research trips not covered in our budget, paying expenses to conventions where we read papers, and paying for fellowships not covered in the budget. Having received First Presidency approval, we secured nonprofit status and an IRS number, and by this means we have continued to dedicate our earnings to this fund.

9. The organization of Friends of Church History. Having secured the approval of Dyer and Hunter, Earl Olson, and Don Schmidt, we asked the sanction of the First Presidency for the formation of a church history support group that would hold monthly meetings to hear papers by those doing research in the Church Library-Archives. Despite bright prospects this organization was never created.

10. The awarding of $1,000 summer research fellowships.

11. The assignment of various trained associates to work on specific topics: Jill Mulvay Derr (later replaced by Susan Staker Oman) and Carol Madsen on a history of the Primary, Bill Hartley on priesthood quorums,

Richard Jensen on immigration, Jill Mulvay Derr and Maureen Ursenbach Beecher on women in church history, Bruce Blumell on the Church Welfare Plan, and Dean Jessee on the Prophet Joseph Smith.

The members of the First Presidency gave their oral approval, and we received written approval in a letter dated September 13, in which my associates and I were commended "for the excellent way in which you have been fulfilling the assignments given to you."[1] Joined by Marion G. Romney and Howard W. Hunter, President Lee, at the August 8 meeting, pronounced a personal blessing on my head, which, among other things, declared: "Brother Arrington . . . the Lord will bless you and enlarge you and will open new doors to you to enable you to amass material and write histories and prepare necessary documentation for the benefit of generations yet unborn so that [all] will know what has gone on before."[2] The following is from the entry I made in my diary that evening.

> In the blessing that President Lee gave me today he spoke of the importance of capturing the fleeting impressions of the Spirit and of embodying those impressions in the policies we follow and the words we write. These impressions *are* fleeting—they are not there as a bank deposit available for us to draw from as we will. We may solicit them by prayer, by living worthily, by preparing ourselves spiritually to merit them and to be receptive to them. They are also impressions for which we must also be professionally prepared. They may counsel us to improve our professional craftsmanship as well as the spiritual phases of our endeavor. They may counsel us to be honest and fearless in reporting aspects of our history that are, perhaps, not understood by the faithful, just as they may counsel us to be careful about upsetting the faith of members who are marginal. My prayer is that the Lord will give me discernment; that He will bless me to be honest, frank, and courageous when those are required, and to be discreet, understanding, and sensitive when those qualities are appropriate.
>
> From my first interviews with church authorities I have been assured that I should work to improve the quality of history writing within the Church and continue to write with such craftsmanship, credibility, and probity that it will win and deserve the respect of professional historians. This is difficult for the historian because, while his contribution toward building testimonies is recognized and expected by officers and members of the Church, his task of helping to build the reputation of the Church in the professional field of history is not as well recognized or appreciated.

Always impeccably dressed, Lee called me to his office at least three times after this blessing to discuss the work of our History Division. He favored our doing a general history directed at members of the church. Lee reiterated that our history should be written by professionally trained historians and that he supported the programs that we had outlined. He thought we should aim for such an honest history that it would be equally acceptable to church members and nonchurch members.

The Oral History Program, under the general direction of Davis Bitton, was inaugurated even before the August meeting with the First Presidency. It was imperative that, as time, resources, and personnel were available, we continue to document LDS history with oral dictations that would furnish personal accounts of experiences and activities that otherwise might never be available to researchers and writers. We invited Gary L. Shumway, a professor of history at California State University in Fullerton and an active Latter-day Saint, to spend the summer of 1972 getting the program started. He gave us lectures, trained the staff in interviewing, and established a workable program. We appointed Bill Hartley to direct the program that fall; under his energetic leadership we interviewed general authorities, administrators of church programs, heads of auxiliaries, general board members, church architects and building supervisors, social welfare leaders, returning mission presidents and missionaries, stake presidents, bishops, Relief Society presidents, and many oldtimers with interesting stories to tell and articulate members with insights worth preserving. As time went on, we interviewed members with a distinct perspective: chaplains, African Americans, Native Americans, Mexican Americans, leaders in Europe, and others. From the original tape a transcription was made by a department secretary and given to the interviewee for editing. It was then typed in final form, a bound copy given to the interviewee, and another bound copy retained with the original tape in the archives. In the case of persons with a long history of connection with an important church enterprise, we conducted many interviews with the same person to get a full chronicle. These personal life stories and insightful recollections proved to be not only a memorable and thoughtful experience for the person being interviewed but also a valuable source for writing the history of the church in the twentieth century. For the benefit of the interviewers and interviewees, Gary Shumway and Bill Hartley wrote a manual, *An Oral History Primer,* that we published in 1973. One of the interviewees, George P. Lee, a Navajo who was sustained as a member of the First Council of the Seventy from 1975 to 1990, was interviewed for fifty-four two-hour sessions, and he used these in preparing his autobiography, *Silent Courage: An Indian Story,* published by Deseret Book in 1987. On September 1, 1989, Lee was excommunicated for disharmony.

When our interviewer went to meet one prominent person at his home, the man asked, "Do you have one of those machines—one of those tape recorders—with you?" Our interviewer replied, "I left it behind this first time, so we could get well acquainted." "Splendid," said the interviewee. "Those people who take down every word never get anything right."

In 1976, in a meeting with Gene Sessions, Bill Hartley, and others, James Moyle and his sister Evelyn Moyle Nelson volunteered to make a generous grant from the James Moyle Genealogical and Historical Association to the Historical Department to fund the program, which we renamed the James Moyle Oral History Program. In 1980, when the History Division was moved to BYU, the program remained with the Historical Department under the direction of Gordon Irving. By then some 1,250 persons had been interviewed and their material typed and stored for use in the library. One of the largest oral history projects in the United States, the program provides an excellent resource for writing twentieth-century Latter-day Saint history. The bulk of the interviews have been conducted in English, but possibly 15 percent have been done in other languages, including French, Spanish, Portuguese, Danish, and German. Interviews have been completed not only in Salt Lake City and Provo but also in many of the other forty-nine states, several parts of Canada, South America, Europe, Asia, and the South Pacific.

Not long after the First Presidency gave written approval for the formation of our Mormon History Trust Fund, Edyth Romney, our manuscripts secretary, was retired. Desiring to consecrate her time to the cause of historical research and preservation, she asked permission to continue her work. It was of enormous importance to us, and we volunteered to supplement her meager social security income with monthly checks from the Mormon History Trust Fund. In her new capacity she began to type the letters of Brigham Young, a project that would require several years but was indispensable if we were to publish, as we expected, a biography of that prominent pioneer leader. Department executives (Joseph Anderson, Earl Olson, Donald Schmidt, and I) agreed that the original ribbon copy of each letter was to be placed in the Church Archives, and because of its financial contribution, the Trust Fund might keep a photocopy of all that she typed. This was bound and kept in my office. When we were transferred to BYU in 1982, these volumes, amounting to thousands of pages of minutes and letters, were lodged with the Joseph Fielding Smith Institute for Church History. Besides Brigham Young manuscripts, these volumes included the diaries of Willard Richards, John D. Lee, and Heber C. Kimball; Brigham Young's office journals; and minutes taken by Thomas Bullock.

Although First Presidency approval was readily given to the formation of Friends of Church History, the public announcement of an organizational meeting on November 30 in our quarters in the Church Office Building caused one cautious member of the Twelve to bring it up for discussion in the weekly meeting. Most of the Twelve favored the organization as a means of encouraging responsible and accurate telling of the Mormon experience, but the one objector warned that *"Dialogue-type historians"* would be permitted to report their freewheeling research on historical topics. Although five hundred persons showed up at the first meeting, we were counseled to delay, delay, and delay a second meeting, and the promising organization never got off the ground. In the face of almost universal approval, the one objector halted a program previously approved by the First Presidency. We were embarrassed and humiliated and we lost public good will.

Although Dyer suffered from high blood pressure, he still maintained a dynamic pace when carrying out his responsibilities as a traveling assistant to the Twelve and holding meetings with Historical Department executives, their advisors, the First Presidency, and the Twelve. In April 1972 he had a stroke, after which he partially recovered and met us on appointed occasions at his car in the church parking lot and occasionally at his home.

Dyer was overjoyed when we moved into our new headquarters in the east wing of the Church Office Building. Although discouraged by Earl Olson, who thought we ought to wait for an official dedicatory prayer by general authorities of the church, we held our own service on November 11, 1972, to pray for God's help as we performed our work in that towering structure. In that service I suggested to the staff some requisites of a good Mormon historian: Sincerely believe that religious experiences are possible; be able and willing to consider ideas and explanations even though they may not be consistent with your values or beliefs; and have a capacity to see events and people in perspective. For their consideration I listed the following as the principal themes of Mormon history:

1. The restoration of the gospel—the emergence of organization and doctrine.
2. The proclamation of the gospel to persons throughout the world—the missionary work.
3. The buildup of cooperative activity—the development of a spirit of community—a spirit of working together.
4. Conflicts with their neighbors, non-Mormon governing officials, and with the federal government.

In December 1972 Dyer, who was much pleased with our spirit but for health reasons was not in a position to maintain effective supervision of the department, was released; Joseph Anderson was appointed managing director.

Joseph Anderson, named after Joseph Smith, was born in Salt Lake City in 1889, youngest of eleven children born to a Scottish immigrant father and an American-born mother. When he was a child, his family moved to Roy, Utah, where his father operated a small farm and was a railroad section superintendent. Joseph went to a one-room schoolhouse through eighth grade and then to Weber Academy, a church-owned high school, of which David O. McKay was principal and English teacher. He fulfilled a mission in Germany. After training in stenography at Weber Academy (now Weber State University), he served as the personal secretary of President Heber J. Grant from 1922 to 1945 and as secretary to the First Presidency from 1945 to 1972. He took down all the general conference sermons and numerous solemn assemblies in shorthand and reported temple dedicatory services in Alberta, Canada; Tempe, Arizona; Idaho Falls, Idaho; Los Angeles, California; and Oakland, California. He met with the First Presidency almost every day, kept minutes of the their meetings, and attended the weekly Thursday meetings of the First Presidency and the Twelve in the Salt Lake Temple. He answered many letters asking for information about the church's doctrines, policies, and history.

In 1970 he was sustained as assistant to the Twelve, and in 1972, at age eighty-three, he became our managing director, ultimately serving five years. As someone who had spent more than fifty years keeping the records of the church, he felt right at home. He was mentally alert and kept himself physically fit by swimming eighteen laps each day in the Deseret Gymnasium. A vigorous leader, he was on the board of Deseret Book for forty-three years and director of several church companies. For more than a third of the church's history, he had recorded events as they occurred. He treasured his close friendship with Heber J. Grant. He had a gentle demeanor and quiet style and his thin mustache was a trademark. When he was first employed, facial hair was not uncommon: Grant, George Albert Smith, and others had beards. As styles changed, he found himself the only general authority with a mustache. He worried about it. When he was called to be an assistant to the Twelve, he asked for advice and was told to shave. His wife Norma objected strenuously but he gave in, and in 1974 he shaved it off. Hinckley said of him: "I think Joseph Anderson knew more and said less than any man I ever knew. . . . He kept the trust that was imposed upon him."[3]

As with Dyer, and under instructions from the First Presidency and advisors Howard W. Hunter and Spencer W. Kimball from the Twelve, Anderson regarded himself as a coordinator, facilitator, and counselor. He held regular meetings with Historical Department executives, insisted that careful minutes be kept so decisions would be recorded and serve as precedents, and took us with him to meetings with the advisors and with the

First Presidency. As he took over management, Anderson asked who read the material that we prepared for publication. I replied that, under an oral agreement with the First Presidency, I read and approved all of the material, and I asked my two counselors, Jim Allen and Davis Bitton, and our editor, Maureen Ursenbach Beecher, to do the same. If we had differences of opinion, we worked them out in a conference. Anderson thought instead that the First Presidency should appoint someone to read each book and article we wrote. Over time, however, he acquired sufficient confidence in us that he did not insist that we send each prospective publication for clearance by the First Presidency or our advisors from the Twelve. Indeed, I brought the matter up in a meeting he arranged with the First Presidency and all accepted our plan to have only History Division members read each projected publication. Anderson wanted to know how each of our newly employed historians was cleared. We explained that each had been personally interviewed by Dyer who, in turn, had cleared them as trustworthy with their bishops and stake presidents. All, of course, had gone through Church Personnel for standard clearances.

Finally, Anderson also told us that he had discussed his assignment with President Lee, who, despite his assurances to me, had cautioned him to be very careful about the materials made available to us and other researchers. These included "sacred" writings, moral transgression and church court cases, financial data, and specific collections that were restricted by the donor or by the church department that created the records. Anderson left the professional work completely up to us—the projects we worked on and the articles and books we wrote. Although he knew more church history than all of us put together, he did not wish to put himself in the position of approving or disapproving anything we were doing. He wisely counseled us against procedures or policies he regarded as extreme or not in line with traditional church policies. Genial and friendly, he frequently told us stories of Heber J. Grant, who had been his closest friend and associate. Anderson did not always permit scholarly access to precious historical documents, but he had confidence in our judgment and loyalty.

I had been invited occasionally to meet with the Historical Arts and Sites Committee of the church, chaired by Mark Petersen. In doing so I became acquainted with Florence Smith Jacobsen, a consultant to the committee, who was appointed curator of the church's collection of art and artifacts in 1974. She felt a kinship with the people in our department and, at her request, was given an office on our floor. Florence, who met regularly with Anderson, Olson, Don Schmidt, and I, had graduated from the University of Utah and served with her husband, Ted Jacobsen, in presiding over the New York Mission. She helped restore the Joseph Smith Sr.

home in Palmyra, New York; the farm homes of Peter Whitmer and Martin Harris; the Nauvoo homes of Wilford Woodruff and Brigham Young; the Forest Farm of Brigham Young; and the Lion House in Salt Lake City. Always interested in cultural improvement, she helped to establish the Young Artists Festival, the Mormon Youth Symphony and Choir, and the Promised Valley Playhouse in Salt Lake City. Her responsibility as curator was to preserve, catalog, and display the historical arts and relics of the church, a massive collection. She was given a budget and some well-trained assistants, and she persuaded the brethren to build the Museum of Church History and Art on West Temple Street, just west of Temple Square in Salt Lake City. Eventually, Glen Leonard left our History Division to become director of the museum, and several of our staff were enlisted to help in the cataloging of paintings, sculptures, and artifacts and preparation for their display.

Intelligent and innovative, Florence was a delight to work with, and part of the reason for sadness in moving to BYU in 1982 was the realization that we would no longer be closely associated with her.

With the written authorization of the First Presidency and the signified approval of Howard W. Hunter and Anderson, our History Division proceeded to work out arrangements with James Mortimer, manager of Deseret Book, for publication of some of the books we were authorized to write: the Heritage Series, the sesquicentennial history, and the one-volume history of the church. Deseret Book's arrangements were also approved by Thomas S. Monson, the church publisher.

These things, however, are never simple. Despite the approvals, those who distrusted the new "hot shot" historians in the department and were opposed to the new "openness" that we were upholding began to throw up roadblocks. An attempt, beginning in 1967, had been made to "modernize" the organization of materials maintained by the old Church Historian's Office. Over the years the office had evolved a system with three kinds of holdings: printed books and magazines, written records (minutes), and manuscripts (diaries, letters, documents). No attempt had been made to maintain the integrity of acquisitions that included all three kinds of items. There were no registers and the principal index was the massive card file of the Journal History of the Church. After 1967 Earl Olson and his assistant archivist, Lorraine Arnell, were encouraged to attend meetings of the Society of American Archivists and to "professionalize" the collection. They employed Janet Jenson and Paul Foulger, trained librarians; Jeffrey Johnson, now Utah state archivist; Max Evans, now director of the Utah State Historical Society; and other professional librarians and archivists. Important changes were made that took old-line, untrained employees out of long-held responsibilities. As our historians began to make heavy use of holdings once restricted to use by general authorities, resentment followed. Traditionally, permission to use rare manuscripts had been inconsistent. Although many loyal scholars at BYU were denied access, others from elsewhere who were neither loyal nor trustworthy were given permission. Inexplicably, approval had been granted to several persons who did subsequent damage to the church—a secret associate of a Salt Lake anti-Mormon group; a writer of sensationalistic fiction; a non-Mormon historian hunting primarily for sensational material; a secret advocate of polygamy; and a nonhistorian who worked through old letters, removed rare stamps, and sold them. The negative results of these unfortunate permissions began to surface through the anti-Mormon underground shortly after our employment, and, although the work had been done months before we were employed, their sensational disclosures were blamed on us and our policy of increased openness. Despite our explanations, in the minds of distrustful hardliners we were responsible for the leaks and exposures. In any case there was a demand for greater control over the access to materials.

Two events showed that we were being watched. The first was a campaign waged by an employee of our library who had misgivings about our "taking over" historical research. We were told by his associates that he submitted to two members of the Twelve, on a regular basis, pages from articles and books we published with "controversial" statements underlined in yellow—statements that, out of context, might have looked questionable to an uninformed or suspicious mind. These and other accusations were circulated by these two to others of the Twelve and were placed in a special file of "questioning liberals" kept by church security at headquarters. We would have been delighted if the members of the Twelve had read all of what we had written, not just the questionable excerpts, and some of them may well have done so. It would not have surprised us if some disagreed with our analyses and interpretations. Some of the rumors circulated may have been born, to use Shakespeare's words, "of surmises, jealousies, and conjectures."

All of us, as believing church members, were confident that we were engaged in legitimate scholarship, that the church approved of the free exchange of ideas, that we were supported by our managing director and by the president of the church and our advisors, and that if we wrote honestly and sensitively our work would be supported by the vast majority of Latter-day Saint readers. Although we were not intimidated, we were watchful. We tried to get the hostile librarian reassigned (other executives of the Historical Department agreed), but perhaps through the intervention of higher authority he remained in his position.

A second instructive episode occurred in the spring of 1973. William G. Hartley, one of our young historians, had published "The Priesthood Reform Movement, 1908–1922" in the Winter 1973 issue of *BYU Studies*. In the article he details the low level of priesthood activity in the early years of the century—the failure to ordain deacons, teachers, and priests; the failure to perform such priesthood functions as ward teaching and collecting fast offerings; the absence of a systematic teaching program; and the failure to hold priesthood quorum meetings. In the article Hartley describes the formation of the General Priesthood Committee that, under the direction of President Joseph F. Smith, was assigned to initiate a church-wide priesthood reform and reorganizing plan that greatly improved the functioning of priesthood quorums.

On April 4, 1973, Thomas S. Monson, Boyd K. Packer, and Marvin J. Ashton of the Twelve wrote to Howard W. Hunter and Bruce R. McConkie, advisors to the Historical Department, noting that Hartley had quoted from meetings of the General Priesthood Committee and from some policy directives of the Presiding Bishopric. They asked whether articles using such materials were approved by the History Division. Anderson replied on May 1, 1973, that, under the direction of Dyer, I had worked out a procedure for approving and clearing articles of a historical nature written by members of our staff. To begin with, I myself approved or initiated each research and writing project of the members of our History Division. I also specifically initialed their requests for use of restricted materials. When the writer had completed the draft of a paper intended for publication, I read it and made suggestions for alterations, deletions, and the inclusion of additional material. The writer then made the suggested revisions. The paper was then retyped and read by James Allen, Davis Bitton, and Maureen Ursenbach Beecher. After our suggestions had been worked on by the author, he or she submitted the paper in final form to me, and I read it again for content and style. Under my direction the article was submitted for possible publication. This procedure was followed, Anderson pointed out, in the case of the article on the priesthood reform movement by Bill Hartley. Admittedly, I had a heavy responsibility in this matter, and had to be prayerful in making judgments. Still Anderson thought I had a right to insist upon high quality work.[4]

Many of our experiences were positive. First of all, the excitement of finding new documents and writing about their significance was energizing. For example, I published "Church Leaders in Liberty Jail" and "Oliver Cowdery's Kirtland, Ohio, 'Sketch Book'" in *BYU Studies* in the summer and fall of 1972, "The Logan Tabernacle and Temple" with Melvin Larkin in *Utah Historical Quarterly* in 1973, and "Lorenzo Hill Hatch:

Pioneer Bishop of Franklin" with Richard Jensen in *Idaho Yesterdays* in 1973. I shared many "finds" and interpretations with audiences in connection with the Commissioner's Lecture Series in Massachusetts, New York, Idaho, and Utah; the Henry Eyring Speaker's Series in Arizona; general Relief Society conference in Salt Lake City; the Know Your Religion Series and Education Weeks in California, Idaho, and Utah; and the Daughters of Utah Pioneers annual meeting in Salt Lake City.

One exciting piece of research was that of Bill Hartley, who wrote the story of Samuel Chambers (1831–1929) and his wife Amanda Leggroan.[5] In 1844, at age thirteen, Chambers, a black slave in Mississippi, was converted. Though he was an orphan, with no further contact with the church, the spirit of God remained with him and he longed to be with the Saints. After the collapse of the Confederacy, he turned to sharecropping to save funds to gather his family to Utah. In 1870, aged thirty-nine, he left Mississippi with Amanda, their seventeen-year-old son Peter, and the family of Amanda's brother, Edward Leggroan. They traveled in a simple ox-drawn wagon and arrived in the Salt Lake Valley in April 1870, settling in the Eighth Ward area southeast of Salt Lake City, where he grew fruits, berries, and vegetables. Tall and trustworthy, he was well received by his white neighbors and was appointed acting deacon. His responsibility was the care and cleaning of the ward meetinghouse—washing windows, sweeping floors, dusting benches, making minor repairs, and lighting the fire and tending the stove in the winter. He was also an usher for the summer afternoon meetings in the tabernacle. His tithing record shows donations of eggs, peas, wheat, corn, butter, pork, chickens, cabbage, peaches, cherries, currants, gooseberries, and molasses. He won many prizes for his produce at territorial and state fairs. After 1900 he attended Wilford Ward. Besides a regular tithe, he frequently donated to special church causes. The clerk of the Eighth Ward Deacons' Quorum faithfully recorded verbatim his and other testimonies, of which the minutes show at least twenty-five given between 1873 and 1877. Here is one such testimony in the minutes for November 11, 1873:

> I know we are the people of God, we have been led to these peaceful vallies of the mountains, and we enjoy life and many other blessings. I don't get tired of being with the Latter-day Saints, nor of being one of them. I'm glad that I ever took upon me the name of Christ. It is our privilege to call our families together, and we can sleep sweetly, and rise and thank God in the morning for his care through the night. It is good when we can go about our business, and return again, and find all right. I've a good woman and that is a great blessing. I thank God, for my soul burns with love for the many blessings I enjoy. I've been blest from my youth up, although in bond-

age for twenty years after receiving the gospel, yet I kept the faith. I thank
God that I ever gathered with the saints. May the Lord bless us and help
us to be faithful is my prayer.

He desired to be humble and "active in doing what he could for the
building up of the Kingdom of God." Church service was important to him
because he "did not come here to sit down and be still." He wanted to be
"faithful to the end" and to "always be valiant." Ultimately, he hoped "to
receive an exaltation in the Kingdom of God."[6] Samuel Chambers died on
November 9, 1929, at the age of ninety-eight years; Amanda had died the
year before.

A second exciting experience for Grace and me occurred in August
1973, when we were invited to join Lee and other church officers at the
area conference of the church in Munich, Germany. Grace and I flew first
to Copenhagen, Denmark, where in three days we saw Tivoli Gardens,
several museums, North Sjaelland, Fredericksborg Castle, and Elsinore. In
Munich we enjoyed the three-day conference, on which I wrote a fifteen-
page report; I was especially impressed with the talks of the European stake
presidents. The conference was at the site where the Olympics had been
held the previous year. We also saw the town hall, St. Peter's, St. Michael's,
other cathedrals, the university, museums, the public market, and the six-
teenth-century glockenspiel. We returned by way of Madrid, Spain, where
we saw the Prado; then to Lisbon, Portugal, where we saw a bull fight.

I was impressed with Lee's leadership, with his cordiality, and with his
positive vision of the future of the church in Europe and Africa. Lee was
especially kind to Grace and me and seemed proud to introduce me as "his"
church historian. After the Munich meetings hundreds of people stood in
line, for hours it seemed, to shake hands with Lee. Someone made a remark about this, and Lee was quick to clarify that the people did not want
to shake hands with him personally, but rather the prophet of the church.

Whatever our role as church historians, many persons expected us to
develop the implications of new findings in church history and to convey
new understandings of our history. Some of the material we developed, of
course, might be interpreted by traditionalists as negative. But it was not
difficult to balance revisionist accounts with exciting new sources and
perceptions that were unquestionably positive in their impact on authorities and general church members alike. I suppose we were trying to bridge
the gap between pietistic history and professional history; we anticipated
we could deal with the political problems involved. Tanner had wished us
to represent a professional approach to church history. We had the respect
of other professionals and of most ecclesiastics, and we prayed that the

Lord would continue to bless us in all that we did. As we had hoped, most of what we found and published was positive and reinforcing to thoughtful Latter-day Saints, even when it consisted of new information or a revision of older perceptions based on less in-depth research. That made our experience all the more gratifying.

I should add that we took our responsibility seriously of being *church* historians by showing appropriate discretion in our writing. In going through documents each of us discovered items that we agreed were private, not part of the church story, and not appropriate for publication. We were cautious and careful in what we wrote. On the other hand, as the prophet had instructed, we had to "tell it like it was." We were trying to be accurate but not offensive in conveying private peccadilloes, truthful but not sensational. On at least two occasions Lee, who was well aware of the chuckholes in writing truthful history, complimented me for my use of good judgment. Especially interesting were the many occasions when a person came to my office to inform me of the facts about a certain historical event "so the history will be an accurate record." I kept an account of these visits and the information conveyed but was reluctant to use the information unless the informant urged me to do so.

After Lee's unexpected death the day after Christmas in December 1973, Spencer W. Kimball, president of the Twelve, assumed office.

Although I had heard his addresses in general conference and in at least one stake conference, I was first impressed with Kimball as a spiritual leader on April 6, 1954, when he spoke in general conference on intolerance. Speaking on behalf of Japanese and Chinese peoples, Hawaiians and Indians, Mexicans and many others, he declared, "O intolerance, thou art an ugly creature! What crimes have been committed under thy influence, what injustices under thy Satanic spell!" Speaking of Native Americans, he declared:

> I present to you a people who, according to prophecies, have been scattered and driven, defrauded and deprived, who are a "branch of the tree of Israel—lost from its body—wanderers in a strange land"—their own land. I give you nations who have gone through the deep waters of the rivers of sorrow and anguish and pain; a people who have had visited upon their heads the sins of their fathers not unto the third and fourth generation but through a hundred generations. I bring to you a multitude who have asked for bread and have received a stone and who have asked for fish and have been given a serpent. . . .
>
> It is a people who, unable to raise themselves by their own bootstraps, call for assistance from those who can push and lift and open doors. It is a people who pray for mercy, ask forgiveness, beg for membership in the king-

dom with its opportunities to learn and do. It is a good folk who ask for fraternity, a handclasp of friendship, a word of encouragement; it is a group of nations who cry for warm acceptance and sincere brotherhood. . . .

Let us not spurn these Nephite-Lamanites until we are assured that we, too, have the love of the Savior as did their people when the Lord stood in their midst and ordained them with his own hands, blessed them with his own voice, forgave them with his own great heart.[7]

This powerful sermon inspired me to thank Kimball for such a strong endorsement of the need of sharing the love of Christ. I wrote him of how much the talk had meant to me personally, to my family, to my university colleagues, and to the church. Kimball replied with a friendly letter in which he reaffirmed that if we are to be true followers of Christ, we must cease to prejudge people because of race, religion, nationality, or previous beliefs and lifestyle. He concluded with typical humility, "I pray the Lord will bless my remarks that they may be beneficial to the cause." I was proud that he was serving on the Twelve.

In the following years, Kimball and I shared several experiences. We sat by each other on the stand at the Brigham Young University commencement in May 1969 when he received an honorary doctorate and I received the David O. McKay Humanities Award. He was very modest, could not understand why they were awarding the degree to *him*, and refused to allow any fuss and fanfare in connection with the honor.

When I was appointed church historian in 1972, Kimball was asked to be an advisor to the Twelve on historical matters. He saw this as an opportunity to inform the Twelve of the importance of the Historical Department's task and the need for church support and encouragement. He always stressed our spirit of service and regarded himself as our advocate with the Twelve.

Within two weeks of my call to the Historical Department, Kimball invited me to his office to show me his numerous journals. He opened the first one, which he had begun when he was appointed to the Twelve, and read aloud from the title page: "To My Family: Upon my death I want you to present this to the Church Historian. This is a record of my service in the cause of the Lord's Kingdom, and should be made a part of the Church records and archives." He then asked me to familiarize myself with the diaries for a few hours and instructed me to tell him if I had suggestions for improvement. I spent the rest of the day reading selections from these journals. They had full, informative, honest entries. I reported to my colleagues: "Three great diaries have chronicled the history of the Church. The first is the diary of President Wilford Woodruff, which provides a day-by-day record of the Church from 1834 until his death in 1898. The second is the diary of President Heber J. Grant, which supplies a daily history of the Church from 1882 until 1944. The third is the diary of Elder Spencer W. Kimball, which carries the history of the Church, in painstaking detail, from 1942 until this very day."

Kimball's diary is a marvelous record, and we have benefited from it in the noteworthy biography by Edward and Andrew Kimball Jr., *Spencer W. Kimball: Twelfth President of The Church of Jesus Christ of Latter-day Saints,* published in 1977. It is one of the great books in the history of the LDS Church—well-written, honest, and inspiring.

Spencer Kimball, a short, dark-eyed man, was reared in Safford, Arizona. He had been in the real estate and insurance business and active in Rotary International until appointed to the Twelve in 1943 at the age of forty-eight. Sincere, diligent, straightforward, with no desire to exercise power, he simply wanted to do what was best for the church.

Once I shared a July 24 platform with Kimball. I gave a historical talk, then he presented an incisive message on honoring the pioneers by cultivating such qualities as compassion, faithfulness, and integrity. Following the program, he embraced me, saying that he was fully aware of the complaints being made about the History Division, and urged us to continue to work faithfully. Then he kissed me on the cheek to affirm his feeling of personal warmth and said, measuredly and movingly, "I want you to know that I love you very much, and that the Lord is pleased that you are the historian of His Church." Imperfect and inadequate as our efforts may have been, I was proud that the prophet wanted us to continue doing the best we knew how. Kimball's loving blessing was a treasure to me and an affirmation of our work.[8]

In 1975 Grace and I were privileged to join Kimball and his party on a three-week tour of the Far East. Included in the group were some of the Twelve and their wives, some Seventies and their wives, the church's ambassador and his wife, the director of Public Communications, the president's personal physician, photographers, the president of the Relief Society, and security personnel. I was assigned to make a complete history of our tour, which I did in ninety-eight pages that were duly placed in the Church Archives for future reference. Most impressive for me was hearing the Korean Choir, which sang for all sessions. It was wonderful.

Kimball was concerned about everyone in the party. Each morning he boarded our bus, shook hands with us, inquired about our health, and gave us a personalized greeting. Before we parted each evening, he did the same. He was a good traveler—always cheerful and witty—and he was tireless. While we rested in our rooms before an important meeting, he scurried off to meet with the local missionaries, ward or branch leaders, or reporters and political leaders. His doctor cautioned him to "take it easy." Kimball replied that despite his respect for the doctor's abilities, he would continue to follow the Lord's instructions.

Kimball was a marvelous leader, untiring in carrying out "the Lord's work" and enthusiastic about doing favors for other people. He was a prophet in his official calling; he was also a great human being.

When we received the invitation to accompany the group, Grace and I telephoned Murdock Travel, the firm handling the arrangements, asking what clothes we ought to wear. We were told that we should dress comfortably for the long flight. Grace confirmed that I could wear sport clothes and she could wear slacks—even Camilla Kimball was wearing them. With that assurance, Grace and I dressed accordingly. When we arrived at Tokyo Airport, we were greeted by perhaps two or three hundred Japanese Saints. Grace was the only woman in slacks, and I was the only man in sport clothes. Apparently, we were the only couple who carried out the instructions given us. We were told later that Camilla Kimball had been told by her husband *not* to wear slacks, and Hinckley complained of the improper dress prescriptions by Murdock Travel.

Grace and I had one opportunity to share a meal with Camilla Kimball and her daughter Olive Beth Mack. Camilla related one delightful experience. In 1936 Spencer was elected district governor of Rotary, and the district voted to pay his travel expenses to the international convention in Nice, France. The Kimballs used some of their savings to pay Camilla's way. They had a marvelous trip, going by way of Montreal, Canada, where their oldest son was serving a mission. They also took in England, the Netherlands, Belgium, France, Switzerland, Austria, Italy, and Germany. Each convention meal in Nice featured goblets of wine from the principal departments of France. Spencer routinely passed these up—after all, he was a stake president. But Camilla had never tasted wine, was curious, and dared to try a sip. This event was mentioned in a draft of *Spencer W. Kimball: Twelfth President of the Church*. When she read the manuscript Camilla said that although she had no objection to being considered a drinker, Spencer appeared more self-righteous than was the case.

My call to be church historian gave me important responsibilities. I was not only a church appointee; I was also leader of the community of Mormon historians. I was given the authority and budget to employ a few; I might assist others with summer fellowships and internships; and I was convinced, rightly or wrongly, that we could follow an organized program of research and writing that would enhance our understanding of the past.

Perhaps because I was an economist, I began to think of myself as a historical entrepreneur—someone who organized people and resources to produce books and articles needed by the church and desired by its members. But without the guide of a price system, how could I and my colleagues make decisions? A given manuscript could take anywhere from one to ten years. A ten-year book, presumably definitive, would be costly in terms of human resources; but would it be worth it? Could a work be as good as necessary and be written in three years? Or one year? As church historian, I could assign a staff member to write a thirty-page essay on the Waldensians who became Mormons and came to Utah in the 1850s. A definitive treatment would require the writer to exhaust all archival sources, contact each descendant, and conduct searches in other archives. But how much effort is such a study worth? Should the researcher spend one month or two on it? Suppose one of the descendants has a period diary in French. Is it worth the expense to have the diary transcribed and translated? And what if the diary is twenty pages long? Two hundred pages? Two thousand pages? Should someone go to Italy to investigate official records? Could someone already in Italy conduct a search? What about staff resources? Should we concentrate on producing books or essays? Editing documents or writing monographs? Writing multivolume works or single volume histories? Narratives or biographies? Hire a specialist in juvenile history to popularize discoveries already made or hire a serious scholar?

I did not suppose that I was smart enough to make these decisions; I had gathered around me two professional historians, James Allen and Davis Bitton, who represented different points of view, and they willingly gave their advice. I also got plenty of advice from Mormon research and writing historians, both those employed by the Historical Department and those employed elsewhere. And of course I also received counsel from ecclesiastical leaders and sentiment from the general public. Nevertheless, decisions had to be made by someone.

The need for collective work had produced the following operational methods:

1. Each of our three senior historians (Arrington, Allen, and Bitton) was given a full-time research assistant. These assistants had at least a master's degree and usually were persons working part-time on a Ph.D. The three of us determined that we would use them only half-time on departmental projects so they could be working part-time on an approved project that they could publish under their own name.

2. Each person was assigned to work on a book but would be interrupted from time to time to work on chapters of other approved books or articles for historical journals or for church magazines.

3. One of our staff members, Maureen Ursenbach Beecher, with a

Ph.D. in English and experience in publishing a scholarly quarterly (*Western Humanities Review*), was assigned to be our editor. She read everything that any of us wrote for publication. She made substantive comments on the tone, style, content, and reader interest needs, as well as performed copyediting. Because she could not review everything we produced, we allowed her to hire an assistant editor as well. The two of them divided the work so that each had some free time to work on her own history projects. Jill Mulvay Derr edited diaries of women Latter-day Saints; Beecher wrote biographical articles about Eliza R. Snow.

4 The division had five secretaries: one transcribed original documents, one transcribed oral histories, one served as my secretary, one served as secretary to Allen and Bitton, and one served as secretary to the rest of the staff.

5. Everything that was written for publication by any member of the staff had to be read by me; and if it was sufficiently important or controversial, it was read by the two assistant church historians as well.

6. We spent long hours discussing the proper division of income received by us for our lectures, books, and articles. Many of our books, of course, were church publications that carried no royalty. But occasionally one of us did get some royalty or an honorarium on work that was not strictly an individual product. We had the help of a research assistant—should we share with him? The editor had contributed to the quality—should we share with her? A member of the archival staff had suggested some rare documents that "made" the article—should we share with him or her? What is fair? In general, we established the Mormon History Trust Fund for such special income. This fund was used to support fellowships to work in our archives and for other agreed-upon purposes. In this way we avoided the problem of determining what was a just way of sharing—nobody profited individually, but the work was forwarded.

7. Staff members and I disagreed over the content and wording of articles and books. Suppose that, upon reading a manuscript, I felt that a given paragraph should be deleted, but the writer insisted that it remain. Did he or she have any recourse? This happened rarely; in that instance, I asked my two assistant church historians and our editor to express their opinions. The staff member could have somebody else read it and, if he or she agreed, attempt to persuade me that the paragraph was both necessary and in good taste. Nobody was laying a job on the line by such a demonstration of stubbornness, and we usually ended up with some kind of compromise: the paragraph was modified and left in, or a sentence or two conveying the same information was incorporated in a preceding or subsequent paragraph. We had no confrontations in the department, even when we had a staff of twen-

ty, each of whom was inevitably a person of strong convictions. We certainly had no wish to dampen the creative energy of our professional staff. We employed them all primarily because they were creative, imaginative, and resourceful and because they had pride in their craft.

8. We employed persons who were intelligent, creative, and well-trained. How should we handle the problem of objectivity in a center that was funded by the church? How should we "tell the truth of history" and at the same time not offend those who controlled the purse strings of our operation? This, we believed, was not as much of a problem as many might suppose. Most of our material would not offend. Unavoidably, however, in the process of writing up a given event it was necessary to tell of the unpraiseworthy action of someone's grandfather. That particular someone might not wish that information to be published. What to do?

At this time I felt that those who charged the church with censorship propensities exaggerated the reality or generalized on the basis of one or two unusual experiences. Usually, I thought, scholars who complained were scared off by some two-bit bureaucrat who had no idea whether the president of the church would object or not. One had to use judgment—be intelligent and prayerful and discreet and then be willing to stand by the work even if one or two people, even in high places, yelled.

9. Under what circumstances were we justified in making confidential material available to professional historians? Letters to presidents of the church confess everything from adultery to burglary. If such materials were available, was the deceased's (or living person's) right of privacy being violated? What about minutes of meetings where statements made in the heat of passion but probably regretted later were included?

Some scholars are anxious to get their hands on such documents and emphasize the public's right to know. Others would like to consider the information but feel no necessity to make public the names of the participants. Still others prefer not to know or make known what was in confidential sources. Whether such material should be made available to outside scholars was one question; whether my colleagues and I should see them another. And if we should, inadvertently or not, see such materials, to what extent were we justified in using them? These questions faced us and our ecclesiastical advisors every day.

Personally I had no wish to suppress useful and relevant information. On the other hand, it would not have been proper for me—nor would I have wished—to expose the church, its leaders, and its members to unfair or sensational disclosures about their personal lives. Inevitably, by nature of my position, I occasionally felt like the Grand Inquisitor in *The Brothers Karamazov*. Not only were the administrative problems weighty; the ethical problems required soul-searching. Fortunately, I was able to counsel with my understanding colleagues, as well as Elders Anderson, Hunter, and Tanner.

Happily, the richness of our archives and the complex, exciting events of Mormon history assured that there were many topics of undeniable importance unaffected by such ethical complexities. These occupied most of our research attention. Even in areas where the source materials raised questions of privacy, I was optimistic that we were discovering ways of writing what we needed to say and of using our findings in a responsible way, often by means of a quantitative approach that provided a good sense of what was going on while avoiding the sensationalism of individual exposure typical of some popular publications.

After two years on the job, I wrote in my diary: "I would not change places with any historian in America; nor, as a Mormon, would I change places with any church official with a different assignment. I am proud that all my work in the documents has increased my love for the church and my faith in its divine mission."

## Notes

1. Harold B. Lee, N. Eldon Tanner, and Marion G. Romney to Leonard J. Arrington, James B. Allen, and Davis Bitton, Sept. 13, 1972, copy in Leonard J. Arrington Collection, Special Collections and Archives, Utah State University Libraries, Logan.

2. Blessing by Harold B. Lee on Leonard J. Arrington, Aug. 8, 1972, copy in Arrington Collection.

3. Gordon B. Hinckley quoted in "Elder Joseph Anderson Eulogized," *The Ensign* 22 (May 1992): 105.

4. Joseph Anderson to Thomas S. Monson, Boyd K. Packer, and Marvin J. Ashton, May 1, 1973, copy in Arrington Collection.

5. See William G. Hartley, "Samuel D. Chambers," *New Era* 4 (June 1974): 46–50. The article was originally written in September 1972.

6. Deacons' Quorum minutes, Nov. 11, 1873, quoted in William G. Hartley, "Samuel D. Chambers," *New Era* 4 (June 1974): 48–49.

7. Spencer W. Kimball, "The Evil of Intolerance," *Improvement Era* 57 (May 1954): 423–26.

8. See Leonard J. Arrington, "Spencer W. Kimball, Apostle of Love," *Dialogue* 18 (Winter 1985): 11–13; and the many articles about Kimball in *BYU Studies* 25 (Fall 1985).

# Our First Publication: *Brigham Young's Letters to His Sons*

Two things I am very anxious all my sons should be: faithful servants of our Heavenly Father, and useful members in his Kingdom. Integrity to the truth and ability to do good are qualities which I hope will characterize you all.
—Brigham Young, July 25, 1871

SHORTLY AFTER MY APPOINTMENT as church historian, I learned, primarily as a result of the probing of D. Michael Quinn, that the basement of the Church Administration Building was filled with cartons of Brigham Young's papers and other historical materials that were still in the boxes in which they had been placed for removal during the Utah War of 1857–58. The documents, we learned, had originally been kept in the home of George A. Smith, who had been church historian from 1854 to 1871, and whose home, across the street from the Beehive House and president's office of Brigham Young, had been built in 1858 expressly to serve as an archive. With the completion of the Church Administration Building in October 1917, the material for general use was placed on the third floor, and documentary material not yet approved for general use was placed in the basement.

When I first saw this rich and precious archive, not previously examined by any historian, I supposed I was in the Garden of Eden. As I touched the precious documents, I felt like Archimedes, who, finding the answer to a problem that had puzzled him, shouted "Eureka, I have found it!" When we informed the First Presidency of our discovery, they suggested that we assign a team to uncrate and catalogue the documents. We had approximately 150 boxes of Brigham Young materials, including twenty-nine letterpress copy books with exact replicas of about 30,000 letters he had dictated and signed; forty-eight volumes, about 50,000 pages, of a manuscript chronicle of his daily doings as president of the church; four diaries written mostly in his own hand during the years 1837 to 1844; ten diaries dictated by him, 1846–77, but in the hands of his private secretary; and thousands of pages of office journals, correspondence, published and unpublished speeches, ledgers, and telegram books. The collection was so vast that, considering other assignments, the task took us several years. We did not finish until 1977, a century after Brigham's death. The register was seventy-seven pages, single-spaced.

We could now flesh out the life of Brigham Young. A member of the church since 1832 and of the Twelve after 1835, Young served as president of the Twelve after the death of Joseph Smith in 1844 until December 1847, when he was sustained as president of the church; he served until his death in 1877. Acknowledged to be one of America's great colonizers, Young was also governor of Utah Territory from 1850 to 1858, superintendent of Indian affairs from 1851 to 1858, a founder of about 350 communities in the far West, and founder of several score business enterprises.

A believer in the principle of plural marriage practiced by the Saints during his lifetime, Young was the head of one of America's largest families. Sixteen of his wives bore him a total of fifty-seven children. Of these children, forty-six, seventeen sons and twenty-nine daughters, grew to maturity. The Church Archives had copies of more than one hundred letters written by Young to his children, including correspondence to sons proselytizing missions for the church, studying at eastern universities, away on business trips, and in the military service. The importance of Young as a letter writer had not previously been appreciated.

Having the responsibility of making available materials in the archives that would be edifying and informative, the Historical Department sponsored the preparation and publication of Young's letters to his sons as the first volume in the Mormon Heritage Series. Enjoying a warm relationship with his sons, Young gave them fatherly counsel through these letters, advice that was as relevant in 1974 as it was when written more than a century earlier.

The heartwarming letters to his sons were full of information about the weather, church affairs, and social and economic developments in the territory and in the church generally; news of the family, of friends, and of the livestock; and counsel and advice. They may not have been as witty or as finely phrased—and certainly not as pompous or cynical—as Lord Philip Chesterfield's *Letters to His Son* (1774), but they were informative, splendidly written, and contained the sincere endearing sentiments of a father to a son.

Most of the letters were dictated and the secretary provided the correct spelling, punctuation, capitalization, paragraphing, and grammar.

Occasionally, Young would add a postscript in his own handwriting at the bottom of the letter. We felt very close to Young as we held in our hands original letters with his personally inscribed postscripts. Since Young had only eleven days of formal schooling and had learned to read from his mother and from the Bible, his spelling was phonetic, enabling us to know how he pronounced words.

Under the superb editorship of Dean Jessee, ninety-five letters to the thirteen sons written between 1854 and 1877 were published by Deseret Book in 1974. The book was beautiful—dignified binding, excellent paper, elegant printing, fine photographs. We were very proud—and still are. It was a fine example of the bookmaker's art. The book contained a biography of each son and explanatory footnotes for references to people, places, and events.

Through these letters Brigham Young is shown to be both a deeply religious man and also a sensitive, loving, and understanding father. His advice to his sons contains his own philosophy of life: the importance of acquiring practical knowledge and skills, the obligation to be of service to others, and the need for total dedication to the kingdom of God.

In one of his first letters, that to his son Joseph Angell Young, then a missionary in England, he appended the following personal handwritten message:

My Dear Son Joseph
    It is now late at nigh, the male has arived this evening and I have heard your letter red, and it rejoice my hart to here sush good knews frm you. May the Lord Bles you for ever and ever, is my Prayr for you. We are jest movin in to our new house. I suepose Mary and the Chldren will give all the famely knews. You can hardly emagen the joy it gives me to here such good knew from you. My sole leaps for joye. Be faithful my son and the Lord will Bles you and I Bles you. Remember you are my oldest son, the arc of the famely. I want you to be faithful that you may [be] worthe of your stashon in my Kingdom. Give my love to all the Brethern. God Bles you Brigham Young[1]

For us in the office there was visual pleasure and excitement—thrill—in observing the shapes of the letters on the page and witnessing the quality of his perceptions, background, and character. The postscript enables us to hear the voice of the loving father.

Spelling, of course, was not standardized at the time Young wrote. During this period Ulysses S. Grant used the following spellings frequently: "asaid" (aside), "forever," "fals," "spleanded," "fer," "poarch," "voise," and "shure." Joseph Smith, who also grew up before spelling became standard, wrote as well as most of his contemporaries, but in his holographs one finds "git," "brotheren," "ritious" (righteous), "betraid," and "durty." Washington Irving, who was highly educated and knew six languages, still wrote "smoak."[2]

*Brigham Young's Letters to His Sons* sported a ten-page introduction by Jack H. Adamson, a popular Mormon-born professor of literature at the University of Utah who was familiar with Mormon history as well as with Shakespeare, Spenser, and Milton. He had written outstanding biographies of Sir Walter Raleigh and Sir Harry Vane and was working on a biography of Chief Joseph of the Nez Perce. Jack's introduction to *Brigham Young's Letters* was masterful, from historical and literary standpoints. He was clearly delighted with Young and his letters. We discussed the possibility of him writing a biography, and he agreed to do so if we would give him full access to the papers. We were in the process of working this out with church authorities when Jack suddenly died of a heart attack, on September 9, 1975, when he was only fifty-seven. He called Young's letters "beautiful and strong." His introduction ended with, "Sleep well, Brother Brigham. You left more sons and daughters than the children of your flesh. They hear you now. They understand."[3]

Let me give selections from Young's letters. He told his son Joseph Angell, who was on a mission to England, to observe his surroundings, as Young had done when a missionary there in the early 1840s:

> While you are absent from the Valley I wish you to lose no opportunity of making yourself familiar with all that is useful and likely to benefit you, for to be able to function in the world we must make ourselves acquainted with the ways of the world. This can only be done by keeping your mind constantly on the alert and when in society never allow anything to escape your notice, listen attentively; and observe minutely the manners, customs, and remarks of all, for, from the most humble of our fellow creatures an observing man can learn something that will be useful to him in after life, such has been my course and, from daily and hourly experience of its benefits I recommend you to pursue the same.
>
> There are many things you can inform your mind upon, the Laws of England, her form of government; lose no opportunity in your travels of visiting her manufactures, her works of art, her grand and spacious buildings, and all that is worthy of note, not from a mere idle curiosity but to store your mind with that which will benefit yourself and your brethren in after years. Use every endeavor to improve your address, and always exert yourself to be agreeable, and no matter whether poor or rich, treat them with equal courtesy, do not be pompous to the needy, nor condescending to the wealthy, but show by your manner that you do not respect a man

just because of his money, by this you will gain the love and admiration of those worthy of your esteem, and at comparatively little expense, for it costs but little labor and attention to be polite and civil to those around you.[4]

He signed his letter "Your Affectionate Father."

Joseph Angell later became a railroad contractor and president of Sevier Stake in southern Utah before his death at age forty-one.

Young's son Willard was appointed to the U.S. Military Academy at West Point, New York, in 1871, and there are many letters to him. The first letter expressed the hope that he would be an exemplary cadet:

> We hope yet to see you a pattern for all of them [the cadets]. By exhibiting your character and the principles you profess in your daily walk and conversation, and by refraining from every appearance of evil, you will not only be admired by the good and the upright, but you will command that respect that even the most unvirtuous are willing to accord to those who truly deserve it. There is no question but you can do a great deal of good among your fellow students and we hope to see you accomplish it. No matter what the world at large believe, or say about the Latter-day Saints, if we do our duty, and live for it, we will be found, among the children of men, at the head, and not at the tail.
>
> With regard to your attending Protestant Episcopal service, I have no objections whatever. On the contrary, I would like to have you attend, and see what they can teach you about God and Godliness more than you have already been taught.[5]

Later, as Willard was about to graduate, Young wrote:

> I admire your determination to use your leisure hours in studying, especially of our holy religion. I am desirous that you should also give especial attention to engineering, chemistry, minerology, and geology. If there are works on these sciences in the library of your post, I think it would be wise of you to use them to the best advantage, and read up on these branches. Amongst the pleasure of my life at the present time is the thought that so many of my sons are acquiring experimental and practical knowledge that will fit them for lives of great usefulness. And with this thought I associate the hope that by God's mercy that knowledge will be applied in striving to save the souls of men, and building up the kingdom of heaven on the earth. This knowledge and this work will prove your happiness, for every human being will find that his happiness very greatly depends upon the work he does, and the doing of it well. Whoever wastes his life in idleness, either because he need not work in order to live, or because he will not live to work, will be a wretched creature, and at the close of a listless existence,

will regret the loss of precious gifts and the neglect of great opportunities. Our daily toil, however humble it may be, is our daily duty, and by doing it well we make it a part of our daily worship. But, whatever be our labor, calling, or profession, we should hold our skill, knowledge, and talents therein, subservient to the accomplishment of the purposes of Jehovah, that our entire lives, day by day, may be made to praise Him, and our individual happiness secured by the consciousness that we are fulfilling the purpose and design of our presence here on the earth.[6]

Willard later became a well-known American engineer and president of the Logan Temple.

To his son Brigham Jr., who was a missionary in England in the 1860s, Young gave some practical advice:

In all probability you will be able to entirely omit the use of tobacco while on your mission, if you have not already done so. In such case I trust you will be wise enough to not resume its use on your return, either while crossing the ocean, passing through the states, nor upon the plains, but permit us to welcome you home with your mouth and breath free from the use and smell of tobacco. It is now going on two years and a half since I have used a particle of tobacco, and I guess a little resolution and faith on your part will also enable you to dispense with its use, in doing which you will ever feel strengthened, prospered, and blest.[7]

Brigham Jr. later joined the Twelve and was its president at the time of his death in 1903.

In searching through the Brigham Young papers, we also found a letter to his daughter-in-law Clara Stenhouse Young, whose husband, Joseph Angell, had just died. Although this was not appropriate to include in the *Dear Son* volume, it offers an example of Young's solicitude, compassion, and regard for women.

Mrs. Clara Young, My dear Daughter: I am not greatly surprised that you occasionally have spells of low spirits, but I hope before this reaches you that you will have entirely got over your down heartedness, and are feeling happy and comfortable. Do not trouble yourself about the future, remember that sufficient is the day for the evil thereof, and the same God who has preserved you and provided for you in days past still lives, and still cares for you, and that your friends have not deserted you, neither do they intend to do so. Half our troubles arise from the anticipation of evils that never take place, and dangers that never reach us. But be contented, seek to train your little ones in the nurture and admonition of the Lord, and prepare the minds of your children to become men of honor, and fit them for lives of usefulness on the earth, You will then find enough to do to fill your mind with happy thoughts and the realization that you are doing your duty, and that the Lord is well pleased with you will be ever present, and by seeking for His spirit you will have joy and peace in your heart constantly. As I have told you before I am always pleased to hear from you and to learn your feelings, your prospects and condition, and try to still believe that I am your friend and have your welfare at heart.

May God bless you, comfort you, and strengthen you and yours is the prayer of Yours affectionately Brigham Young.[8]

Three days after the appearance of *Letters of Brigham Young to His Sons*, we were given a copy of a four-page letter from Boyd K. Packer to the First Presidency, stating his concern, "expressed on several occasions," about historians' "orientation toward scholarly work." He cited as examples a reference to litigation brought against the executors of Young's will by disgruntled family members and the letter to Brigham Jr. suggesting that he stop using tobacco. Packer also "winced" at Jack Adamson's references to "Brigham" in the introduction because a biography of Harold B. Lee would not speak of him as "Harold."

He concluded his letter by saying that he found the book "on balance . . . all right" and thought "there is a warm and wonderful message to be drawn from President Young's letters to his sons." He also gave permission for his letter to be shown to us and added, "If we determine that we should continue to publish information such as this, that itself will be an interesting bit of history, for the brethren who have preceded us were very careful to do just the opposite." The book was good, in other words, but it would have been better if we had not volunteered the information about certain Brigham Young family foibles.[9]

Hunter told me that the letter had been read and discussed at the meeting of the Twelve on November 14, 1974, when McConkie was absent and Hunter, caught unprepared, could not answer some of the questions the Twelve put to him. He could only tell Packer that his letter should not have been sent to the First Presidency but instead to himself or to me.

Nervously, we asked Hunter if Packer's closing query ("I . . . wonder if these projects ought to be carefully reviewed before they continue") meant that proposed publications should be cleared by the Correlation Committee, which had been appointed to reduce and simplify the church program, or whether they should be reevaluated by appropriate authorities for propriety? Hunter thought Packer meant both; this upset Hunter because he was strongly opposed to either form of review. We admired Bruce McConkie, our other advisor, despite his rigid doctrinal stance because he was a valiant defender of what he thought was right. McConkie declared with strong emphasis that Latter-day Saints could not avoid the responsibility to write history, so we might as well use professionals and do it right. McConkie also said that the Correlation Committee was assigned to oversee doctrine in manuals—and if our books were to become manuals, no doubt the members would have some suggestions. Our works, however, should be approved by professionals, not by committee members with no training in history. The Correlation Committee, after all, was appointed to effect a reduction and simplification of the church program, not to be a final authority on what could be said in a history book.

Joseph Anderson added that since first names had been traditionally used for Joseph Smith and Brigham Young, he saw no problem in following this form. Further, he thought that including Young's admonishment to his son was perfectly appropriate. Young had phrased it well, the advice would have positively affected his son, and no doubt it would similarly affect current readers. I mentioned that we had received a letter from another of the Twelve, now dead, specifically congratulating us on Jack Adamson's introduction.

Clearly, although our managing director and advisors from the Twelve were satisfied with our work, we had to limit our contributions to *Dialogue, Exponent II,* and *Sunstone;* increase our visibility with church periodicals and *BYU Studies;* keep a steady flow of positive articles to balance the potentially controversial ones; keep reassuring people about the reviews done by our screening committee; and carry on as usual in a guarded manner. I wrote in my diary after the stir created by Packer's letter:

> It is inevitable that Church historians should have some problems. I sometimes feel like a football coach deciding to punt instead of trying for a first down; or a basketball coach fouling in hopes of getting a rebound. There are always people in the stands who feel they understand the situation more clearly and are eager to express their dissatisfaction. President Kimball, particularly after he became our Prophet, has gone out of his way to let us know that *he* supports us and appreciates our efforts. He is willing to acknowledge that he thinks we are valiant servants who should not be deterred by uninformed or unfair criticism.

Packer, who continued to be critical of our work, was a native of Brigham City, Utah, had earned a doctorate in education from Brigham Young University, and had served as mission president in New England during the student revolt of the 1960s. His views on the writing of church history are articulated in a chapter in his biography by Lucile C. Tate.[10] Influenced by the scriptures, by the "unwritten" history told to him by his fellow general authorities, and by his experiences as a student and teacher in seminary, he believed that historians tend to emphasize secular explanations, are prone to mention the foibles of church leaders to prove that they are human, and are guided more by the principles of their profession than by the revealed word of God. The focus, he contends, should be on the "inspiring works" of leaders.

In a later speech to seminary and Institute of Religion teachers, Packer voiced four cautions:

1. There is no such thing as an accurate, objective history of the church without consideration of the spiritual powers that attend this work.

2. There is a temptation for the writer or the teacher of church history to want to tell everything, whether it is worthy or faith promoting or not.

3. In an effort to be objective, impartial, and scholarly, a writer or a teacher may unwittingly be giving equal time to the adversary.

4. Just because something is already in print is no reason to assume it is suitable for use in writing or speaking or teaching.[11]

In noticing the research and writing done in the archives of the church, Packer believed that he and his colleagues were "watching over the Church, defending the Lord's anointed, and protecting a sacred stewardship."[12]

## Notes

1. Dean C. Jessee, ed., *Brigham Young's Letters to His Sons* (Salt Lake City: Deseret Book, 1974), 12. See also Dean C. Jessee, "The Writings of Brigham Young," *Western Historical Quarterly* 4 (July 1973): 273–94.

2. See Elinore Hughes Partridge, "Nineteenth-Century Spelling: The Rules and the Writers," *The Ensign* 5 (Aug. 1975): 74–80.

3. Jack Adamson, introduction to *Brigham Young's Letters to His Sons,* xx.

4. Letter to Joseph Angell Young, Feb. 3, 1855, *Brigham Young's Letters to His Sons,* 14.

5. Letter to Willard Young, July 25, 1871, *Brigham Young's Letters to His Sons,* 170–71.

6. Letter to Willard Young, Nov. 11, 1875, *Brigham Young's Letters to His Sons,* 190–91.

7. Letter to Brigham Young Jr., Oct. 11, 1862, *Brigham Young's Letters to His Sons,* 32–33.

8. Letter to Clara Stenhouse Young, Jan. 24, 1876, bound typescript copy of Brigham Young letters, Manuscripts Division, Harold B. Lee Library, Brigham Young University, Provo.

9. A major portion of the letter, together with comments on Packer's perspective on church history, is given in Lucile C. Tate, *Boyd K. Packer: A Watchman on the Tower* (Salt Lake City: Bookcraft, 1995), 244–45. The letter is dated October 24, 1974.

10. See Tate, *Boyd K. Packer.*

11. These and other comments about history are in Boyd K. Packer, "The Mantle Is Far, Far Greater than the Intellect," *BYU Studies* 21 (Summer 1981): 259–78. See also Packer, *Let Not Your Heart Be Troubled* (Salt Lake City: Bookcraft, 1991).

12. Packer, *Let Not Your Heart Be Troubled,* 247.

8

# Other Early Studies and Publications

Brigham Young: "Well, I suppose you are going to go off and
  apostatize."
Bishop Edwin D. Woolley: "No, I won't. If this were your church I
  might, but it's just as much mine as it is yours."
  —*From Quaker to Latter-day Saint*

It is the duty of the Lord's clerk . . . to keep a history, and a general
church record of the . . . things that transpire in Zion . . . and also their
manner of life, their faith, and works.
  —Doctrine and Covenants 85:1–2

IN THESE EARLY YEARS in the History Division my colleagues and I published other books and task papers. Some of them had their origins in the universities with which we had been connected.

## Manchester Mormons

The first of these was *Manchester Mormons: The Journal of William Clayton, 1840–1842*, published in 1974 by Peregrine Press and edited by James Allen and Thomas Alexander, both at Brigham Young University. One of the earliest daily journals of a Mormon official born in England, William Clayton's diary made significant contributions to an understanding of the human side of Mormon history. Clayton, who is perhaps best known for writing the words of the famous Mormon hymn "Come, Come, Ye Saints" and for chronicling the journey of the pioneer company's emigration to Utah in 1847, was converted in 1837, at age twenty-two, and began his journal in 1840. *Manchester Mormons* is a marvelously sensitive account of life among the new Saints in the factory town of Manchester in the midlands of England as well as a testimony to Clayton's personal dedication to his calling as second counselor in the British Mission. The early English Mormons are seen as real people—not an idyllic community of highly spiritual, loving and fully cooperative Saints, but rather people struggling with everyday problems and displaying the weaknesses of all human beings. However, they were people whose lives were characterized by genuine religious devotion.

## Wit and Whimsy in Mormon History

A second book, by Davis Bitton, was *Wit and Whimsy in Mormon History*, published by Deseret Book in 1974. A volume of Mormon humor, it is a compilation of selections drawn from early Utah newspapers and from material in the archives designed to show that early Mormons were not insufferable bores. Some accounts are hilarious. Perrigrine Sessions records in his diary of 1853 that Sarah Kirkman rattled a chain at night to frighten her husband into believing he was being punished for failing to say his prayers. A story from an 1880 *Juvenile Instructor* describes playful boys teasing a sleeping member in church and Priddy Meeks's colorful advice on dress standards—tight lacing and corsets cause "weakness, emaciation, nervous irritability, shortness of breath, headache, and faintings." The *Deseret News* of January 25, 1851, argues that hot drinks are not for the body or belly: if a person drinks hot coffee or tea, it will relax the stomach and food may lie dormant until "putrefaction commences." Priddy Meeks must have had good medicine; he lived to be ninety-one and his wives died at ages ninety-five and ninety-six. The categories included in *Wit and Whimsy* were courtship, pioneering, preaching, church meetings, dress, Word of Wisdom, persecution, pot pourri, and subscription blurbs.

## Charles C. Rich: Mormon General and Western Frontiersman

A third book was my biography of Charles C. Rich, published in 1974 by Brigham Young University Press under the title *Charles C. Rich: Mormon General and Western Frontiersman*. In 1970 Roland Rich Woolley, a prominent attorney in southern California, arranged for me to write a biography of his grandfather under a grant to Utah State University. To facilitate my research, I was able to employ several student assistants.

Born in Kentucky the same year and in the same region as Abraham Lincoln, Rich was also tall (six feet four inches), possessed a dry humor, and was a strong leader. He was converted in 1832 when he was twenty-three by John Corrill, Lyman Wight, and George Hinkle, three itinerant missionaries. Like most early converts, he alternated between proselytizing and farming. He took part in the Zion's Camp expedition. After five years he decided, at age twenty-nine, for doctrinal reasons if for no other, that he ought to marry. "I could not do much good without a wife, and without posterity," he wrote; "I therefore concluded to marry."[1] Not wishing to interrupt his missionary work to court, he asked his missionary friends and acquaintances to watch for a likely prospect. Several persons recommended a twenty-three-year-old convert in southern Illinois, Sarah DeArmon Pea. At the same time, missionary friends told Sarah, "We have got a good young Elder in the Church picked out for you for a husband."[2] Too busy with his missionary work to visit her, Charles finally mailed Sarah a letter. Copied into his missionary diary, the letter read as follows:

> Miss Sarah Pea . . . although a perfect stranger to you, however, I trust that these few lines may be . . . the beginning of a happy acquaintance with you. . . . Elder G. M. Hinckle and others have highly recommended you as a Saint of the Last Days as being worthy of my attention. . . . I think I should be happy to get a good companion, such a one as I could take comfort with through life and such a one as could take comfort with me. As you have been recommended to me as such, I should be very happy to see you and converse with you on the subject. . . . If these lines is received with the same feeling that I write them, I trust that you may be single and unengaged. . . . After you read and meditate upon it, I should be glad you would write me an answer to it. If so you can direct your letter to me at Liberty, Clay County, Missouri. Charles Rich.[3]

Sarah read the letter, prayed about it, and decided to let the Bible give her direction as to what she should do. Opening the Bible at random, she was immediately greeted with these lines: "Whither thou goest, I will go; and where thou lodgest, I will lodge. Thy people shall be my people, and thy God my God" (Ruth 1:16). She copied this verse on a sheet and sent it to Charles without any comment. Thus began a correspondence that lasted six months, when her father sold his land in Illinois and moved to Missouri. Two weeks later, she wrote in her diary: "In a public meeting today I saw, for the first time, Charles Rich. Our eyes rested on each other, we knew each other at sight."[4] They were married shortly thereafter. Because of his strength and height, he became a brigadier general of the Nauvoo Legion. He was a member of the select Council of Fifty. As they left Nauvoo he presided over the cholera-stricken Saints at Mount Pisgah, Iowa, then led one company of Saints across the Great Plains to the Salt Lake Valley. He was immediately installed as a counselor in the presidency of Salt Lake Valley Stake, and Sarah established a home at Centerville, Utah. The home has been moved to Pioneer State Park near the Pioneer Monument at the mouth of Emigration Canyon on the east bench of Salt Lake City.

Sustained as one of the Twelve in 1849, Charles was cofounder of the Mormon colony at San Bernardino, California, and in 1863 directed the colonization of sixteen settlements in Bear Lake Valley in the Utah-Idaho area, a far cry from balmy southern California. He was president of the

European Mission in the early 1860s. Sarah, who faithfully looked after the home front, bore nine children, most of whom, like their parents, were community builders. One of them, Ben E. Rich, was one of the great missionaries in the history of the church. With six wives, Charles Rich had fifty-one children.

While working on the history I discovered that Sarah Pea's grandfather, Joshua Pea, was a soldier in the Revolutionary Army. On his tombstone in the Martha's Vineyard cemetery is the following epitaph:

> *Under this sod and under this tree*
> *Lie the remains of Joshua Pea.*
> *Oh he is not here but only his pod.*
> *He shelled his peas and went to God.*

*Charles C. Rich: Mormon General and Western Frontiersman* is more a "history" than a "biography" or "life." Readers were brought tantalizingly close to Rich's experiences without ever feeling that they knew the man. His life is detailed, but few insights are given by interpretive analysis. Rich was a fine leader, but how he won people's confidence is not clear save that he was careful and considerate. This is partly the result of his taciturnity. He was often a preacher and chairman of meetings, but his journals usually told what he did and what he saw but ignored the "how" of things he did. He was in charge of many church projects yet made little mention of his concerns as an administrator. The biography suggests that he subordinated the role of women in his life. He loved his wives and children yet was always being dispatched on some new mission for the church, leaving his wives to fend for themselves under conditions of grueling hardship. In writing his life I did not speculate about why Rich agreed to go. He could be farsighted but also stubborn and literal. The book would have been better if I could have looked into the mind and soul of this fascinating leader of a heroic era.

## David Eccles: Pioneer Western Industrialist

In 1971, when I was still in Logan, Nora (Nonie) Eccles Treadwell Harrison, a sister of financial magnates Marriner and George Eccles, proposed that I write a biography of her father, David Eccles. Although I had previously been co-author of *William Spry* and principal author of *Charles C. Rich,* I did not fully appreciate that biographies are something different from histories. As it turned out, the Eccles project helped me learn to improve. Nonie financed the project by making a grant to Utah State University, which, in turn, set up an expense account for me and reduced my teaching assignments.

Nonie, of course, was from the Logan family of David and Ellen Eccles, and no one in that family, that I could find, had sufficient material to put together the story of David Eccles's life. I soon discovered, however, that Cleone Eccles, widow of Royal Eccles of the Ogden family, had substantial material. A resident of Ogden and a member of the Relief Society General Board, she was willing to share her materials with me. With her gracious hospitality, she permitted me to spend weeks, working in her home—searching through letters, clippings, ledgers, books, photographs, and other documents. Royal, a lawyer, had apparently considered writing a biography at one time and in the 1920s and 1930s had collected a large block of manuscripts and documents. He had interviewed several dozen people who had known David, and these had all been typed and certified.

With the assistance of George Daines, one of my students, who traced each of the business enterprises of David and provided the material for the appendix on the Eccles businesses, I finished the first draft about the time of my appointment as church historian and furnished a copy to Nonie, who circulated it among some of the family. She lived in Los Altos Hills, California, in the same neighborhood as Wallace Stegner, the Pulitzer Prize–winning novelist who taught creative writing at Stanford. Stegner had lived in Salt Lake City several years, was interested in Mormon history and culture, had been acquainted with my work, and had visited me in my office while writing *Gathering of Zion*. On April 25, 1973, he wrote me a fifteen-page critique of my draft that was, in many respects, a miniature manual on how to write a good biography. He had suggestions for reorganization, gave pointers on making it more lively, and copyedited it.

By the time the critique arrived I was immersed in the running of the Historical Department, and so I asked Maureen Ursenbach Beecher to help me. She worked on the manuscript for several weeks, and her creative revision gave it new life. She is a wonder. We completed the book in 1974 and Gerald Sherratt, then vice president at Utah State University, arranged for the university to publish it, the first book for what became the Utah State University Press. The book was splendidly printed, bound, and illustrated, a credit to the university, to the Eccles family, and to me. When the School of Business at the University of Utah was renamed the David Eccles School of Business, Spencer Eccles, a grandson of David, bought the unsold copies of the book and presented copies to the faculty.

I was delighted to do the biography of David Eccles. He was an excellent example of the American success story; as much as anyone he was responsible for bridging the gap between Mormon and non-Mormon businessmen in Utah in the 1880s, 1890s, and early 1900s; he founded several dozen enterprises in Utah that gave the state a boost at a critical time in its history; and he came to the rescue of LDS leaders when the church was financially strapped due to the federal confiscation of its properties under the Edmunds-Tucker Act in 1887.

The William Eccles family, with seven children, lived in a poor section in Paisley, near Glasgow, Scotland, where William was a half-blind woodturner, making spools for weavers. The family members were converted by Mormon missionaries in 1842 but, because of their poverty, were unable to migrate to Utah until 1863 and only then because of the support of the Perpetual Emigrating Fund. David was fourteen at the time. They settled in Liberty in Ogden Valley. Their crops were destroyed by grasshoppers, and friends persuaded them to migrate to Oregon City, Oregon. There William furnished spools for a new textile factory and David and his brothers worked in lumber mills and on railroad construction. Upon their return to Utah in 1869, David opened a lumber business, contracting to cut and finish timber, and gradually extended his operations to Wood River, Idaho, where an influx of miners created a demand for lumber; then to northeastern Idaho, where Mormons were building a railroad from Ogden to Montana. When the Oregon Short Line Railroad was being constructed from Cheyenne to Portland in 1882, David furnished ties and lumber for buildings. Seeing opportunities for lumber extraction and manufacturing in the Northwest, he and some Mormon partners organized the Oregon Lumber Company, earned good profits, and invested in businesses in Utah. David eventually became Utah's first multimillionaire. He helped to found a host of enterprises: Ogden First National Bank that formed the basis for the First Security Corporation, milk products manufacturing, the Utah Construction Company, canning plants, and railroads. He was the mayor of Ogden, started the Ogden Chamber of Commerce that included both Mormon and non-Mormon businessmen, and had a large plural family: twelve children by Bertha Jensen, a Danish immigrant, and nine children by Ellen Stoddard, a daughter of a Scottish immigrant who was one of David's partners. On one occasion, being informed that the church was in financial straits, David wrote out a personal check for $100,000. He was a person worth writing about and I very much enjoyed the assignment.

## Latter-day Patriots

The fourth volume was written in preparation for the bicentennial celebration in 1976. National leaders encouraged states, churches, and private groups to make suitable contributions. At early meetings of the Church

Bicentennial Celebration Committee, chaired by L. Tom Perry, our History Division volunteered to prepare a book on prominent Mormons and their Revolutionary heritage. Although Latter-day Saints appropriately dwell on the stirring scenes of Mormon history in western New York, Ohio, Missouri, Illinois, and crossing the Plains, they are also partakers of a much larger inheritance rooted deep in the soil of early America. Joseph Smith, for example, had ancestors who came on the *Mayflower,* and both of his grandfathers and his paternal great-grandfather served as soldiers in the American Revolution. The plan was to illuminate some of the breadth of our American heritage while telling the story of Mormonism as it affected the lives of a few descendants of participants in the Revolution.

We asked Gene Allred Sessions, a new member of our staff who was well read in the history of the Revolution, to write the volume. He had just completed a life of James Moyle from papers in our archives and in the collection of the Moyle family. At the end of 1975 Deseret Book and the Historical Department jointly published *Latter-day Patriots: Nine Mormon Families and Their Revolutionary War Heritage,* a handsomely designed and well-written volume with essays on Joseph Smith, Brigham Young, Daniel Wood, Ezra Taft Benson, Daniel H. Wells, Edward Bunker, John Brown, Christeen Golden Kimball, and Hartman Rector Jr. The individuals were selected on the basis of their ancestors' experiences in the war and of their own part in the growth and development of the church. The nine cases, therefore, involved many significant topics of both Revolutionary and Mormon history loosely woven together into a fabric of people, their kinship, and their time. The sketches demonstrated the affection of many pioneer Mormon leaders for America and furnished a recollection of the sacrifice in the War for Independence by the ancestors of many people prominent in the Latter-day movement.

## *Professional Articles*

President Tanner had instructed us in explicit terms to undertake the writing of church history. It was not only that the Church Historian's Office had not written any history since B. H. Roberts completed the *Comprehensive History* in 1930 but also that the materials had not been available to outside and inside researchers since the deluge of postwar graduate students caused archives administrators to limit access beginning in 1952. To utilize the available sources, we initiated a series of much-needed projects, and with the approval of the Committee on Expenditures built our staff to undertake them. In addition to those mentioned in the previous chapters, the following are examples of our research and writing.

1. Studies of the priesthood and church organization. Using minutes of priesthood meetings and other sources, Bill Hartley wrote articles on the Priesthood Reform Movement, 1908–22, deacons through church history, teachers, the Seventies' quorums, and the priesthood reorganization of 1877. D. Michael Quinn wrote on the evolution of presiding quorums, on prayer circles, and on LDS religion classes. Scott Kenney, under a fellowship, wrote on the history of the Mutual Improvement Association. Jill Mulvay, Susan Staker Oman, and Carol Madsen wrote on the history of the Primary. Bruce Blumell wrote on church welfare. Dale Beecher wrote on the office of bishop. Ronald Esplin wrote on the Twelve in a historical context. Maureen Ursenbach Beecher and Jill Mulvay Derr wrote on the history of the Relief Society.

2. Studies of the history of LDS women. Maureen Ursenbach Beecher, Jill Mulvay Derr, and Carol Cornwall Madsen each published studies of individual LDS women, of the Relief Society, of historical aspects of women's activities, and of the history of Mormon women.

3. Studies of different phases of LDS history. Each of us prepared articles for special issues of *BYU Studies, The Ensign, Dialogue,* and other magazines and journals that dealt with different phases of LDS history: New York, Kirtland, Missouri, Nauvoo, crossing the Plains, early Salt Lake Valley, and colonization. Similarly, we undertook studies of the histories of various LDS communities: Franklin, Paris, Blackfoot, and Oakley, Idaho; Ogden Valley, Utah Valley, Logan, St. George, Cedar City, Carbon and Emery Counties, and Salt Lake City in Utah. We also prepared histories of many wards and stakes for local audiences where we were asked to speak and studies of LDS colonies in Nevada, California, Arizona, New Mexico, Colorado, Wyoming, Idaho, Utah, and Canada.

4. Studies of the histories of Mormon national and ethnic groups. These included articles on Scandinavian, English, Welsh, Swiss, American southern, and Hawaiian Mormons. There were also articles on African Americans, Native Americans, and a general article by Dean May on Mormons as an ethnic group for *The Harvard Encyclopedia of American Ethnic Groups.*

5. Short and extended biographies of many Latter-day Saint personalities. These included Joseph Smith, Brigham Young, Wilford Woodruff, Heber C. Kimball, Heber J. Grant, Harold B. Lee, Joseph Fielding Smith, Eliza R. Snow, Emmeline B. Wells, Edwin D. Woolley, John Pack, Lorenzo Hill Hatch, N. L. Nelson, Margaret Judd Clawson, Samuel D. Chambers, Juanita Brooks, Sarah M. Kimball, Edward W. Tullidge, and many others. In addition, David Dryden, under a fellowship, prepared biographical essays on three general authorities of the early twentieth century:

Anthony W. Ivins, George F. Richards, and Stephen L Richards; he wrote similar biographical essays on four general authorities of the twentieth century: Charles A. Callis, Albert E. Bowen, Adam S. Bennion, and Matthew Cowley. These were published in our Task Papers series as numbers 11 and 12.

6. Assistance in research. Through fellowships we were instrumental in the preparation of several books that made important contributions to LDS history, including not only those mentioned elsewhere but also Donna Hill's *Joseph Smith, The First Mormon* (1977), Dallin H. Oaks and Marvin S. Hill's *The Carthage Conspiracy: The Trial of the Accused Assassins of Joseph Smith* (1975), Stanley B. Kimball's *Heber C. Kimball: Mormon Patriarch and Pioneer* (1981), and Merlo J. Pusey's *Builders of the Kingdom: George A. Smith, John Henry Smith, and George Albert Smith* (1981).

## Studies of Joseph Smith's Writing Style

From any point of view, Joseph Smith is the central figure in Mormon history. Many of our efforts, by our staff or by recipients of our fellowships, were devoted to exploring primary materials in the archives that related to his life in western New York, in Kirtland, and in Nauvoo. Articles from these sources were published in *The Ensign, New Era, Brigham Young University Studies,* and *Dialogue.* Perhaps one of the most significant of these studies was done by Elinore Partridge, a professor of English at the University of Wisconsin at Milwaukee.

Which of the *Lectures on Faith* that were once used in the Doctrine and Covenants were delivered by Joseph Smith and which by others? Were the sermons attributed to him in the *History of the Church* edited by B. H. Roberts in Joseph Smith's style or were they "edited up" by his secretaries and recorders? What were the particular elements of his style? Which of the works attributed to the prophet were actually written or spoken by him? In searching for help, we discovered that Partridge, a fellow church member, had studied writing styles of many Americans. We offered her a fellowship in 1975 to spend a summer studying the holograph letters, diaries, and "histories" of Joseph Smith and to give us some analysis of his style.[5] Her work was helpful to the biographers of Joseph Smith, to the students of Mormon doctrine, and especially to Dean Jessee, who was working on articles related to early church history and who edited volumes on the writings of Joseph Smith.

Although he did not speak with the eloquent, precise articulation of one highly educated, Joseph Smith was fervent and could hold audiences spellbound for hours.[6] While he possessed "a rough eloquence," Partridge found that the prophet shared four important characteristics with some of the finest writers of the English language:

1. He was nurtured on the King James Bible, a source of eloquence for Abraham Lincoln and for many writers from Milton to Melville to William Faulkner.
2. He had an acute sense of detail. He knew how to create visual descriptions that enabled the audience to picture what he was saying.
3. He had a good narrative sense, selecting the events of an experience in a way to hold the interest of his audience.
4. He wrote as he spoke, in a style more familiar than formal.[7]

What did his style tell about his personal qualities? His writings, Partridge reported, were those of a spiritual leader giving advice, shaped by a definite sense of authority, to his people. Yet, his writings revealed a humble, unhesitating man, seeking divine comfort and assurance. "He shows courage and forbearance, but he also sometimes complains that he is lonely and wishes to hear from family and friends." Many of the letters, she wrote, clearly reveal the lonely husband and the concerned father. "He mixes eloquent idealism, concerned with spiritual welfare, with homely advice, designed to improve physical welfare, sometimes in the same sentence; for example he tells Emma: 'I am happy to find that you are still in the faith of Christ and at Father Smiths.'"[8] Partridge concludes:

> In this close study of Joseph Smith's language, the personal quality which most impressed me was the tremendous sense of joy and vitality. . . . In contrast to the dark visions of Calvinism and the dry, rational theology of Unitarianism, Joseph Smith's pronouncements emphasize the wonder of existence and the love of humanity. Likewise, in contrast to the threats of wrath, judgment, and damnation, which one can find in the statements of some of the early church leaders, there is an undercurrent of understanding and compassion in those of Joseph Smith. Moments of discouragement and anger do occur; however, even at times when he laments the state of mankind, he tempers the observations with trust in God, love for his family, and hope for the future. The love of others, the pleasure in variety, and the joy in living which is apparent in the language of Joseph Smith give us some real sense, I believe, of what he must have been like as a leader and a friend.[9]

## Pioneer Economy

Way back in 1952 my good friend George Ellsworth told me of some records of the old Cache Valley Stake that were located in an abandoned building. Upon investigation I found hundreds of ledger books, day books, and letter books that had been used by the Cache Valley Tithing Office in the nineteenth century. Recognizing the church policy of not giving public access to tithing records, I prepared a paper on the general operations of the tithing office, making sure that I did not use from that source any individual tithing accounts. I voluntarily submitted the manuscript to A. William Lund of the Church Historian's Office and to the First Presidency for clearance. The article was eventually published as "The Mormon Tithing House: A Frontier Business Institution" in *Business History Review* in 1954. I received many letters from scholars and church officials complimenting me on the article, in which I demonstrated that the tithing house played a major role in the economic life of the Mormon community. The tithing house was a communal receiving and disbursing agency, warehouse, weighing station, livestock corral, general store, telegraph office, employment exchange, and social security bureau. These functions extended the reach of the tithing house into banking, the fixing of official prices, and bulk selling.

The Cache Valley Tithing Office also served as a center for distributing goods to traveling groups of Native Americans; I used the data in the "Indian Account" to show the extensive trade with these groups. An article with this information was published as "How the Saints Fed the Indians" in *Improvement Era* in 1954.

When we moved into the Church Historian's Office in 1972, we found ledgers with the accounts of the General Tithing Office in Salt Lake City, 1849 to 1900. Recognizing again the church policy of not making individual tithing records available, we thought a scholarly study of tithing records, leaving out names, would tell us much about the distribution of income and wealth in pioneer Utah. We therefore obtained permission from our managing director, our advisors, and the First Presidency to make the records available to trustworthy scholars for summary studies of the pioneer economy. We first granted permission to Lee Soltow, of Brookings Institution, not a member of the church, who made use of the material in his book *Men and Wealth in the U.S., 1850–1870* (1975). He also published, with the help of Dean May of our staff, "The Distribution of Mormon Wealth and Income in 1857" in *Explorations in Economic History* in 1979.

We also approached some BYU economists about a more detailed study. Those involved were Larry Wimmer, Clayne Pope, and James R. Kearl of the department of economics. Their first publication was "The Distribution of Wealth in a Settlement Economy: Utah, 1850–1870," which appeared in 1980 in the *Journal of Economic History*. Basically, they concluded that the pioneer Mormon economy was more egalitarian than that of the American economy generally and most other Western communities as well.[10] These and other studies in such publications as *Journal of Economic History, Journal of Interdisciplinary History, Review of Economics and Statistics*, and *Journal of Labor Economics*, and in such books as *Studies in Income and Wealth*, volume 51, edited by Stanley Engerman and Robert Gallman (1986), and *Strategic Factors in Nineteenth Century American Economic History*, edited by Claudia Goldin and Hugh Rockoff (1992), have garnered plaudits from several disciplines for their scholarly craft and for the church's willingness to make the original material available for study.

## *Mormon Sisters: Women in Early Utah*

In 1972 a group of Mormon women in the Cambridge, Massachusetts, area began to meet together to discuss their lives. As they looked for models who combined a dedication to the faith with a spirit of individual action, they discovered a special edition of the *Utah Historical Quarterly* that I had edited, published as the Winter 1970 issue, commemorative of the beginning of woman suffrage in Utah—and in the United States. The discussion group was invited to present a class on Mormon women for the LDS Institute in Cambridge. Because of the class's enthusiastic reception and the widespread desire for copies of the material presented, the lecture notes and quotations were turned into written papers. Our division historians reviewed the essays, suggested additions and corrections, and in some cases rewrote sections. Under the editorship of Claudia L. Bushman, founding editor of *Exponent II,* they were published in 1976 under the title *Mormon Sisters: Women in Early Utah*. The original edition was quickly sold out and at least three additional printings were required. Maureen Ursenbach Beecher was invited to submit an article on Eliza R. Snow and Jill Mulvay Derr prepared one on teachers. Carolyn Person, a granddaughter of Susa Young Gates, wrote a splendid piece on that formidable personality. Other articles featured women as mystics, healers, midwives, politicians, and feminists as well as analyses of women as characters in Mormon fiction.

Well received, the book was used immediately as reading material for study groups, family home evening groups, sacrament meeting talks, Relief Society presentations, and seminary and Institute of Religion classes. Instructors who taught college classes about women, even those in state universities, put the book on their reading lists. I felt honored by the book's dedication: "To Leonard Arrington: He takes us seriously."

## From Quaker to Latter-day Saint: Bishop Edwin D. Woolley

Finally, we published biographies of some "middle wagon Saints" in Mormon history, those who were not general authorities and who illustrated Mormonism in action at the grass-roots and "second echelon" level. Davis Bitton wrote *The Redoubtable John Pack;* Gene Sessions published *Mormon Democrat: The Religious and Political Memoirs of James H. Moyle;* Maureen Ursenbach Beecher wrote several essays on influential women that were later published under the title *Eliza and Her Sisters;* and, with help from Rebecca Foster Cornwall Bartholomew and others, I published the life of Bishop Edwin D. Woolley.

In 1973 I began researching pioneer Mormon wards and their bishops, soon focusing on the Thirteenth Ward in the center of Salt Lake City for its wealth of economic and statistical records. I found extensive information available on its bishop, Edwin D. Woolley. A prominent merchant, farmer, and stockman, Woolley was Brigham Young's personal business manager for a period and, as proprietor of the "church store," one of Edward Hunter's chief assistants in establishing and carrying out the economic practices of all the bishops in the LDS Church. He was a respected committeeman, chairman, and editor during his several terms in the Utah territorial legislature; a member of the first church high council in the Salt Lake Valley; an incorporator of the Deseret Telegraph Company; and for several terms Salt Lake County recorder.

He was also a spiritual leader in the community. Though he was known for frankness and even obstinacy, his judgment was respected by ward members and superiors alike. Many of those who distrusted the church trusted Woolley, while his fellow Mormons knew his devotion to the church to be unquestioned and thought his habit of blunt speech made duplicity impossible.

Roland Rich Woolley, a grandson who had sponsored the Charles C. Rich biography, offered to defray the costs of a scholarly biography of Woolley, who was also the grandfather of J. Reuben Clark Jr., counselor in the First Presidency from 1933 to 1961, and of Spencer W. Kimball. Such a biography seemed to be consistent with my responsibilities as the church historian, and Kimball was aware and approved of this project, although he did not read the final manuscript.

With the funds generously provided by the Roland Rich Woolley Foundation, I employed Rebecca Foster Cornwall Bartholomew as a research assistant and writer, and she worked with me on the project for more than a year. Her research was competent and thorough and her task papers carried an animated style. Her work was tantamount to collaboration. Indeed,

I did my level best to persuade Roland Woolley to allow me to list her as coauthor, but for reasons of his own he adamantly refused.

Thanks to Becky, the book is filled with engaging anecdotes, colorful details, strong descriptive writing, and plenty of good humor. When Edwin Woolley's diary contained no interesting material about his trip from Pennsylvania to the Ohio River Valley in 1830, Becky turned to diaries of other travelers for tidbits of adventure on those frontier thoroughfares. Many light touches kept the narrative lively. The book provides capsules on home building and homemaking in the Salt Lake Valley, the barter economy, the administration of public works, the Utah expedition, the Godbeite schism, and the duties of a nineteenth-century bishop. It portrays the growing irascibility of Brigham Young, the turbulence of polygamy, and the strange excesses of the reformation of 1856–57.

We found Edwin Woolley to be a sincere, hardworking, honest, straight-talking person. He had an innate spirituality, was a good manager of the Salt Lake Thirteenth Ward, and was an independent spirit. Articulate and outspoken, he was an easy subject. We were able to learn much about his mind and reactions, as well as the events in which he participated. We included a treatment of the Thirteenth Ward as well as its bishop. It was also one of the few biographies of a male pioneer that included a great deal of material about women and children. We featured ordinary family life in Nauvoo, while crossing the Plains, and in the early Salt Lake Valley. We described the cattle drive to California and the immigration of 1848; we also gave a portrait of Brigham Young with whom Woolley had a close personal, not always harmonious, relationship. After one dispute, Young remarked caustically: "Well, I suppose now you are going to go off and apostatize." "No, I won't," retorted Woolley. "If this were your church I might, but it's just as much mine as it is yours." That was the kind of response Brigham Young respected, and they continued to remain close friends. Young commented, "If Bishop Woolley should fall off his horse while crossing the Jordan River on the way to his pasture, those searching for him should not expect him to be floating downstream; they would more likely find him swimming upstream, obstinately contending against the current."[11]

A native of West Chester, Pennsylvania, Edwin Dilworth Woolley was born to a well-to-do farmer in 1807, two years after Joseph Smith. He received a good common school education. His mother died when he was nineteen and his father when he was twenty-five, so Woolley, the oldest in the family of seven, had the responsibility and care of his six brothers and sisters, the youngest of whom was only seven. In 1831, a year after his father's death, he reestablished his family in East Rochester, Columbiana County, Ohio, where he married Mary Wickersham.

While living in East Rochester, Woolley heard of Joseph Smith and journeyed some ninety miles to Kirtland to meet him. Since the prophet was away at the time, Woolley instead met his father and invited him to spend the winter of 1837–38 in East Rochester, which Smith did. On December 24, 1837, Woolley was baptized and confirmed a member of the church and the following day was ordained a high priest. He was set apart to preside over the branch of the church at East Rochester. On an early mission for the church to Pennsylvania, he was instrumental in converting Edward Hunter, of West Chester, who served for thirty-two years as Presiding Bishop of the church in Utah. In 1839 Woolley moved his family to Quincy, Illinois, where he finally met Joseph Smith and Hyrum Smith. The next year he moved to Commerce, Illinois, later named Nauvoo. In addition to serving several missions for the church, he was a Nauvoo merchant and a business leader in the Mormon capital.

Woolley was among the first to adopt the principle of plurality; he ultimately married six women and fathered twenty-six children. Joseph Smith often visited the Woolley home, and it was there in June 1844 that he called prior to going to Carthage Jail and uttered the words, "I am going like a lamb to the slaughter; but I am calm as a summer's morning. I have a conscience void of offense towards God and towards all men. I shall die innocent, and it shall be said of me, 'he was murdered in cold blood.'"[12] Indeed, on June 27, 1844, Joseph and Hyrum Smith were murdered by a mob while they were at Carthage Jail.

During the winter of 1846, Woolley and his family fled with other Latter-day Saints to Winter Quarters, Nebraska, and in the summer of 1848 they crossed the Great Plains to the Valley of the Great Salt Lake. The Woolleys settled in what became the Salt Lake City Thirteenth Ward. Woolley succeeded Edward Hunter as bishop of that ward in 1854 and served as bishop until his death in 1881.

The presentation of the biography at the Woolley family reunion in 1976 was an agreeable affair. I shared the podium with President Kimball and signed autographs for about 250 books. "So far," I noted in my diary, "the book is being well received." There was also no nonsense about its being "controversial." The *Church News* included a photograph of Roland Woolley, Kimball, and I smiling over a presentation copy as well as a long book review lifted straight from the jacket copy and the table of contents. My comment at the time: "Good publicity, but it is clear that the reviewer had not read the book—even a few pages." I prized more a brief note from S. Dilworth Young praising "the value and expertise" of the biography. It was the first letter I had received from any general authority complimenting me on one of our books.

The ultimate accolade, however, came from Camilla Kimball, who made a point of stopping me at the monthly Cannon-Hinckley Church History Group dinner to tell me how much she enjoyed the biography and in fact had constantly laughed at its humor. With a sigh of relief, I breathed, "So I guess I passed the inspection of the prophet's family."

A year or two after the biography was published, I was in Deseret Book Company offices talking with its general manager, James Mortimer. Always very friendly because we had known each other in Logan, he asked if I would be interested in touring the warehouse west of town. When we got there, he showed me the assembly line along which workers wrapped, boxed, and mailed off books to wholesalers and bookstores. He introduced me to one of the workers, who said, "Brother Arrington, we all just loved your biography of Bishop Woolley." I took that as a great compliment to both Woolley and myself, and I thought what a nice thing to have a readership even among warehouse employees. Then the worker went on to say, "We just loved it. It was the perfect size for packing."

### Notes

1. Leonard J. Arrington, *Charles C. Rich: Mormon General and Western Frontiersman* (Provo: Brigham Young University Press, 1974), 55.

2. Ibid., 55.

3. Ibid., 56.

4. Ibid., 57.

5. Two products of that fellowship were "Nineteenth-Century Spelling: The Rules and the Writers," *The Ensign* 5 (Aug. 1975): 74–80, and "Characteristics of Joseph Smith's Style and Notes on the Authorship of the Lectures on Faith," Task Papers in LDS History no. 14, Historical Department of the Church, 1976. More recent is Charles D. Tate, ed., *The Lectures on Faith: In Historical Perspective* (Salt Lake City: Bookcraft, 1990).

6. Dean C. Jessee, "Priceless Words and Fallible Memories: Joseph Smith as Seen in the Effort to Preserve His Discourses," *BYU Studies* 31 (Spring 1991): 33–40.

7. Partridge, "Characteristics of Joseph Smith's Style," 19.

8. Ibid.

9. Ibid., 20.

10. See J. R. Kearl and C. L. Pope, "Wealth-Mobility: The Missing Element," *Journal of Interdisciplinary History* 13 (Winter 1983): 461–88; J. R. Kearl, C. L. Pope, and L. T. Wimmer, "Household Wealth in a Settlement Economy: Utah, 1850–1870," *Journal of Economic History* 40 (Fall 1980): 477–96; and his unpublished paper "Wealth in Nineteenth Century Utah: Distribution, Determinants, and Mobility," copy in my possession. See also Clayne L. Pope, "The Church and the Secular World, Freedom and Equality," in *Mormonism: A Faith for All Cultures*, ed. LaMond Tullis (Provo: Brigham Young University Press, 1978), and "Households on the American Frontier: The Distribution of Income and Wealth in Utah, 1850–1900," in *Markets in History: Economics Studies of the Past*, ed. David W. Galenson (Cambridge: Cambridge University Press, 1989), 148–89.

11. Leonard J. Arrington, *From Quaker to Latter-day Saint: Bishop Edwin D. Woolley* (Salt Lake City: Deseret Book, 1976), 449; Leonard J. Arrington, *Brigham Young: American Moses* (New York: Alfred A. Knopf, 1986), 200.

12. B. H. Roberts, ed., *History of the Church of Jesus Christ of Latter-day Saints, Period I: History of Joseph Smith, the Prophet, by Himself,* 2d ed. (Salt Lake City: Deseret News, 1950), 6:555; Arrington, *From Quaker to Latter-day Saint,* 124.

Leonard, age three.
(Author's collection)

The Noah W. and Edna Corn Arrington home, circa 1930. Leonard and his
eight brothers and sisters grew up here, three miles east of Twin Falls, Idaho.
(Author's collection)

Leonard at eighteen. He had just graduated from high school and was elected first vice president of the Future Farmers of America. (Author's collection)

USU Stake president Reed Bullen speaking at the 1963 groundbreaking of the new USU Stake Center. Behind him are Leonard; High Councilman Eldred Waldron; Wendell Rich, first counselor in the stake; USU president Daryl Chase; his wife Alice Chase; Assistant Apostle Alma Sonne; and architect Sterling Lyon. (Author's collection)

The Leonard and Grace Arrington family in 1969, just before oldest son James left on a mission to Brazil. *Left to right:* Susan, Carl, Grace, James, and Leonard. (Author's collection)

First Presidency of the LDS Church at the time Leonard was sustained as church historian in January 1972. *Left to right:* N. Eldon Tanner, second counselor; Harold B. Lee, first counselor; and Joseph Fielding Smith, president and former church historian. (Used by permission, Utah State Historical Society, all rights reserved)

Leonard Arrington, church historian, and his two assistant church historians, James B. Allen (*right*) and Davis Bitton (*left*), in front of the Mormon Temple in Salt Lake City, July 1972. (Author's collection)

S. George Ellsworth, professor of history at Utah State University. He taught Leonard historical methods and literature in the early 1950s. (Used by permission, Utah State Historical Society, all rights reserved)

The four administrators of the LDS Historical Department in 1973. *Left to right:* Earl Olson, church archivist; Joseph Anderson, managing director; Donald T. Schmidt, church librarian; and Leonard Arrington, church historian. (Author's collection)

Howard W. Hunter, lawyer, apostle, church historian from 1970 to 1972, and church president from 1994 to 1995. (Author's collection)

Thomas G. Alexander, one of Leonard's students at USU, who was Leonard's associate at the Charles Redd Center at Brigham Young University. (Used by permission, Utah State Historical Society, all rights reserved)

Alvin R. Dyer, assistant apostle and managing director of the Historical Department, 1972–73. (Used by permission, Utah State Historical Society, all rights reserved)

Leonard working in the Church Historian's Office, 1972. (Used by permission, Utah State Historical Society, all rights reserved)

The History Division in 1976, in front of the Salt Lake Temple. *Front row, left to right:* Edyth Romney, Debbie Liljenquist Biggs, Nedra Yeates Pace, Jill Mulvay Derr, Maureen Ursenbach Beecher, and Cathy Robison. *Second row:* Davis Bitton, James Allen, Bruce Blumell, Gene Sessions, Gordon Irving, Dean Jessee, and Glen Leonard. *Third row:* Leonard Arrington, Bill Hartley, Richard Jensen, Jim Kimball, Ron Esplin, and Dean May. (Author's collection)

G. Homer Durham, educator, president of the Seventy, and managing director of the Historical Department from 1977 to 1985. (Courtesy of the LDS Church Archives, used by permission)

Spencer W. Kimball, apostle from 1943 to 1973 and president of the church from 1973 to 1985. He revealed that all worthy males may hold the priesthood. (Courtesy of the *Deseret News*)

Edyth Romney, who voluntarily transcribed thousands of pages of manuscript minutes, diaries, and speeches of Brigham Young and other Mormon leaders. (Author's collection)

Leonard and Harriet Horne at the time of their marriage in 1983. (Author's collection)

Leonard in 1997. (Author's collection)

# 9

# Story of the Latter-day Saints and Building the City of God

> How the Church maintained its constant commitment to certain central religious truths and at the same time remained flexible enough to adapt to the ever-present but always changing challenges of the world is an essential part of its history.
> —*Story of the Latter-day Saints*

IN SEPTEMBER 1972, two months after the death of Joseph Fielding Smith, James Mortimer, then managing director of Deseret Book Company, invited me to his office to discuss replacing Joseph Fielding Smith's *Essentials in Church History* with a new one-volume history of the church. He pointed out that while Deseret Book sold approximately ten thousand copies of *Essentials* each year, it received many complaints about the volume from seminary, Institute of Religion, and Sunday school teachers, not to mention Mormon and non-Mormon historians. *Essentials* was published in 1922 as a priesthood manual, which meant it was a teaching tool of church doctrine as well as history. Introductory chapters on the gospel in ancient and medieval times emphasized "the falling away," and various historical facts were evidenced by scriptures. Theologically oriented, the narrative covered the opening of the dispensation of the fullness of times; the Ohio, Missouri, and Nauvoo periods; and the settlement of the Rocky Mountains. The chapters on more recent church history were organized by presidential administrations: John Taylor, Wilford Woodruff, Lorenzo Snow, and Heber J. Grant. Subsequent editions were updated with chapters on the administrations of George Albert Smith and David O. McKay. Although Mortimer recognized the need for a new narrative volume, this would take two or more years. In the meantime he planned to publish a twenty-sixth edition in 1973 and wished us to write chapters on the administrations of Joseph Fielding Smith and Harold B. Lee. By the time that edition was exhausted, he hoped to publish a volume that we would prepare.

Originally written in 1921, *Essentials* could not incorporate the new information and interpretations presented in the 1930 edition of B. H. Roberts's six-volume *Comprehensive History of the Church*. Nor could it be based on source materials uncovered by scholars in the thirties, forties, fifties, and sixties. Moreover, the book was written from a polemical rather than an analytical point of view. Primarily an account of the recurring conflict between the church and its "enemies," *Essentials* was a morality play. There was no acknowledgment that some of the persecutors may have been sincere and had good cause. Even the Mountain Meadows massacre was deemed the horrible crime of an individual, John D. Lee, "a fanatic of the worst stamp."[1]

No attempt had been made to relate Mormon history to contemporary national developments. Of most importance, many developments in the church since 1922 had not been taken into account. Other weaknesses and errors in the book made it out of date. We wanted to write a book that would be historically accurate and balanced and that would be written from a friendly, pro-Mormon point of view, but that would acknowledge other points of view.

There were four purposes for a new one-volume history:

1. To prepare a history that might serve the same needs that *Essentials in Church History* had provided for many years.
2. To use the new materials acquired by the Church Archives.
3. To record the important events that had taken place in the past five decades.
4. To offer, principally in narrative form, a compact, introductory overview of the exciting, often controversial, history of the Church.[2]

In their preface to *Story of the Latter-day Saints,* authors James Allen and Glen Leonard listed the four outstanding themes in Mormon history that would mark their story:

1. The Latter-day Saints were a religious people, not motivated largely by personal economic or political considerations.
2. The Church was always influenced to some degree by the events of the world around it.
3. The Church as a religious body expanded to claim an international membership, so the narrative tells the how and why of its worldwide growth.
4. The dynamics of change exist within the Church, hence there is interest in the how and why of new programs, the operations of continuing revelation, as well as the things that have remained constant.[3]

In writing the book the authors consulted primary sources in the Church Archives, published books, church and nonchurch articles, theses and dissertations, diaries, and official church publications. The twenty-one chapters were divided into five periods, and the book, including the index, was 722 pages in length. It was priced at $9.95. Supplemental material included 10 maps, 144 photographs, and an ample 62-page bibliography. As with *Essentials in Church History*, the emphasis was on happenings at church headquarters and the doings of church leaders, and so the book was not really the story of the Latter-day Saints and their activities but of leaders at church headquarters.

The book was intended for a Mormon reading audience and so, as one reviewer wrote, in educating the reader to a broader and truer view of the Latter-day Saint past, "the treatment has been softened to accommodate delicate feelings. Many accounts fall short of telling the whole truth, and subjects controversial in some minds are handled with tact and a certain gentleness, softened rather frequently with concluding expressions of confidence, faith, and moral lessons to be drawn from the telling."[4]

In his thoughtful review, George Ellsworth wrote that it made a distinct contribution to Mormon historiography by showing "the divine operative in human affairs while fearing not the human element in religious history."[5] The hows and whys were not emphasized as much as the "story," and there was little theological exposition. Changes in beliefs and practices were only a minor theme in the new history.

Groundwork had to be laid in preparation for *Story of the Latter-day Saints*. As early as June 26, 1973, the Historical Department executives, including our advisors, met with the First Presidency to discuss the project. The minutes of the First Presidency show that this one-volume history was approved. My own record for that date, written immediately after the meeting, contains the following paragraph: "Brother Anderson then brought up the matter of the one-volume history of the Church and explained it very briefly—he didn't ask me to comment, and he said he understood that the First Presidency approved it, was that correct? . . . Lee, Tanner, and Romney all nodded their heads in approval."

On August 8, 1973, this project was the focus of a subsequent conversation with Lee. I had gone to the office of D. Arthur Haycock, Lee's assistant, to pick up corrected galley proofs of the chapter I had written about Lee and his administration for the 1973 edition of *Essentials in Church History*. As I walked in, the door to Lee's office was open and Lee was at his desk alone. Seeing me, he asked me to come into his office. I told him why I had come. Lee said had finished the galley proof and generally approved it, but had some minor corrections. He explained these corrections to me.

Lee then began talking about the problem of having general authority committees read books prepared by members of the Twelve and the Seventy. He told me of some experiences that did not end happily. There were bitter words, and the books had to be rewritten.

Lee also referred to the histories we were writing. He expressed his feeling that I should establish a screening committee of professional historians who were loyal to the church, and that this committee should help assure that our books were accurate and readable. He did not believe that the Correlation Committee was equipped to evaluate our history books. He then concluded by telling me how much he appreciated my work. He remarked on how grateful he and others in the church were for my honest, well-researched, and compelling work.

I reported this conversation at our next executive meeting with Anderson, which was held on August 14, and stated that the one-volume history would be authored by James Allen and Glen Leonard, under my direction.

Unfortunately, Lee died before we were able to present a formal proposal on the screening committee. This proposal was finally submitted to the members of the new First Presidency—Spencer W. Kimball, N. Eldon Tanner, and Marion G. Romney—on May 29, 1974, when Hunter, McConkie, Anderson, Earl Olson, Don Schmidt, and I met in a special meeting. The First Presidency, after an extended discussion, did approve a screening committee consisting of the church historian, the two assistant church historians, and the editor of the Historical Department. My notes also show that Kimball counseled us to get some outside reviewers of the manuscript as well as some LDS people. He wanted to be sure that the volume was written in such a way that it would be purchased by libraries around the country.

By 1976 more than two years of effort were culminating in the publication of *Story of the Latter-day Saints*. Much of that year was consumed with the business of publishing—galleys, page proofs, and indexing. On January 11, 1976, Deseret Book had accepted the manuscript and put it into production by February 27. I did the final proofreading in March. John Carr of the Translation Department agreed to prepare its German, Spanish, and French versions.

*Story of the Latter-day Saints*, a handsomely designed, abundantly illustrated volume with an invaluable bibliography and a thorough and detailed narrative of church historical events, came off the presses in July after a brief delay from a paper shortage. It officially went on the shelves on July 12. Knowing the way in which one of the Twelve had received *Brigham Young's Letters to His Sons*, I experienced frequent twinges of anxiety. I wrote in my diary: "It looks fine. We'll now see how the Church will react to the first published history that treats in a professional manner its history in general, and a full treatment of the twentieth century in particular. I am anxious, but the die is cast and I feel good about what we have done, proud of it." Almost a month of total silence followed, except for the private pleasure of the staff and a few friends and a phenomenal sale—ten thousand copies in four weeks. Church Public Communications ordered five thousand copies to place in U.S. libraries. One month after the publication, I reported to our advisors that "the book has been well received and many favorable comments have been made by those who have read the book."

Historians were particularly complimentary. "As professional historians and active Mormons," wrote one reviewer, "the authors have achieved a remarkable blend of the scholarly approach and the religious story. . . . They do not feel constrained to bear testimony, and yet they demonstrate an empathy toward Mormonism that could only emanate from devoted members. It is a pleasant balance."[6]

The first intimation of conflict that would last for the rest of the year and cast its shadow into the future of the writing of Mormon history was a report from a friend that "one or two members of the Quorum of the Twelve" did not like "the absence of inspiration—descriptions of occurrences in Church history without attributing their cause solely to God or to His direction and inspiration." These members of the Twelve went to Ezra Taft Benson, who requested a thorough critique from his executive assistant, William O. Nelson, who was not a historian. Soon the book was up for a full-scale review by the Twelve and the First Presidency. Nelson had been with Benson in Washington, D.C., when he was secretary of agriculture under Dwight D. Eisenhower, 1953–61.[7]

Throughout the history of the church, as my colleagues and I had learned, occasional periods of tension had arisen between the Twelve and the First Presidency. At times, as under Brigham Young, the First Presidency had been dominant; at other times, as under the aged Joseph Fielding Smith, the Twelve had exercised controlling influence. At times some of the Twelve resented the role played by counselors in the First Presidency, including George Q. Cannon during the John Taylor and Wilford Woodruff administrations and J. Reuben Clark Jr. during the Heber J. Grant period. Three members of the Twelve appeared to harbor similar resentment of Harold B. Lee and N. Eldon Tanner during the Joseph Fielding Smith administration. In the foreword to *Story of the Latter-day Saints,* I specifically wrote that "with the approval of the First Presidency" we had asked James Allen and Glen Leonard to prepare the history. Certain members of the Twelve, now feeling an obligation to warn President Kimball of the dangers of our "freewheeling" historical research, demanded that the Twelve have more say in these matters. The implication was clear that if they had made the choice I would not have been church historian and they would not have supported a project to replace *Essentials in Church History*. This assertiveness of some members of the Twelve grew ever stronger as Kimball's health declined during his last years. As Gordon B. Hinckley explained, "The president, after all, is just one of the fifteen prophets, seers, and revelators, so when the president is not functioning, we simply carry on with the remaining apostles." As he said, "there is abundant 'backup,'" and when the Saints sing "We thank Thee, O God, for a Prophet," they are expressing their joy in being led by not just one man but by a council of fifteen.[8] Problems arose, however, when any one or two of the Twelve made a pronouncement or took an action, because the remainder felt obligated to give support, rather than to interfere. Obviously there would be differences of opinion among the general authorities on questions of administration and policy. After all, church history was no longer the preserve of one of the Twelve, as it had been for Joseph Fielding Smith and Howard Hunter. From my point of view, that inspired men and women might maneuver to have their influence felt illustrated how human agents interact in their efforts to do God's work. Not every statement or act of church leaders is inspired, since they disagree among themselves. Not every conclusion is right, since they occasionally backtrack. That the Lord is in charge does not mean that he inspires or approves everything done in the church. That he is in charge *does* mean that our leaders will get a lot more right than wrong. In the meantime, a follower like me, trying to do a job under conflicting instructions or pressures, was like a mouse crossing the floor where elephants are dancing.

Of course, from their point of view these people were trying to *defend* faith and tradition and heroes against what they perceived as attacks by modern professionals with no respect for traditional values. And I think they would probably wish to say that ours was a kind of history that they found offensive, perhaps especially galling when produced by people on the church payroll. On March 28, 1976, Ezra Taft Benson, president of the Twelve, spoke at BYU, attacking historians and biographers who had "humanized" national leaders. He was specific about the same pattern in church history, denouncing it as an attempt "to underplay revelation and God's intervention in significant events." He branded such efforts as "tarnishing church history and its leaders." He repeated the same sentiments six months later to a group of religious educators at BYU. There he specifically denounced those who "inordinately humanize the prophets of God so that their human frailties become more evident than their spiritual qualities." He suggested that temple covenants should discourage teachers from such an approach to "our prophetic history" and went out of his way to caution those who "feel you must write for the scholarly journals." He also instructed the seminary and institute teachers not to purchase the writings of "apostates." We did not feel that our historians were meant by this criticism because our research and writing projects, all along, had been approved by the First Presidency and our apostolic advisors. And, of course, we had no intention of "underplaying revelation" or "inordinately humanizing"—although we might disagree on what was underplaying and what was inordinate.[9]

In a meeting with one of our Historical Department advisors, Delbert Stapley, I asked if there were complaints about *Story of the Latter-day Saints*. He affirmed there were complaints of inaccuracies. I responded that if we could obtain further information as to which statements were inaccurate, we would be happy to make corrections in the next edition. Within a few days I heard from a friend, who read to me the eight-page single-spaced critique, which had comments from William Nelson and Gary Bennett, neither one a historian. Basically the critique made eight assertions.

1. The "traditional" book, Joseph Fielding Smith's *Essentials in Church History*, should be continued in print.
2. The bibliography mentioned works that were antichurch: Brodie, *No Man Knows My History;* articles in *Dialogue,* particularly those by Richard Poll and Duane Jeffery.
3. The story of the crickets and seagulls did not bring God into the picture.
4. The account of Zion's Camp implied that it was a failure.
5. The account of BYU's firing the evolutionists in 1911 was not sufficiently antievolution.
6. The book failed to mention the doctrinal contributions of Joseph Fielding Smith.
7. The book was basically a secular history and did not have enough of the spiritual to be a "true" account of LDS history.
8. All of our history publications should be routed through the Correlation Committee to ensure that they were doctrinally and historically accurate and had the right tone and impact.

This critique had been given to the Twelve at their meeting on September 2, and they were supposed to discuss it at a special Sunday meeting called for September 5. My diary entry was as follows:

Although several members of the Twelve have been aware of the existence of the critique, and of the support for it of Elder Benson and Elder Mark Petersen, not a person has called me up or written me, or made other contact to ask me (or Drs. Allen or Leonard) how I would defend the book, and our history writing in general. Elder Howard Hunter told me, as he walked out of our advisors meeting on Wednesday, September 1, that he wanted to talk with me sometime on the subject of running all our works through Correlation, but he has made no attempt to discuss this with me.

Who might defend history? Hunter? McConkie? Probably Packer would agree with the critique. I found the prospect cheerless:

> Shall I retain the job of Church Historian (assuming they don't release me) and try to write history that will be approved by Correlation? Or shall I resign and continue to write "real history"? And what would this do to my associates?
>
> I am not clear in my own mind as to the best course but feel discouraged. It has been a tough few days for me since I do not dare mention this to a soul. I recall that Andrew Jenson went through several such episodes and stuck to it for the good of the Church. But can I retain my integrity and my reputation, whatever it is worth, with the "intelligentsia" of the Church and remain on the job under conditions that will almost certainly be imposed upon me?

My first "official" encounter came on September 7, when Stapley called me to his office and reported that the Twelve had discussed my responsibilities and activities at considerable length, particularly *Story of the Latter-day Saints*. The line of questioning was ominous: Did I have a letter of appointment outlining my duties? Had I been told to have somebody approve our publications? Would I agree to have members of the Twelve review manuscripts? (The members of such a committee had already been tentatively named.) Stapley added that some members of the Twelve insisted that we exclude any information from our publication that might put the church in a bad light. The only example he could think of, however, was that Brigham Young used tobacco and that example did not appear in *Story of the Latter-day Saints*.

The interview terminated with Stapley's disquieting statement that he was going to "talk further" with some unnamed parties and then would get back in touch with me. The call came late that afternoon. Were royalties paid on *Story of the Latter-day Saints*? No. Were royalties paid on the Brigham Young book? I pointed out that it wasn't even written yet and that no arrangement had been made one way or the other. Would royalties be paid on the sixteen-volume sesquicentennial history? I again reviewed the agreement that had been approved to pay the authors a fee in lieu of royalties. Would I be willing to submit my manuscripts to the Correlation Committee? To the latter, I countered: the First Presidency has already decided against this on the grounds that history ought to be screened by people who know history; the First Presidency had already picked an advisory committee. Would I be willing to have a member of the Twelve go over my manuscripts? "Of course."

On September 20, I received a phone call from Francis Gibbons, secretary to the First Presidency, inviting me to an 8:30 A.M. meeting with the First Presidency. What was the meeting about? What materials should I bring with me? What issues should I be prepared to discuss? Gibbons gave me no details. The meeting was well attended. The members of the First Presidency were present, and Benson and Petersen were smiling as if in triumph. Hunter and McConkie bore puzzled expressions because they had been given no warning of what was about to take place.

Kimball began by saying that *Story of the Latter-day Saints* had raised some concerns. Benson admitted that he had read only portions of the book but that at least one of the Twelve had read all of it. Calvin Rudd, an institute teacher, had given him a two-page list of his concerns in very general terms: the book would make young people "lose faith," it "demeaned" Joseph Smith, it gave only sixteen lines to the founding of the church. For five or ten minutes Benson continued his "grave warnings" about "the problems and dangers and risks" of the existence of such a book. I responded. Then Petersen expressed his concerns very strongly and openly. I again responded. Then both Benson and Petersen took another turn. I defended myself by making four points: they might not like the book, but given the responses I had received, they were in the minority—most readers did not feel it damaged their faith; since the book would be read by non-Mormons and scholars as well as by Latter-day Saints and general readers, the historians had tried to provide evidence for events based on facts instead of only prophecy; criticism of contextualism had missed the point of the book, that "the Lord was preparing the people to receive the restored gospel"; certain well-known historical events could not be ignored (the Mountain Meadows massacre, different versions of the First Vision, African Americans in the church, the polygamy underground) and it was best to treat them in a place where LDS scholars could control the tone and the proper presentation of evidence.

Kimball then asked me if I would agree to have the manuscripts read before publication by a person assigned by him from the Twelve. I said I "welcomed" such an arrangement but felt it wise to keep this private "for the purpose of not diminishing our credibility as historians and raising the cry of censorship." Kimball agreed, but those at Deseret Book, when informed, shared the information freely. Kimball expressed his further concern that we were paying too much attention to outside audiences and too little to the church audience. I bore my testimony as to my belief that a person could write for both audiences successfully. Kimball seemed to be persuaded, as was Tanner.

The meeting adjourned after an hour and forty-five minutes. I felt very good, as I recorded at the time, "in having the opportunity of responding personally to the criticisms that had been made of our publications; that they did not require us to clear our things through Church Correlation; that President Kimball seemed to be supportive and friendly, as were his counselors. All were cordial and genial as we disbanded. I think I managed to quiet some of the criticism or at least match some of the criticism with some favorable responses."

On October 21 in a meeting with the advisors, Stapley again questioned me about the publication program, access to sources, approval of projects, and royalties. Again Stapley pronounced the necessity of writing faith-promoting works. I assured him that we had been preparing articles for church magazines and writing books that met this objective. Once again I prepared a description of how scholars use sources and what restrictions govern the use of archival materials.

On October 22, I recounted in my diary events of the previous weeks and added new information. Benson's observation to Ernest Wilkinson that the Zion's Cooperative Mercantile Institution, a church-operated business, had received more attention than the founding of the church had come originally from an instructor in the Salt Lake Institute of Religion. Petersen, during the First Presidency meeting, had been "even more critical in his tone and more vigorous and dogmatic in his assertions" than Benson and had singled out contemporary intellectual and social origins of the law of consecration and stewardship as evidence that the authors of *Story of the Latter-day Saints* were denying "the revealed nature of the program." Clearly, both Petersen and Benson were unfamiliar with the contents of the book they were attacking.

At about the same time, I learned that at least two other members of the Twelve did not like *Story of the Latter-day Saints*. Both felt that it was too "secular"—that the history was not flavored or balanced sufficiently with spiritual experiences and faith-promoting stories. They recognized that although the book contained such passages, these were insufficient to make it well-balanced for Latter-day Saints.

Marvin J. Ashton, president of Deseret Book's board, privately provided the best news: After finishing his copy, Kimball remarked that he thought *Story of the Latter-day Saints* was a great work and could not comprehend why anyone would think otherwise. I was exultant. I was further reassured to learn about a week later that Hunter was "especially displeased" that

Petersen and Benson had gone directly to the First Presidency instead of bowing to his authority as an advisor. The final insult had come when he was invited to the September 20 meeting with the First Presidency, Benson, Petersen, and I without knowing its purpose.

Hunter confined his support, however, to a privately expressed personal reassurance. Kimball, for all his pleasure with the book, was not willing to curb Benson and Petersen, either in their public disapproval of the book before audiences of church members or in their private instructions to entities at BYU and Deseret Book. Even though those at Deseret Book were "definitely" willing for the History Division staff to continue writing in the same vein, they were relying on the report of Kimball's approval. It would be interesting to know why Kimball did not make that approval public, at least within the Twelve. Of course he was very busy and his health soon deteriorated sharply. More likely, he never got accurate information about the methods being used to suppress our history. Sometime later, Kimball's sister-in-law told me that Kimball had been alarmed about the scandalous way Jim Allen had been treated by some religion instructors at BYU for having been the principal author of *Story of the Latter-day Saints*. Kimball, she said, openly wept at this recital, and declared this was not a Christian way to treat someone who had honorably performed an approved assignment. A strong believer in free moral agency, Kimball told his sister-in-law and her husband that Benson and Petersen did not have the authority or the right to interfere with the sale of the book.

I realize that the general authorities who were alarmed by our publications did not think it appropriate to discuss matters directly with me, and I can understand why. I thought candor and openness were healthy; they thought forthright history was dangerous to the faith of the weak and provided ammunition for those who made anti-Mormon arguments by taking facts out of context. I thought that providing context for problem quotations and episodes was the best solution; they believed such explanations would never catch up with the use of snippets by the opposition. Further, the First Presidency had approved our general enterprise and had set up advisors as liaisons and directors. If the general authorities perceived that those in the First Presidency and the Twelve did not understand what we were doing or did not appreciate fully the dangers, it was their responsibility to go to those in a position to redirect us. Although the members of the First Presidency had instructed us to produce a one-volume history of the church, they could not know in advance just how our authors would treat specific events. The critics sought to prevent what they saw as inappropriate writing, even by people who had good intentions.

My observation recorded in my diary in November 1976 was that the prophet is not always a determining force in church government. What we really have is a form of collective leadership consisting of the three members of the First Presidency and the twelve members of the Quorum of Apostles. This collective leadership had determined that they must be essentially unanimous. Despite the inevitable wide-ranging diversity of views, the presiding quorums agreed early in church history to maintain a public posture of unanimity so as to minimize dissent and factionalization within the general membership. If any particular person expresses a strong feeling about a particular matter, his views will normally prevail through the courtesy of the others. Thus, although President Kimball indicated he liked very much *Story of the Latter-day Saints* and would approve it for the widespread distribution among and use by the Saints, strong negative feelings had already been expressed by Elders Benson and Petersen and President Kimball did not wish to embarrass them or go against their wishes with the result that their wishes prevailed. If they had waited until the prophet had expressed his own view then that would have held sway.

Clearly, we should have expected some readers to second-guess our approach. There were legitimate concerns about how we had treated history, since some historians attribute most of it to God and others attribute most of it to natural and human forces. Our historians might choose one place to draw the line and others might draw the line in a different place. It was proper for us to defend our writings, just as it was proper for others to urge a different approach. Since there was disagreement among general authorities themselves as to where to draw the line, it was obviously a matter of human judgment, not of "religious truth."

## Building the City of God

In September 1976, just a few weeks after the publication of *Story of the Latter-day Saints*, Deseret Book issued *Building the City of God: Community and Cooperation among the Mormons*, with Dean May, Feramorz Young Fox, and me as authors.

During the early years of the Great Depression of the 1930s, Feramorz Young Fox, grandson of noted Mormon pioneers, a Ph.D. in economic history from Northwestern University, and president of LDS Business College in Salt Lake City, made a comprehensive study of Mormon efforts to solve the problems of want and inequality. Beginning with Joseph Smith's Law of Consecration and Stewardship, introduced in 1831, the Latter-day Saints had experimented through much of their history with idealistic economic arrangements. Some scholars had studied the Law of Consecration and Stewardship; others, the group-sharing proposals by which the Saints migrated to the West. Still others had investigated Brigham Young's United Order of the 1870s and John Taylor's Board of Trade movement of the 1880s. But no one had written in depth of the entire span of Mormon economic idealism when Fox wrote his treatise in the 1930s.

"Experiments in Cooperation and Social Security among the Mormons: A Study of Joseph Smith's United Order," a 426-page typescript that Fox completed in 1937, was never published. Perhaps publishers determined that the market in those depressed years was not sufficient to justify the expense of publication.

When I began my studies of Mormon economic activities in the summer of 1946, I found a bound copy of Fox's typescript in the Church Archives and was immediately impressed with its sound and thorough approach. I made a point of meeting Fox and discussed the various research projects in which he had been engaged relating to Mormon history. Always generous and helpful, he loaned me a copy of his manuscript to microfilm for the library at Utah State University. He also furnished me with a bibliography of his personal works, which included articles in the *Deseret News, Improvement Era,* and other journals and periodicals.[10]

Unsuccessful in encouraging Fox to publish part or all of his monumental study on cooperation prior to his death, I did have the opportunity to edit his chapter on the Richfield United Order for publication in the *Utah Historical Quarterly* in its Fall 1964 issue. Five years later, Karl A. Fox, son of Fox and at the time head of the department of economics at Iowa State University, after consultation with Richard Thurman, director of the University of Utah Press, asked me to prepare Fox's typescript for publication under a collaborative arrangement. I accepted, although my responsibilities at Utah State University prevented me from completing the task immediately. As I worked with the material, the assignment broadened, and I recognized that we were not just reworking; we were expanding. My former secretary, JoAnn W. Bair, worked on the rewriting, as did my research assistant, Richard Daines, an honors graduate of Utah State University, who drafted a preliminary chapter on the Church Welfare Plan. Dean May, who had a Ph.D. in economic history from Brown University and was a senior historical associate of the Historical Department, helped me through the last few months of revision and enrichment. His contributions to the volume included original drafts of the introduction; the United Orders in Utah Valley, Cache Valley, Bear Lake Valley, Kanab, Arizona, Nevada, and Mexico; and the concluding chapter. My contributions consisted of the chapters on the Law of Consecration and Stewardship, Orderville, Brigham City, Zion's Board of Trade, and the Mormon welfare system of the 1930s, in addition to substantial contributions to the chapters of the other two authors.

Readers acquainted with the Fox manuscript observed that May and I relied heavily on Fox for the information presented in the chapters on the consecration movement of the 1850s, cooperative mercantile and manufacturing associations of the 1860s and 1870s, the St. George United Order, and the Richfield United Order. May and I made substantive changes in all the chapters, and the entire manuscript, including the material from Fox, was run through our own typewriters at least twice. By this merging and reworking we sought to create a unified work and a uniform style.

Although we were active and believing Latter-day Saints, we tried to present a well-researched and accurate history and analysis. *Building the City of God* detailed the Mormon cooperative enterprises that were unique for America in the last half of the nineteenth century. Most prominent of these was the United Order, a bold experiment in economic idealism initiated by Brigham Young regionwide in 1874. Though its immediate effects were short-lived, it remained a powerful symbol for Latter-day Saints, a vivid expression of the reform impulse that had been a recurring aspect of Mormonism since its founding.

*Building the City of God* traced the development of Mormon communitarianism and cooperative experiments from 1831, when Joseph Smith announced the Law of Consecration and Stewardship as part of a design for building a city of Zion in Jackson County, Missouri. These plans were cut short by persecution, but the Missouri experience of the 1830s set an archetype that helped to define for Mormons the appropriate relationship of individual, community, and economic processes. This study of communitarian and cooperative experiments interpreted such episodes as part of the ongoing process in which faithful Latter-day Saints were schooled through all-embracing church activity in those very qualities needed to make a success of cooperative endeavor.

I was anxious to see the scholarly reviews of the book, even though they would not appear for another quarter. Meanwhile, the book was tarred with the same condemnatory brush as *Story of the Latter-day Saints*. Early in November, I heard from a staff member of the *Church News* that those at the publication had been instructed, presumably by one member of the Twelve, not to review *Building the City of God*.

What was objectionable about *Building the City of God?* Apparently, some leaders feared that the book might encourage unauthorized communal endeavors. Also, it called attention to the apparent failure of a major initiative of church leaders between 1874 and 1877. The treatment was balanced; that is, there were explanations of programs and policies that were couched in temporal terms. We had not used the traditional explanation of historical processes that everything extraordinary was an action of God. Finally, they reacted against the word *communitarian,* which appeared several times in the book and on the dust jacket. A term popularized by Arthur Eugene Bestor in *Backwoods Utopias: The Sectarian and Owenite Phases of Communitarian Socialism in America, 1663–1829* (1950), communitarianism was a movement, particularly of the 1820s and 1830s, that employed small experimental communities as the agency of social reform. I had used the term in my article on such early Mormon communities in the Autumn 1953 issue of *Western Humanities Review,* so the word was well known among Mormon and Western historians and was even the title of a symposium at BYU. Somehow, Benson and Petersen, or, more likely, their consultants, thought it was easily identified with communism and for that reason it caused them to shudder.

The scholarly reviews, however, were almost entirely favorable. Jonathan Hughes of Northwestern University, in *BYU Studies,* called it "stunning." "With a wealth of detail, guided by their sure knowledge of classical Mormon principles, and the impact of differing personalities in Church leadership, these authors have restored the fabric of Mormon historical reality." With its "careful scholarship, extensive reliance on primary information sources, illuminating quotations, solid writing style, and balanced judgment," the book "is a model of microhistory. . . . It is a tradition of thinking, sacrifice, and achievement of which the Mormon people can be justly proud. . . . The old-fashioned Mormons created a sense of community upon which their religion survived and modern Mormons can build. . . . These authors have restored the fabric of Mormon historical reality for Mormon readers, and for non-Mormon readers provided a fascinating introduction to a rich and largely unknown epoch in American social history. . . . In this book a valuable lesson is found that adversity has its positive uses, failures of one generation can inspire another."[11]

In 1976, the year that *Story of the Latter-day Saints* and *Building the City of God* appeared, some young Latter-day Saint intellectuals founded *Sunstone,* an independent quarterly journal that dealt with the modern problems of Mormonism in a less scholarly atmosphere than that supplied by *Dialogue* and *BYU Studies.* Spearheaded by Mormon students attending the University of California at Berkeley, *Sunstone* sought to "provide an opportunity for young people and older amateurs to express their views and meet their peers in an atmosphere more compatible with their informal lifestyle and more conducive to their participation—an arena for lively discussion with a high [school] student, rather than professional, academic and literary standards. . . . *Sunstone* sees itself more as a companion than a competitor of *Dialogue.*"[12] The image of the sun, the editor wrote, was a rich metaphor: "the radiating of light, truth, knowledge, and beauty; the democratic blessings of God to humankind; the dispelling of falsehood and the uncovering of hidden truths; and the seeing of things by new light. In Mormon temple iconography the sun is a symbol for the celestial kingdom, and fuses heaven and earth, the divine and human, the visionary and practical." *Sunstone* editors sought to explore the interplay between the human and the divine, a difficult task, something we historians were very aware of.[13] Many of our historians, including myself, published in *Sunstone*, something we were later admonished to discontinue.

In May 1977, however, another land mine was laid that later exploded. A senior honors student at the University of Utah turned in a ninety-eight-page paper for an project supervised by James L. Clayton. In this inaccurately documented work, he traced the rise of "secularism" in church history through such landmark events as the formation of *Dialogue,* the organization of the Mormon History Association, and the professionalization of the Church Historian's Office, all of which, he claimed, set the stage for "the traditional conflict between the secular and the spiritual."[14] He footnoted "interviews" with several Mormon scholars that contained such frank and damaging statements that it is unlikely they would have made such pronouncements to a student and especially improbable that they would have made them for publication. Falsely, the young scholar asserted a connection between professional LDS historians and the career apostates Jerald Tanner and Sandra Tanner.

Reportedly, he also interviewed Mark E. Petersen, who, turning the tables, interviewed *him* and wanted a copy of the paper. The student provided him a copy; Petersen provided copies to the Twelve. At about the same time, our "observer" in the library was highlighting pertinent lines in these copies for the Twelve. With great sadness, I catalogued evidences of anti-intellectualism in the church in a July diary entry: Eugene England and Lowell Bennion were not permitted to publish with Deseret Book or Bookcraft by direct intervention of two members of the Twelve. Carol Lynn Pearson was blacklisted from church publications until she was able "through prayers and tears" to get one of the Twelve to reverse the decision. Jim Allen was viewed with suspicion because of *Story of the Latter-day Saints.* The *Church News* could not review *Building the City of God* or any other book by our History Division employees without specific clearance from the Twelve. Claudia Bushman and Scott Kenney could not be published or mentioned because of their connection with *Exponent II* and *Sunstone.* Several Mormon intellectuals were publishing under pseudonyms.

In August I spent a weekend doing a background study on John D. Lee and the Mountain Meadows massacre for the First Presidency, alternately frustrated because they wanted the report in four days and flattered, pleased, honored, and delighted that they had asked me to prepare it. It was the first—and only—time I received a direct request to be a resource to the First Presidency's office.

I was told on August 11 that a subcommittee consisting of Petersen, Hinckley, and Packer, formed to investigate our publications and actions, had met at least once with Stapley and twice with our new managing director, G. Homer Durham, to express their complaints, most of which Durham regarded as misapprehensions. The investigative subcommittee did not talk to anyone in the division under scrutiny.

As I look back on the period I see a diary entry that suggests how I envisioned magnifying my calling. Clearly, my expectations as church historian were not being realized:

1. I had expected to be a consultant in helping the general authorities prepare talks to dedicate historic sites, celebrate historic events, and review texts for accuracy or completeness. With the exception of two talks for Packer, one for Tanner, and one for David B. Haight of the Twelve, I had received no requests for service.

2. I had expected to provide historical background on church organization and for public relations. Our records showed that our office was consulted about one-tenth of the time it ought to have been, and even then it was sporadic, occasional, and ad hoc.

3. I had expected to be used as an appropriate speaker for historical anniversaries. Many general authorities, of course, received such invitations, but I was aware of no cases where the general authority suggested that I might be a suitable complementary person. The invitations I received seemed to originate on the local level from the speaker's committee that had tried general authorities without success and could not find a suitable replacement.

4. I had expected to be consulted by the Curriculum Department on lessons for the Sunday school on church history. Not only was I not invited to join the planning committee but I was also never asked for background information or for an expert opinion on a particular question. Occasionally a staff member would be consulted by a personal acquaintance serving on the curriculum committee, but there was no official representation or participation.

5. I had expected to prepare a new church history. Despite our commission from the First Presidency, that assignment merely created, on the part of some, animosities, suspicion, and incredulity that we would dare to do so.

I noted that my recent public appearance as an official church spokes-man—defending the Book of Mormon manuscript against attacks on the basis of handwriting analysis—was at the request of a Public Communi-cations staff person and that some general authorities "resented what I did and were surprised that I was invited to make a statement."

That fall I reflected: "At the time of my appointment as Church Historian, . . . I had an unshakable conviction that it was possible, if a man was clever enough, to write professional history that would be accepted as such by the profession, and at the same time be acceptable to the intel-ligent LDS reader. My confidence in that conviction has been shaken dur-ing the past few months." I gave up thinking there was any way to reach the extreme conservatives who saw a "liberal" in every intelligently writ-ten "fair" book. Some general authorities concerned with protecting the young and bureaucrats fearful of being censured for liking the wrong thing refused to sanction any of our writings and publicly criticized works they deemed controversial. I had failed to appreciate their belief that many of the problems of our culture were not the incidental consequence of "lib-eral" ideas but were the actual agenda of "liberal" activists. As historians, we were not liberals in that sense, of course, but it might have been difficult to avoid confusing us with them.

I summarized, "it is not that they disapprove of *me* as Church Histo-rian; they would disapprove of any professional historian, any intellectu-al, any independent-minded writer. They want someone who (1) has writ-ten little history; (2) saturates history with scriptural allusions and references; and (3) obstinately refuses to mention controversial episodes."

Although the tone of this entry comes close to bitterness and discour-agement, it suggests my overwhelming desire to feel "approved" at a time when I was clearly on a collision course with vocal elements among our superiors. It would have helped me if I could have observed hurts and humiliations more impersonally, as points in a game between two very unequally matched opponents, and to find moral victories in decisive tac-tical losses.

### Notes

1. Joseph Fielding Smith, *Essentials in Church History,* 26th ed. (Salt Lake City: Deseret Book, 1973), 419.

2. Leonard J. Arrington, foreword to *Story of the Latter-day Saints* by James B. Allen and Glen M. Leonard (Salt Lake City: Deseret Book, 1976), vii–viii.

3. Allen and Leonard, *Story of the Latter-day Saints,* ix–x.

4. S. George Ellsworth, review of *Story of the Latter-day Saints, BYU Studies* 17 (Winter 1977): 243.

5. Ibid.

6. Dennis L. Lythgoe, review of *Story of the Latter-day Saints, Dialogue* 10 (Autumn 1977): 135.

7. See also a reference to Nelson in D. Michael Quinn, "Ezra Taft Benson and Mormon Political Conflicts," *Dialogue* 26 (Summer 1993): 76.

8. Gordon B. Hinckley to seminary and institute teachers, Aug. 22, 1986; notes in my diary for that date in Leonard J. Arrington Collection, Special Collections and Archives, Utah State University Libraries, Logan.

9. Ezra Taft Benson, "This Nation Shall Endure," lecture at BYU, Mar. 28, 1976; Ezra Taft Benson, "The Gospel Teacher and His Message," lecture at BYU, Sept. 17, 1976.

10. Especially important were Feramorz Y. Fox, "The Consecration Movement of the Middle Fifties," *Improvement Era* 47 (1944): 80–81, 120–21, 124–25, 146–47, 185, 187–88; "United Order: Discrimination in the Use of Terms," *Improvement Era* 47 (1944): 432, 459, 461–62; and "Consecration: Some Distinguishing Features," *Improvement Era* 49 (1946): 368–69, 404–5.

11. J. R. T. Hughes, review of *Building the City of God, BYU Studies* 17 (Winter 1977): 246–49. See also James L. Clayton, "Equality and Plain Living," *Dialogue* 10 (Autumn 1977): 132–34.

12. Scott Kenney, "Letter to the Editor," *Dialogue* 9 (Summer 1974): 5.

13. Elbert Eugene Peck, "A Cornucopia of Things," *Sunstone* 16 (Mar. 1993): 8–10.

14. "The New Mormon History," typescript in the Arrington Collection.

# 10

# A New Pharaoh and New Directions

My son, despise not the chastening of the Lord; neither be weary of his
correction. For whom the Lord loveth he correcteth; even as a father
the son in whom he delighteth.
    —Proverbs 3:11–12

AT 4:00 P.M., ON FRIDAY, April 29, 1977, the staff members of the Historical Department convened in the conference room, where they found
N. Eldon Tanner, Joseph Anderson, and G. Homer Durham. Tanner announced that the First Presidency and the Twelve had released Anderson
from his position as managing director of the Historical Department and
they wished us to sustain the release with upheld right hands. After words
of praise for Anderson, he then asked if we could sustain the First Presidency in appointing Durham to that position. All hands went up. After
further words of appreciation for Anderson, Tanner asked him to speak.
In a voice filled with emotion, Anderson expressed his profound appreciation for the opportunity to work with the department the past four years;
stated his respect and love for the personnel, especially the executives; and
testified of the harmony, unity, absence of bickering, and dedication to our
positions and to the church among that group.

Tanner then asked Durham to speak. He stated his pleasure in the assignment, declared his love for history, complimented us on our work in
the past, and expressed earnest hope for the future. He pledged untiring
service in helping the department carry out its mission. Tanner added that
Durham had been his home teacher and stake president and he had great
appreciation for Durham's dedication to the church. Tanner asked Earl
Olson, as an old-timer in the department, to speak on behalf of us all. Earl
expressed our love for Anderson and for Marjorie Golder (his secretary)
and pledged our support for Durham. Tanner then dismissed us. Recognizing she was leaving good friends, Marjorie wept a good deal. As we
shook hands with Anderson at the end of the meeting, he also wept as he

expressed appreciation for the opportunity to work with us and his regret at leaving the Historical Department.

G. Homer Durham, born in 1911 in Parowan, Utah, grew up in Salt Lake City, where his father was a professor of music. In England on a mission he became well acquainted with Gordon B. Hinckley, who remained his lifelong friend and associate. After his marriage to Eudora Widtsoe, daughter of the mission president, John A. Widtsoe, Durham attended the University of Utah, took a Ph.D. in political science at the University of California at Los Angeles, and taught for periods at Swarthmore College, Utah State University, and the University of Utah. At the latter institution he headed the political science department, edited the *Western Political Quarterly,* and served as academic vice president, 1953–60. He was president of the American Society of Public Administration, 1959–60. Selected president of Arizona State University in 1960, he served nine years before resigning to become Utah's first commissioner of higher education. In April 1977, at age sixty-six, he was sustained as a member of the First Council of the Seventy, and shortly thereafter he was assigned to replace Joseph Anderson as our managing director.

Durham had a serious interest in church history. He wrote a monthly column for the *Improvement Era,* 1946–70, and compiled several books, including *Joseph Smith: Prophet Statesman* and selections from the writings and addresses of John Taylor, Wilford Woodruff, Heber J. Grant, and David O. McKay. He served as president of Salt Lake Central Stake, as a regional representative of the Twelve, and as a long-time member of the General Sunday School Board. He was a popular and effective teacher and persuasive speaker. Outwardly calm and even-tempered, distinguished looking, a lover of music, Durham was a brilliant leader who did not feel bound by the policies of his predecessor.

I had known Durham since 1947, visited him occasionally, and exchanged correspondence with him about my research and writing. In political science journals he had published two seminal articles that I had used in *Great Basin Kingdom* and other works: "Political Interpretation of Mormon History" and "Administrative Organization of the Mormon Church." Stimulating and resourceful as he was, we supposed that he would enthusiastically support our staff and programs. Though his position was not entirely his choice, we were hardly prepared for the extent of his cutbacks.

Durham had been president of Arizona State University during a stormy period of protest and political activism. Politically independent, he did not bow to the John Birch Society and was considered "too liberal" by con-

servatives even as he kept radicals under control. In the eyes of conservative authorities upset by our galloping historical program, he was the perfect person to rein us in.

A firm administrator, Durham was very different from Joseph Anderson, who had made no attempt to enter into our professional decision-
making. Every matter we took up with Anderson, he simply said we should
discuss with our advisors or with the First Presidency, and he arranged the
meetings. He was not daunted by the criticisms and threats of those who
disliked or opposed what we had done or were doing. He thought we were
doing just fine; he was sweet and kind and helpful. Durham, however, with
different instructions, wanted to *run* the department: to set goals and objectives and means of attaining them. For our own and the church's good,
we were expected to obediently acquiesce.

Durham acknowledged to us that several members of the Twelve had
instructed him to turn things around "by ninety degrees." The department,
he was told, was like a locomotive, speeding along in one direction. Durham
must make the ninety-degree turn so it would chug along in the right direction. In making the turn a few might fall off, and there would inevitably be a diminution in the speed of the train. Clearly, our work must be
reduced, controlled, constricted. Durham declared to Earl Olson and me
that our History Division was suspect, that we had very little standing
among the general authorities, and that he would try to "save" us by keeping
a tight control on our operations. He claimed that with our broader approach we did not fit well into other church programs. He insisted that he
approve each research project, staff assignment, and proposed publication
and curtailed the number of projects we would write. Clearly he wanted
to place us on a short leash, effectively replacing me as church historian.

The changes were implemented at once. I submitted to Durham a detailed report on each staff member's projects and notes on every change
in assignment or new assignment except for the vignettes we wrote for the
*Church News*. Every article, manuscript of a talk, and preliminary book
manuscript he went over as a professor goes over term papers, theses, and
dissertations. This is no doubt what his advisors had asked him to do.
When Durham ordered Olson to administer our privately created Mormon
History Trust Fund, keep its books, and approve of its transactions, however, I promptly and strongly resisted. I was willing to give him a copy of
the annual report and, if he insisted, an annual CPA auditor's report, but
this was a private bank account and I intended for it to stay private. It was
not his business. Durham pushed. I pushed back. Durham questioned. I
held firm. Durham protested that he would be "held responsible." I pointed

out that he could hardly be held responsible for something outside his department. Reluctantly, he agreed.

Equally upsetting was Durham's attempt to cope with the "suspicion and displeasure" expressed by some general authorities over the "opening of the archive" by instructing me to limit references to those materials. Astounded, I pointed out that we did not use material not available to other scholars and that we already, as a matter of professionalism, gave source citations by location if original manuscripts were preserved in other depositories. Couldn't we, Durham asked, cite a letter of Brigham Young by addressee and date without giving the location? At this proposal from a former university president, my hopes collapsed that Durham would be an ally in a division dedicated to responsible historical scholarship. I asked for an opportunity to explain to the general authorities that the church would "lose face" with historians by the enforcement of this policy. The request was denied. We had never sought to carry out a nonapproved program, but we did hope to foster a climate of understanding.

Having been advised to act as church historian and recorder in the Joseph Fielding Smith style, Durham did not have regular meetings to discuss policies and procedures with our executive council but simply met, usually once a week, individually, with each division executive. No minutes were kept and his decisions were ad hoc. He did not regard himself as bound by any previous counsel or decisions. Instead of including us in meetings with the advisors from the Twelve, as Dyer and Anderson had done, he went alone, or with Earl Olson, whom he appointed assistant managing director. He did not arrange for us to meet with the First Presidency; he went alone. His principal advisor was Gordon Hinckley, his fellow missionary in Great Britain in the 1930s. In 1978 he made his position clear by putting up a series of photos of church historians. Mine was excluded, but his was included. For those staff members who objected, he declared that Howard W. Hunter had been replaced by Alvin Dyer, even though he was managing director of the Historical Department and not church historian. Earl Olson's photo was also included even though he was the assistant managing director and not church historian.

Most damaging to our work were the steps he took to remove all the scholars from the department. Originally, this meant not hiring replacements for those who left—Glen Leonard, Bruce Blumell, James Allen, and Jill Mulvay Derr. Indeed, he served as a midwife to get some of them transferred—Glen Leonard to the Arts and Sites Division, Jim Allen to BYU as history department chair, and Bruce Blumell to law school in Calgary.

When reminded that certain things had been done or decided by Anderson, Durham would remark that Anderson was sweet but unaware. My reaction was that Anderson, because he listened and had the experience of witnessing church government for many years, was quite aware of what was going on and respectful of what we were trying to do.

Durham explained that he came under very different instructions from his superiors, who told him to strictly supervise our work and make it conform with the teachings of other programs. The First Presidency no doubt approved his subsequent actions, based on information he gave them, but his was the only voice. He wrote the basic memoranda, the letters outlining policies. Despite the latter-day revelations counseling us to "keep our history," some authorities apparently preferred that we have no history except that kept by public relations writers.

Of course, Durham was entitled to do what he did; he was called for that purpose. He was doing his job in a way he understood to be for the good of the church. It would have been improper for the division to be in the hands of revisionist historians with an agenda. We did not regard ourselves in that sense, nor did we believe the First Presidency thought so. If we had been, we *should have been* "reined in." My reaction at the time was simply that we had been instructed by Tanner, Dyer, Anderson, Lee, and Kimball to follow the revelations (Doctrine and Covenants 21:1; 47:1, 3; 69:3; 85:1–2): "to keep a history and a general church record of all the things that transpire in Zion . . . and also their manner of life, their faith, and works." This is what we had undertaken to do, we had been assured that the Lord was blessing us in doing this, and if we kept our minds and souls open, we should continue to do this in righteousness.

In many ways I felt defenseless. I was not a relative of any general authority nor had any of them been my mission president, bishop, or stake president. I did not have anyone I could call on for help. If I had problems, to whom should I go? In the early years I could have taken misunderstandings to Hunter, Kimball, McConkie, and Stapley. But Durham did not give me that liberty. He alone discussed our work with them. Tanner had told me in 1972 that I should feel free to go to him with problems that might arise, but by 1977 he and Kimball, another supporter, were in poor health and I could not, in good conscience, burden them with our concerns.

Some have suggested that we would have done better to have cleared our writings with the Correlation Committee. This committee, which was first established in the 1960s under the direction of Harold B. Lee, was intended to coordinate the work of the various organizations of the church and, according to Lee's comments to me in 1972, was never intended to censor subject matter except that occurring in instructional materials. I had a revealing conversation in 1973 with Wendell Ashton, chairman of Public Communications. I asked Ashton if he submitted his releases for publication for clearance through the Correlation Committee. Ashton claimed that such a submission would "ruin everything." He explained that he had previously been a member of the committee and objected to the members' reading for subject matter. The committee makes so many suggested changes, he said, and it is difficult to get certain matters approved by them. Auxiliary leaders sponsoring manuals gave up their responsibility and assumed that a task was completed if it had passed the committee. Ashton said a manuscript could pass muster with the committee and still not be well written or stimulating or instructive or thought-provoking or accomplish any of the goals set up by the auxiliaries for their manuals. In short, something could pass the Correlation Committee and still be dull; in fact, if it was dull it usually passed with speed and high praise. I had observed the same thing.

I talked frankly to Wendell about the problems we had in writing good biographies, regretting that we had not produced better ones. I said that I doubted we could do very much about it as long as family members and church officials were so sensitive about realistic treatments. Ashton's wife broke in to say that we ought not to employ church people to write biographies and histories. They should instead be left for independent persons who could write honestly. She asked me if in writing history and biography we had to consider what the church leaders and members would think. I replied affirmatively. She countered that our work would always be compromised because we had to do this. She greatly preferred to rely on Juanita Brooks, a fiercely independent writer with acknowledged probity. She remarked that if she wanted to get a straightforward account of something, she would read Juanita's publications instead of the church historian's accounts.

I defended our work: "What is wrong with letting our own people have the freedom to write things honestly so that the members of the church can depend on what they say?" She apparently felt that this balance was impossible to attain.

Apparently many LDS readers agreed that they wanted the history of "real" people. An amazing number of persons were reading *Nightfall at Nauvoo* (1971) by Samuel W. Taylor, an experienced Mormon novelist (*Absent-Minded Professor, Heaven Knows Why, Family Kingdom*) and grandson of John Taylor, third president of the church. Entering imaginatively into the minds of historical Latter-day Saint figures, Sam explained how the small anti-Mormon minority effectively forced the expulsion of the Saints from Nauvoo. He saw the Saints as human beings, with individual flaws that made their Illinois neighbors distrust their intentions and sincerity and prepared the way for the murder of their prophet and their ultimate expulsion. Sam's literary ability brought Nauvoo and its residents alive. He described real people, not just pious celestial saints. The reader had the feeling of being there, of actually participating in the fast-moving events. Although the book was a sympathetic view, there was also a tone of innuendo that caused some resolute officials to regard it as sensationalist. Sam's writing was imaginative and entertaining, and I personally did not see that he had done any damage to the church's image.[1]

The popularity of *Nightfall at Nauvoo* suggests how starved members of the church were for dramatically written historical material, and their curiosity to know "the real story" of what took place. Clearly, many members were not buying the time-worn "seminary version" of church history.

Word had gotten to some of the general authorities that I had opened the archives to Raymond Taylor, Sam's brother, who had spent years doing research on the life of their grandfather, John Taylor, and that he had fed the information to Sam, who used it in writing *Nightfall at Nauvoo* and *The Kingdom or Nothing: The Life of John Taylor, Militant Mormon* (1976). Ray died in December 1972, and Sam spoke at the funeral in Provo. In his talk, a little more humorous than one normally given at a funeral, Sam thanked *me* twice for allowing Ray access to the materials. Word of this sped back to church headquarters. The truth was that in 1969 Joseph Fielding Smith, A. William Lund, and Earl Olson had given Ray Taylor permission to use the archives—three years before my appointment— and Ray had almost completed his research before I arrived in 1972. Moreover, it was not my prerogative to give approval to work in the archives; this had to be done by Don Schmidt and Earl Olson. So I was graciously, but wrongly, given credit for something I might have done but didn't do. As I wrote in my diary, President Ernest Wilkinson of BYU, who was at the funeral and with whom I was working on a four-volume history of BYU, was personally concerned, telling me that when word of Sam's talk got around, "you will be hearing about it." "You," he said, "will be needlessly blamed for all the unpleasant material Ray found and conveyed to Sam. This is unfortunate. As Church Historian you are too important to all of us to have your image tarnished with 'the Brethren.' We must not allow you to be controlled or removed."[2]

Approximately a year after Durham took office, on April 5, 1978, he prepared a memo, duly endorsed by the First Presidency, suggesting that church history could be written by many scholars both within and without the church. The point was that the church no longer needed to sponsor history. The work of the History Division should be focused on maintenance and refinement of the Journal History of the Church (since my appointment, I had spent an hour each morning on this work); maintenance of a growing archives and the ever-increasing body of historical data pertaining to the church (of what use were growing archives if no one could use them?); providing assistance to the First Presidency, general authorities, and church agencies (we had always done this on the rare occasions we were asked); undertaking such research and publication projects as directed and specifically authorized by the First Presidency (since 1972 every research project and publication had been cleared by our managing director, advisors, and by the First Presidency). The First Presidency used the letter to acknowledge that there would be budgetary restraints and personnel adjustments. The letter thanked us for our past activities.

Durham wrote the letter, I thought, as a way of changing the image of our division in the minds of a few powerful members of the Twelve by giving the impression that we would now follow what they would like us to do. But it also gave the mistaken impression that we had previously failed to consult our superiors.

In the spring of 1979 Durham called me in to express his feelings about the future of our division. He said that Hinckley, though sympathetic with what we were doing, felt strongly that the research and writing of church history ought to be turned over to independent scholars not in the employ of the Historical Department. In the magisterial manner suggested by his advisors, he spoke of our historians one by one and suggested those that ought to be moved into a university or other employment. He said since Kimball remained in ill health, Ezra Taft Benson would likely become president soon. Unfortunately, the president of the Twelve was not sympathetic to those of us in the History Division.

Durham sincerely believed he was protecting our best interests—or the best interest of church history. He said that shortly after his appointment he asked Joseph Anderson what land mines to avoid. Anderson assured him there were none, that things were going along very well with the department and with the manner in which the department was being received by others. But when Durham was called in by a few members of the Twelve who expressed grave concern about the History Division, he knew that there were plenty of land mines.

## The Sesquicentennial History

The sixteen-volume sesquicentennial history of the church was scheduled for publication in 1980 by Deseret Book. We signed agreements with sixteen persons chosen by us and approved by the First Presidency to write the volumes.[3] The project got underway in the fall of 1972 at a dinner meeting sponsored by Deseret Book and attended by each of the sixteen authors. The speaker was Thomas S. Monson, a member of the Twelve, chairman of the executive committee of Deseret Book, and president of Deseret News Publishing Company. We proudly mentioned the project in articles in *The Ensign* and elsewhere, and we were pleased that a full history from 1830 to 1980 was underway. Fellowships enabled most authors to spend a summer or more working in our archives. The fellowships were likewise available to their research assistants. Annual letters reported progress, and we were hopeful we would have the books in print by the sesquicentennial year.

I was visited during this period of preparation by Daniel Boorstin, librarian of Congress, who had just completed the editing and publication of a thirty-volume history of American civilization for the University of Chicago Press. The hour-long conference was of great personal interest to me—not only for Boorstin's cautions about the sesquicentennial history project but for other comments as well. He had entered Harvard at fifteen and graduated in law with highest honors at eighteen. He took a doctorate at Yale and went on to become an outstanding Rhodes Scholar at Oxford. I congratulated him on his many books that I had read: *The Lost World of Thomas Jefferson* (1948); *The Genius of American Politics* (1953); *The Image* (1962); the prize-winning trilogy *The Americans: The Colonial Experience* (1958) that won the Bancroft Prize; *The Americans: The National Experience* (1965) that was awarded the Parkman Prize; and *The Americans: The Democratic Experience* (1965) that was a Pulitzer Prize winner. I discovered that we had much in common: he was sixty and I was fifty-eight; we both had been trained for a separate profession (he in law and I in economics); we both used mechanical typewriters; and we both wrote history because we enjoyed it. We both had the pleasure and opportunity of teaching, we did not make our living by writing, we never had a literary agent, and we wrote what we wanted to write. Neither of us had an ideological agenda that imprisoned our writing. Boorstin was fascinated to hear about our sesquicentennial history project and thought it was much overdue, but he suggested the difficulties in completing it. Some of the assigned volumes, he predicted, would never be completed; the best volumes would be finished first.

Only later did we learn that Durham and Hinckley had secretly decided in April 1978 not to go ahead with sesquicentennial history, even though it had been authorized by the First Presidency. At Hinckley's direction, the church's attorneys were requested to determine the legal status of the contracts with the authors. Wilford Kirton sent a long legal opinion to Hinckley stating that the church could not avoid publication of the volumes even if the various authors did not turn in their manuscripts on time. Deseret Book had never defaulted on a contract because an author failed to meet a deadline, and in any suit Deseret Book would not be able to substantiate it as an excuse for not publishing. Moreover, the brief stated that Deseret Book had an affirmative responsibility to publish the manuscripts after a reasonable period of editing, designing, printing, and binding. Deseret Book and the Historical Department had a legally defensible right to insist upon a proper length, to edit the manuscripts, and to require changes and alterations in language, style, and content. This, of course, the sixteen authors had always known and expected. Authors displeased with alterations suggested by us or by Deseret Book would have a weak case in court because they all had known who the publisher was, the attitudes of its officers, and company editorial policy. With this opinion, privately related to us, we continued to push the project exactly as before.

Five manuscripts came in by 1979: Richard Bushman's, Milton Backman's, Thomas Alexander's, Richard Cowan's, and LaMond Tullis's. These were read by Jim Allen, Davis Bitton, Maureen Ursenbach Beecher, and me. Copies were then given to Durham, who, after his reading, took them to the members of the First Presidency for reading by a person they designated.

When it became clear that all of the manuscripts would not be finished by 1980, let alone published, the concept of a sixteen-volume set was abandoned by Deseret Book as not realistic. With the build-up of antagonism among the Twelve and the new direction launched by Durham, Hinckley and Durham finally decided to abandon the project as a church-sponsored enterprise and allow each author to find his own publisher. Deseret Book paid each author for the work he had done on the project, and most of them parted with good feelings. Since I was the editor without a stipulated compensation, though I expected a share of the royalties, I was not reimbursed. But I regarded my editorship as part of my job as church historian and did not make it an issue.

Some books have since been published, others are completed and await publication, and others are still in preparation.[4] In addition, a number of splendid articles have been published in professional and church publications. Since all authors were active Latter-day Saints, we did not anticipate any problems with the tone of the manuscripts and that has proven true thus far.

Durham was disappointed that we did not have all volumes completed by 1980 and began to make remarks about the dilatory nature of historians. Indeed, he decided he would show us how a good history could be written in a few months by directing an ingratiating biography of N. Eldon Tanner. At first he considered doing it himself, and we watched with enormous interest. On January 23, 1981, he convened Glen Leonard, Steven Olsen, Paul L. Anderson, Dale Beecher, Donald Enders, William Kehr, Ronald Barney, James L. Kimball Jr., and Gordon Irving. He presented an outline and sample materials for a biography of Tanner, who at the time was eighty-two years of age and in failing health. The product of this hurried-up group effort, compiled from drafts of chapters and memoranda, was published in 1982 shortly before Tanner's death. Tanner certainly deserved a biography, but although the volume was an important contribution to LDS history in many ways, it did not compare with the major two-volume biography of J. Reuben Clark Jr. published by Brigham Young University Press in 1980 that was written by Frank Fox and D. Michael Quinn, skilled Mormon historians and writers.

## Two Commissioned Books

In 1972, with the approval of our managing director, advisors, and the First Presidency, we commissioned two scholars not connected with the Historical Department to write books that in our opinion would benefit the church. The first, Spencer J. Palmer, was to write about missions to Asia and developing countries, and the second, Kenneth Godfrey, was to prepare a book giving firsthand insights of pioneer women into historical events in the church. These two publications would cover new territory; historians had traditionally focused on the American church and on male leadership.

Spencer Palmer, a native of the Gila Valley in Arizona where Spencer Kimball, after whom he was named, had lived, earned degrees from Brigham Young University and the University of California at Berkeley. With a Ph.D. in Asian history, he had served as a Mormon chaplain in the U.S. Army in Korea and Japan and was president of the church's Korean Mission, 1965–68. He had been a member of the board of directors of the Research Institute of Korean Affairs and of the Royal Asiatic Society. He had been a bishop, stake high councilor, counselor in a stake presidency, and regional representative of the Twelve. He had published *The Church Encounters Asia* (1971) and many articles in professional journals on aspects of Far Eastern history. Aware that Mormonism was on the threshold of becoming a world-embracing faith, we asked him in the fall of 1972 to prepare a book that would present the experiences of missionaries "to every nation, kindred, tongue, and people." Deseret Book agreed to publish the book. The result was Palmer's *The Expanding Church*, published in 1978. In the edited collection, four representative families in Switzerland, Japan, Guatemala, and Tonga told of problems they faced in reconciling the teachings of Mormonism with their nationality and heritage. The reflections of the Karl Ringger family, the Masao Watabe family, the Pablo Choc family, and the Vaha'i Tonga family attested powerfully to the internationalism of Mormonism. Of special interest were chapters by Bruce R. McConkie on the expansion of the church in Asia; by David M. Kennedy, ambassador-at-large for the church, who discussed the universality of its appeal; and by Soren F. Cox, the church's first mission president in Singapore.

The book received fine reviews. Truman Madsen, in *BYU Studies*, welcomed this narrative of historical and doctrinal footings for the mandate to "penetrate every clime." With its recitation of church programs and procedures that cross cultural divides, the book demonstrated that Mormonism is not a community of blood but a community of faith. Noel Reynolds, reviewing it for *Dialogue*, said that Palmer was able to deal realistically with serious problems facing the church and its individual members without wearing the dark glasses of cynicism. The sensitive book correlated prophetic statements on the international responsibility of the church. [5]

Strangely, this completely positive, faith-promoting book faced the same distrust and suspicion that *Story of the Latter-day Saints* and *Building the City of God* did. While the work was still in the manuscript stage, those in our office were reading it, Deseret Book editors were reading it, and, as we learned, a member of the Twelve had been assigned by Kimball to read it for the First Presidency. After his first reading, the member of the Twelve asked to speak with Palmer, who was under the impression that he was "being called on the carpet." As I was informed by a private source, the apostle told him that he was very unhappy about my leadership and the work of the History Division, that he thought we were disobeying counsel, that we were guided more by professional motives than religious motives, and that we were more anxious to please our peers in the history profession than our superiors in the church. He told Palmer that he thought the first section of the book by David Kennedy would cause problems for the church and that he should not have expected to publish intimate details about the church's relationship with foreign powers. There were things that even he, as a member of the Twelve, did not know. Palmer explained to him in some detail how he was assigned to write the book, how the approval to do so had come from the First Presidency, and how at every stage in writing the book he had received the encouragement of me and through me of our advisors and of the First Presidency. He explained that the idea of having a section by Kennedy had been suggested by me, that I had mentioned it to Kennedy, that Kennedy had checked with Kimball, and that Kimball had urged him to write it. After a number of weeks passed with nothing being done, Palmer then made contact with Kennedy and asked him if we might expedite the project by having him dictate his story on tape to Palmer, who would then transcribe it, edit it, and take it back for his approval. Kennedy checked with Kimball; Kimball urged him to do it. He then granted the taped interview and it went through Palmer's editorial hand. Palmer submitted the manuscript to Kennedy, who corrected and amplified it and then submitted the manuscript to Kimball. Kimball read it, made suggestions, approved it, and gave it back to Kennedy, who forwarded it to Palmer.

Listening to the explanation, the assigned reader countered that the manuscript contained quotations from others, and why weren't these cleared with them? Palmer explained that he had received the permission of McConkie and William Bangerter, an assistant to the Twelve, to use their statements. The apostle, always wanting to be sure that proper protocol was followed, seemed to be very surprised that Palmer had secured approval all the way along for the project and also that we had gone over the manuscript carefully several times before the manuscript had finally been submitted to the First Presidency. Apparently my covering letter in submitting the manuscript to Hunter for conveyance to Kimball had never been forwarded to the assigned reader. It was surprising to me that the member of the Twelve would not have discussed the matter with me before he sent a memo to the First Presidency and before he called in Palmer.

In a subsequent call to Palmer, the member of the Twelve was pleasant, affable, and encouraging. He told Palmer that he had discussed the manuscript with Kimball, that he was recommending a few changes in the manuscript, and that when those had been made he would be pleased to approve the manuscript. He thought the changes could be made within a week. Basically he recommended that the reports from the various countries be summarized in the introduction and that they be omitted in the text. He thought Palmer could do this rather easily. When Palmer resubmitted the manuscript to him he would then take it to the First Presidency and the members of the First Presidency would send it on to Deseret Book with their full endorsement and request that Deseret Book publish it.

In concluding the telephone conversation, the member of the Twelve added that he was pleased to be associated with this project, that he thought it would be a tremendous contribution to the church and its missionary work, and that Palmer was to be congratulated for preparing such a useful and exciting book. He also told Palmer that he should get in touch with me and be sure that I agreed with these modifications and procedures. He also encouraged Palmer to let me know that the Twelve loved and supported me. Palmer was pleased with this completely different attitude—as were we all. But we wondered why general authorities approached our work with such suspicion and mistrust.

On December 19, 1978, we held in the Historical Department conference room a party for *The Expanding Church*. Kimball was present with his assistant, D. Arthur Haycock, as was David Kennedy and about sixty other persons, including faculty members from BYU, persons from church headquarters, and our research historians. Lowell Durham, president of Deseret Book, conducted; Joe Christensen, director of the LDS Institute of Religion at the University of Utah, gave the opening prayer; and James Mortimer, manager of Deseret Book, formally presented the book to Kimball, who proudly declared that Spencer Palmer was from his stake in Arizona. As a little boy, he said, Spencer and other boys once sat on the front row during his visit to their ward and mimicked his actions on the stand, crossing their legs when he crossed his, moving their hands when he moved his, and so on. Spencer Kimball obviously loved Spencer Palmer.

Our experience with the second of our two commissioned books was completely positive: *Women's Voices: An Untold History of the Latter-day Saints, 1830–1900* by Kenneth W. Godfrey, Audrey M. Godfrey, and Jill Mulvay Derr, published by Deseret Book in 1982. In the fall of 1972, I wrote to Ken Godfrey, then director of the LDS Institute adjacent to Utah State University in Logan, asking him to write a book containing selections from the letters, diaries, and journals of Mormon women. There had been a glaring lack of material regarding LDS women in the major histories of the church. A few weeks thereafter Ken and his wife Audrey decided to do the book together. In January 1974 the Church Educational System granted Ken a leave to do the research. Working in the Church Archives, Ken and Audrey read more than 250 women's diaries, letters, and journals and selected moving, important, and informative passages. When they received a call from the First Presidency in 1975 to preside over the Pennsylvania-Pittsburgh Mission, we arranged for Jill Mulvay Derr to work on the manuscript and selection of materials.

Ken received his bachelor and doctorate degrees from Utah State University and Brigham Young University. Audrey is also a graduate of USU. Jill earned a B.A. at the University of Utah and a master's degree from Harvard before joining our History Division staff.

*Women's Voices* was a significant addition to the increasing number of published memoirs and journals of Mormon women. The authors divided the seven decades of Mormon history into nine sections, presented chronologically and introduced by brief historical notes that skillfully set the stage for the ensuing excerpts. Each section featured two to five excerpts from the journals, letters, and diaries of women "anxiously engaged" in the momentous events of the era. Each of the twenty-five featured women was introduced biographically, literarily, and historically. Common themes of the excerpts were a strong commitment to the gospel, persecution, hardship and discomfort, heartache at the frequent loss of children and loved ones, ill health, and the drudgery of farming, building, midwifery, home industry, constant cooking, church service, and sending husbands on missions. There are also accounts of ward dances, concerts, plays, clubs, debates, politics, and an endless round of visits. The book tended to accent the spiritual aspect of the women's lives. In his review Richard Cracroft concluded:

> Well-documented and edited, *Women's Voices* is an important volume—for the library, the Western- or Mormon-history buff, the historian. The voices heard in this volume remind us that every life is laden with the stuff of drama, but such drama is more certain when that life is one of steadfast devotion to a cause, especially when that cause means changing one's beliefs, leaving one's home, enduring persecution, adopting a new and generally unacceptable lifestyle, fleeing into a wilderness, and building a community—all the while teaching and rearing a family, attempting to promote some vestiges of culture—and sending the family breadwinner on repeated, unremunerated missions to convert the very people who had caused the upheaval. These voices, in various tones, and at various amplitudes, murmur, speak, sometimes shout to us from the past with such vigor and realism as to lend these accounts literary as well as historical importance, for in these powerful records of personal lives we see enacted and recorded day-by-day, year-by-year, those little human acts which add up to important literary expression about individuals whose lives came to mean "Mormonism or nothing," and whose lives, thanks to this fine volume, now mean so much more to many.[6]

Perhaps because of the focus on women's spirituality, the absence of historical analysis of women's problems, and the obvious dedication of the women whose writing was included, the book received not a word of criticism from any general authority—or at least none that we heard. Deseret Book marketed the volume enthusiastically and it was a best-seller. This was one of our products that pleased—or did not displease—church leaders.

A friend of mine has speculated that my experience as a soldier in World War II was a precursor of what I would experience working for the church, another authoritarian institution. The army, in those years, followed a caste system: officers enjoyed a different status than enlisted men. Officers frequented an officers' club, ate different food rations at a separate mess, and were given privileges denied to enlisted men like myself. We saluted officers, were often assigned to carry their suitcases and duffle bags, and were also assigned to clean up their club. Something similar was true in the church. General authorities usually ate in a different cafeteria, used a different men's room, and, of course, out of respect, we tipped our hats to them when we saw them on the street. Once, without realizing it, I made use of the wrong men's room. A janitor discovered my trespass and gave me a stern lecture forbidding me to do it again. Because I had dealt with sergeants, lieutenants, captains, and colonels in North Africa and Italy, in a setting where resistance was natural but risky and useless, I was prepared for a church position that required confrontation with many old-line officials who by virtue of their kinship and personal relationships with each other and their lifetime appointments did not welcome my intrusion. They saw no need for me and my fellow staff members to update or retell the church's story, as the revelations of Joseph Smith would require. Indeed, they were not merely satisfied with church history as it had been written years before but, despite the explicit instructions given to me by the First Presidency, determined to place every obstacle in our path and use every opportunity to cast suspicion on our many endeavors.

## Notes

1. See the review by Frederick G. Williams in *Dialogue* 6 (Autumn–Winter 1971): 117–20.

2. See my diary entry for December 18, 1972.

3. Here is a complete list of the projects and those assigned to them: introduction and background to 1830, Richard L. Bushman; the Ohio experience to 1838, Milton V. Backman Jr.; the Missouri experience to 1839, Max Parkin; the Illinois period, 1839–46, T. Edgar Lyon; the crossing of the Plains, Reed C. Durham Jr.; the early pioneer period, 1847–69, Eugene E. Campbell; the later pioneer period, 1869–1900, Charles S. Peterson; the early twentieth century, 1900–1930, Thomas G. Alexander; the middle twentieth century, 1930–50, Richard O. Cowan; the contemporary church, 1950–80, James B. Allen; a history of the Saints in Europe, Douglas F. Tobler; a history of the Saints in Asia and the Pacific, R. Lanier Britsch; a history of the Saints in Mexico, Central America, and South America, F. LaMond Tullis; a history of the expansion of the church, S. George Ellsworth; a social and cultural history of the church, 1830–1900, Davis Bitton; a social and cultural history of the church, 1901–72, John L. Sorenson.

4. As of 1997, the following volumes of the proposed history have been published: Richard L. Bushman, *Joseph Smith and the Beginnings of Mormonism* (Urbana: University of Illinois Press, 1984); Milton V. Backman Jr., *The Heavens Resound: A History of the Latter-day Saints in Ohio, 1830–1838* (Salt Lake City: Deseret Book Company, 1983); Thomas G. Alexander, *Mormonism in Transition: A History of the Latter-day Saints, 1890–1930* (Urbana: University of Illinois Press, 1986); Richard O. Cowan, *The Church in the Twentieth Century* (Salt Lake City: Deseret Book, 1985); R. Lanier Britsch, *Unto the Islands of the Sea: A History of the Latter-day Saints in the Pacific* (Salt Lake City: Deseret Book, 1986), and *Mormonism in Hawaii* (Salt Lake City: Deseret Book, 1990); and F. LaMond Tullis, *Mormons in Mexico: The Dynamics of Faith and Culture* (Logan: Utah State University Press, 1987). Eugene E. Campbell's manuscript was unfinished at the

time of his death in 1986, but was completed by his son Bruce and Gary Bergera and published as *Establishing Zion: The Mormon Church in the American West, 1847–1869* (Salt Lake City: Signature Books, 1988). None of the chapters was read by any member of our editing committee. Ed Lyon died in 1978, but before his death he agreed with our recommendation that Glen Leonard be given his notes and take over the responsibility of completing the volume.

5. Truman Madsen, review of *The Expanding Church*, *BYU Studies* 19 (Winter 1979): 251–53; Noel Reynolds, review of *The Expanding Church*, *Dialogue* 12 (Summer 1979): 131–32.

6. Richard H. Cracroft, review of *Women's Voices: An Untold History of the Latter-day Saints, 1830–1900*, *BYU Studies* 23 (Spring 1983): 244. See also the review by Elouise M. Bell in *Dialogue* 16 (Summer 1983): 138–39.

# The Long-Promised Day

Behold, I say unto you they are made known unto me by the Holy
Spirit of God. Behold, I have fasted and prayed many days that I might
know these things of myself. And now I do know of myself that they
are true; for the Lord God hath made them manifest unto me by his
Holy Spirit; and this is the spirit of revelation which is in me.
—Book of Mormon, Alma 5:46

THE MOST EXCITING single event of the years I was church historian occurred on June 9, 1978, when the First Presidency announced a divine
revelation that all worthy males might be granted the priesthood.

It had been a busy week. I taught a class on Mondays and Wednesdays
at BYU, entertained some Italian visitors in Salt Lake City and Provo on
Tuesday, spoke at the Richfield High School graduation, and accompanied
Hugh W. Pinnock to Kane, Pennsylvania, where I gave a talk on Colonel
Thomas Kane, a great friend of Mormons, for the one hundredth anniversary of the opening of the Kane Memorial Chapel. On Friday I stayed
home from the office with a sore throat and laryngitis.

Just before noon my secretary, Nedra Yeates Pace, telephoned with
remarkable news: Spencer W. Kimball had just announced a revelation that
all worthy males, including those of African descent, might be ordained
to the priesthood. Within five minutes, my son Carl Wayne telephoned from
New York City to say he had heard the news. I was in the midst of sobbing with gratitude for this answer to our prayers and could hardly speak
with him. I was thrilled and electrified. I felt like the Prophet Joseph Smith
said we should feel about the gospel: "A voice of gladness! A voice of mercy
from heaven; and a voice of truth out of the earth; glad tidings for the dead;
a voice of gladness for the living and the dead; glad tidings of great joy"
(Doctrine and Covenants 128:19). For many days I talked with a host of
friends and relatives on the telephone and in person. Everyone was elat-
ed—and sobered.

As a historian I sought to learn the particulars and record them in my private diary. The following account is based on dozens of interviews with persons who talked with church officials after the revelation was announced. Although members of the Twelve and the First Presidency with whom I sought interviews felt they should not elaborate on what happened, I learned details from family members and friends to whom they had made comments. Some of these statements may have involved colorful, symbolic language that was taken literally. It is a common regret among Latter-day Saints that general authorities do not speak openly about their remarkable spiritual experiences in the way Joseph Smith and other early prophets used to do. Although they unquestionably *do* have such experiences, they have said little about this one.

Such a sacred experience that affected us all calls for a sober recitation. Here was indisputable evidence of God's presence and direction in these latter days—divine reaffirmation of the faith and values of our church. The telling of the event expresses the profound wonder and enthusiasm that continues to grip Latter-day Saints in general and historians in particular. I need to emphasize that the following account is mine and might be different from another person's understanding.[1]

Of all general authorities, Kimball was probably the most inclined to disregard ancestry and culture in his dealings with people. George Albert Smith asked Kimball, in his early years as a member of the Twelve, to watch specifically over the Indian nations. Kimball so embraced this assignment that he reached out to all peoples. He was certainly pained that some could not receive the blessings of the priesthood and could not be sealed to their families in the temple. In 1976, two years after he became president, Kimball began a systematic program of prayer, fasting, and supplication, asking the Lord to rescind the rule denying blacks the priesthood. Special emphasis was placed on this effort during the two-month period beginning in April 1978, when every day he put on his sacred clothes and went alone into the Holy Room of the temple for meditation, prayer, and supplication.

When the First Presidency (then consisting of Spencer Kimball, N. Eldon Tanner, and Marion G. Romney) met with the Twelve each Thursday in the sacred upper room of the temple, Kimball spoke of these visits and invited the members to share their feelings.[2] Some sent him private communications of substance, reviewing scriptural allusions and policy pronouncements by church leaders. Others spoke to him privately. Still others spoke earnestly in their meetings. There was fasting and prayer.

On June 1, 1978, at the regular temple meeting of the general authorities, Kimball asked the members of the First Presidency and the Twelve to stay for a private conference. In a spirit of fasting and prayer, they formed a prayer circle. Kimball opened by saying he felt impressed to pray to the Lord and asked their permission to be "mouth." He went to the altar. Those in attendance said that as he began his earnest prayer, they suddenly realized it was not Kimball's prayer, but the Lord speaking through him. A revelation was being declared. Kimball himself realized that the words were not his but the Lord's. During that prayer some of the Twelve—at least two who have said so publicly—were transported into a celestial atmosphere, saw a divine presence and the figures of former presidents of the church (portraits of whom were hanging on the walls around them) smiling to indicate their approval and sanction. Others acknowledged the voice of the Lord coming, as with the prophet Elijah, "through the still, small voice." The voice of the Spirit followed their earnest search for wisdom and understanding.[3]

At the end of the heavenly manifestation Kimball, weeping for joy, confronted the church members, many of them also sobbing, and asked if they sustained this heavenly instruction. Embracing, all nodded vigorously and jubilantly their sanction. There had been a startling and commanding revelation from God—an ineffable experience.

Two of the apostles present described the experience as a "day of Pentecost" similar to the one in the Kirtland Temple on April 6, 1836, the day of its dedication. They saw a heavenly personage and heard heavenly music. To the temple-clothed members, the gathering, incredible and without compare, was the greatest singular event of their lives. Those I talked with wept as they spoke of it. All were certain they had witnessed a revelation from God.

They then discussed the means of announcing the revelation to the world. They agreed that a letter should be written and signed by the First Presidency and that it should be presented to a meeting of all general authorities on June 9. At that meeting, which lasted all morning, there were again tears of joy and jubilation. With their wholehearted, joyous approval, the letter was then released to Heber Wolsey, director of Public Communications, who, in happy tears, released it to the press. The following is the official announcement, dated June 8, 1978, and published without comment in the *Church News* and *The Ensign* and published with considerable comment in the *New York Times* and other national and local newspapers and magazines.[4] The notice is addressed to "general and local priesthood officers of the Church."

Dear Brethren:
   As we have witnessed the expansion of the work of the Lord over the earth, we have been grateful that people of many nations have responded

to the message of the restored gospel, and have joined the Church in ever-increasing numbers. This, in turn, has inspired us with a desire to extend to every worthy member of the Church all of the privileges and blessings which the gospel affords.

Aware of the promises made by the prophets and presidents of the Church who have preceded us that at some time, in God's eternal plan, all of our brethren who are worthy may receive the priesthood, and witnessing the faithfulness of those from whom the priesthood has been withheld, we have pleaded long and earnestly in behalf of these, our faithful brethren, spending many hours in the Upper Room of the Temple supplicating the Lord for divine guidance.

He has heard our prayers, and by revelation has confirmed that the long-promised day has come when every faithful, worthy man in the Church may receive the holy priesthood, with power to exercise its divine authority, and enjoy with his loved ones every blessing that flows therefrom, including the blessings of the temple. Accordingly, all worthy male members of the Church may be ordained to the priesthood without regard for race or color. Priesthood leaders are instructed to follow the policy of carefully interviewing all candidates for ordination to either the Aaronic or the Melchizedek Priesthood to insure that they meet the established standards for worthiness.

We declare with soberness that the Lord has now made known his will for the blessing of all his children throughout the earth who will hearken to the voice of his authorized servants, and prepare themselves to receive every blessing of the gospel.

Sincerely yours,

Spencer W. Kimball

N. Eldon Tanner

Marion G. Romney

The *Deseret News* stopped a press run to get this calm, firm affirmation of revelation in its first edition. *Time* and *Newsweek*, too, stopped their presses to get the story in their current issues. Thousands of people, hearing it for the first time on radio and television, telephoned church offices in Salt Lake City asking if it was true. Members of the church—in Canada, England, South Africa, the American South, the Midwest, the Pacific Coast, Utah, and Idaho—were joyously surprised and teary-eyed. "The Lord has heard our prayers." "The long-promised day has come." On the Sunday that followed the announcement, a number of worthy black members of the church in New York, Chicago, Salt Lake City, and Hawaii were ordained to priesthood offices. Young black men stepped forward to serve missions. The following week a number of black families went to the temple for their endowments and sealings. When Kimball was interviewed after the announcement, feeling a great weight off his shoulders, he simply declared, "Isn't it beautiful?" Jimmy Carter sent a telegram to Kimball: "I commend you for your compassionate prayerfulness and courage in receiving a new doctrine. This announcement brings a healing spirit to the world and reminds all men and women that they are truly brothers and sisters."[5] The revelation was accepted unanimously as "the word and will of the Lord" in the general conference session on September 30, 1978.

The historian is always interested in what led to a certain action—considerations that may have prompted Kimball and his associates to seek God's will on this matter at this particular time. Here are several that I identified in June 1978.

First, from the founding of the church, declarations were made that the gospel would be preached to every nation, kindred, and tongue and that it was the privilege of all peoples to go to the holy temple. The following statement was made by Joseph Smith and the other members of the First Presidency on October 5, 1840: "If the work rolls forth with the same rapidity it has heretofore done, we may soon expect to see flocking to this place, people from every land and from every nation; the polished European, the degraded Hottentot, and the shivering Laplander; persons of all languages, and of every tongue, and of every color; who shall with us worship the Lord of Hosts in His holy temple and offer up their orisons in His sanctuary."[6]

Second, Mormon scriptures contain passages reemphasizing the worth of all souls: "He [Jesus] inviteth them all to come unto him and partake of his goodness; and he denieth none that come unto him, black and white, bond and free, male and female . . . and all are alike unto God, both Jew and Gentile" (Book of Mormon, 2 Nephi 26:33). Statistical studies indicated that, compared with other Christian groups, Mormons, despite what appeared to be a discriminatory policy, did not have a higher degree of prejudice.[7] Perhaps this was because, with their historical experience, the Mormons retained a heritage of concern for the disadvantaged. Further, Mormon leaders had clearly stated that blacks should have full constitutional rights and urged members to help guarantee equal opportunities and protection under the law.[8]

Third, all of us, impressed with the egalitarian ethos of the gospel, understood that someday the priesthood would be made available to all worthy male members. This is the way I was brought up; this is the way the matter was understood by the vast majority of Saints; this is in line with pronouncements of various of our prophets. Consider these:

> And when all the rest of the children have received their blessing in the Holy Priesthood, . . . they will then come up and possess the priesthood, and receive all the blessings which we now are entitled to.[9]

But the day will come when all that race will be redeemed and possess all the blessings which we now have.[10]

This . . . exclusion from the exercise of the rights of the priesthood was pronounced upon these people by the Lord, and it remains in force until He shall see fit to withdraw the decree.[11]

Sometime in God's eternal plan, the Negro will be given the right to hold the Priesthood.[12]

According to Mormon thinking, God's love would not permit an indefinite continuation of exclusion from the temple of any worthy person.

Cognizant of this general doctrine and hope, David O. McKay had prayed earnestly to the Lord for permission to rescind the rule of exclusion. The Lord did permit him to make two "loosening" decisions: first, to permit all black males except those of African ancestry to receive the priesthood, thus allowing the ordination of Fiji Islanders and Australian aborigines; second, to instruct missionaries and local officers that they might ordain persons to the priesthood who did not look "obviously Negroid" and for whom no evidence existed that they had African ancestors. McKay was disappointed that the Lord did not permit him to go farther than this. Later, Harold B. Lee, shortly before his death, spent three days and nights fasting in the upper room of the temple, praying earnestly to the Lord for guidance on this matter, but the only answer he received was "not yet."

Historically the Saints did preach the gospel to blacks. The early Saints, often called Negro-lovers, were driven out of anti-abolitionist Missouri at least partly for their encouragement of blacks. Joseph Smith and his associates then adopted a policy of protecting the Saints from persecution by not alienating Missourians unnecessarily. Although there were never many African Americans in Utah, Idaho, and other centers of LDS population, leaders tried to discourage prejudice and discrimination.

During the social unrest that occurred during and after the Vietnam War, many people demonstrated against the priesthood policy at football and basketball games and wrestling matches in which church-owned Brigham Young University participated. These anti-Mormon demonstrations and riots were an obvious embarrassment.

The church's response to the adverse pressure and publicity was that only divine revelation could authorize a change in policy. Church leaders reminded critics that the issue was a matter of religious faith; pending a prophetic declaration they could do little but continue to encourage individual members to support the principle of full civil rights for all people.

In 1963 Hugh B. Brown of the First Presidency declared at the October general conference:

> We believe that all men are the children of the same God, and that it is a moral evil for any person or group of persons to deny any human being the right to gainful employment, to full educational opportunity, and to every privilege of citizenship, just as it is a moral evil to deny him the right to worship according to the dictates of his own conscience. . . .
>
> We call upon all men, everywhere, both within and outside the Church, to commit themselves to the establishment of full civil equality for all of God's children.[13]

Stewart L. Udall, from a prominent Arizona Mormon family and the secretary of the interior under John F. Kennedy and Lyndon B. Johnson (1961–69), wrote an open letter to *Dialogue* that was published in the summer 1967 issue, in which he complained that "the very character of Mormonism is being distorted and crippled by adherence to a belief and practice that denies the oneness of mankind." Writing that "the time has surely come," Udall called on the church to give men of African descent full fellowship. There were perhaps a dozen responses in subsequent issues of *Dialogue*. One person complained that Udall was "trying to lecture" and "presuming upon the Prophet." Most, however, congratulated Udall for initiating open discussion of this important issue. Some referred to scriptural authority, others mentioned moral, social, and theological considerations. Recognizing that decisions must come from the Lord through the chain of authority, many individual members felt free to make earnest inquiry, express concern, and demonstrate an active moral and social conscience.[14]

On December 15, 1969, as the protests continued, the First Presidency issued another official statement: "Negroes [are] not yet to receive the priesthood, for reasons which we believe are known to God, but which He has not made fully known to man. . . . We believe the Negro, as well as those of other races, should have his full constitutional privileges as a member of society, and we hope that members of the Church everywhere will do their part as citizens to see that these rights are held inviolate. Each citizen must have equal opportunities and protection under the law with reference to civil rights."[15]

Over the years some church leaders had tried to explain the exclusion policy, often by speculating possible differences in the premortal state that carried over into mortality. For all of these, Bruce McConkie had a ready answer. The revelation, verified by powerful confirmations, changed everything:

Forget everything I have said, or what President Brigham Young or President George Q. Cannon or whomsoever has said in days past that is contrary to the present revelation. We spoke with a limited understanding and without the light and knowledge that now has come into the world.

We get our truth and our light line upon line and precept upon precept. We have now had added a new flood of intelligence and light on this particular subject, and it erases all the darkness and all the views and all the thoughts of the past. They don't matter any more.[16]

Several more immediate events may have influenced the change in policy at this particular time.

The Lord may have felt that by 1978 the Latter-day Saints were fully prepared to accept blacks as leaders and prophets. To say this another way, the Lord's refusal to grant the priesthood to blacks earlier may have had as much to do with white members being unprepared to accept those of African descent as with any supposed divine judgment on blacks. Similarly, the Lord may have felt that black men were fully prepared to exercise the priesthood and to serve as leaders.

The opening of the temple in Sao Paulo, Brazil, projected for August 1978, surely enhanced the tension regarding blacks and the priesthood. The Lord in his mercy may have felt that this was an appropriate time to resolve such difficulties and anxieties. In March 1976 Kimball was present at the laying of the cornerstone of that temple. There he was told about Helvécio and Rudá Martins, sincere black members converted in 1972. Helvécio was a prominent professor and businessman in Rio de Janeiro who had saved funds to send his son on a mission. Discovering that the young man couldn't go because he was black, the Martins gave the money to the church to send another person. Helvécio had donated for the construction of the temple, both in labor and money, knowing full well that under existing arrangements he could never enter. At the same time Rudá sold her jewelry and contributed the proceeds to the temple fund. All of this grieved Kimball. After the revelation of June 9, the son, who had been about to marry, went on his mission, his fiancée joined the church while he was gone, and the two were married in the temple, which was dedicated by Kimball in October 1978.

Helvécio Martins, meanwhile, served as a bishop and counselor to two stake presidents, and in 1990, when he was president of the Brazil Fortalezza Mission, he was sustained to the Second Council of the Seventy—the first black to become a general authority. Many other stories paralleled the experiences of the Martins, not only in Brazil but also in New York, California, Utah, and elsewhere.[17]

Various state governments were beginning to refuse to exempt church buildings from taxation on the grounds that the church discriminated against African Americans. This had already been done in Wisconsin, where tithing could not be listed as a tax-exempt deduction. Church lawyers were fearful that this might be followed in Hawaii and several other states.

The Lord may have felt that the continuation of the exclusionist doctrine might lead the Saints to take measures that violated people's civil rights. The Lord may have used this means of reminding the Saints that we were all the Lord's children and that he was displeased with those who acted otherwise.

Kimball had received many letters from devoted church members asking for a change in the policy. One that he allowed me to see was from my friend Chase Peterson, vice president of Harvard University (later president of the University of Utah). A beautiful, sincere, well-expressed letter, it was, as I learned later, carefully considered by Kimball, as were many others.

A special committee of the Twelve appointed by President McKay in 1954 to study the issue concluded that there was no sound scriptural basis for the policy but that the church membership was not prepared for its reversal. Research by Lowry Nelson, Armand Mauss, Stephen Taggart, Newell Bringhurst, Naomi Woodbury, and others, however, had prompted some Latter-day Saints to feel that the church was indeed spiritually prepared for a change.[18] Personally, I knew something about the apostolic study because I heard Adam S. Bennion, who was a member of the committee, refer to the work in an informal talk he made to the Mormon Seminar in Salt Lake City on May 13, 1954. McKay, Bennion said, had pled with the Lord without result and finally concluded the time was not yet ripe.[19]

Less than a week after the revelation, I wrote our children to say that we had all been blessed with a superlative spiritual endowment—a gospel and priesthood that were now clearly for all kindreds, tongues, and peoples. In the winter of our discontent, the sun had shone brilliantly.

### Notes

1. Sources other than those cited below include Gerry Avant, "President Kimball Says Revelation Was Clear," *Church News*, Jan. 6, 1979, 15; James E. Faust, "The Doctrine and Covenants and Modern Revelation," in *Hearken, O Ye People: Discourses on the Doctrine and Covenants* (Sandy, Utah: Randall Press, 1984), 287–97; Bruce R. McConkie, "The New Revelation on Priesthood," *Priesthood* (Salt Lake City: Deseret Book, 1981); LeGrand Richards, *Interview with Mormon Apostle LeGrand Richards concerning the 1978 "Negro" Revelation* (Phoenix:

Bobwitte, 1978); Lester E. Bush Jr., "Introduction," *Dialogue* 12 (Summer 1979): 9–12; Armand L. Mauss, "The Fading of the Pharaohs' Curse: The Decline and Fall of the Priesthood Ban against Blacks in the Mormon Church," *Dialogue* 14 (Autumn 1981): 10–45.

2. On June 1, 1978, the Quorum of the Twelve was composed of Ezra Taft Benson, Mark E. Petersen, Delbert L. Stapley, LeGrand Richards, Howard W. Hunter, Gordon B. Hinckley, Thomas S. Monson, Boyd K. Packer, Marvin J. Ashton, Bruce R. McConkie, L. Tom Perry, and David B. Haight. Absent from the June 1, 8, and 9 meetings was Mark Petersen, who was visiting in Brazil.

3. Gordon B. Hinckley quoted in Mike Cannon, "Pres. Hinckley Urges Youth to Choose Right," *Church News*, Jan. 20, 1996, 14.

4. "Every Faithful Worthy Man in the Church May Now Receive the Priesthood," *The Ensign* 8 (July 1978): 75.

5. "Carter Praises LDS Church Action," *Deseret News*, June 10, 1978.

6. B. H. Roberts, ed., *History of the Church of Jesus Christ of Latter-day Saints, Period I: History of Joseph Smith, the Prophet, by Himself,* 2d ed. (Salt Lake City: Deseret News, 1946), 4:213.

7. Armand Mauss, "Moderation in All Things," *Dialogue* 7 (Spring 1972): 57–70.

8. Statement of First Presidency, Dec. 15, 1969, *Deseret News*, Jan. 10, 1970.

9. Brigham Young, sermon, Aug. 19, 1866, in *Journal of Discourses,* 26 vols. (Liverpool: F. D. and S. W. Richards, 1854–86), 11:272.

10. Matthias F. Cowley, *Wilford Woodruff* (Salt Lake City: Bookcraft, 1964), 351.

11. Heber J. Grant, letter to L. H. Wilkin, Jan. 28, 1928, Archives Division, Historical Department of the Church of Jesus Christ of Latter-day Saints.

12. David O. McKay, letter to Lowell Bennion and students at the University of Utah, Nov. 3, 1947.

13. Hugh B. Brown, "The Fight between Good and Evil," *Improvement Era* 66 (Dec. 1963): 1058.

14. Stewart L. Udall, letter to the editor, *Dialogue* 2 (Summer 1967): 5–7; and letters in subsequent issues by Robyn Sandberg, Vernon B. Romney, Paul C. Richards, Edwin P. Rudel, Gary Lobb, Lowry Nelson, John Phillips, Ramon S. Wilcox, Alexander T. Stecker, William L. Knecht, Grant Syphers Jr., Bruce S. Romney, and Samuel N. Henrie Jr.

15. The full statement is in *Improvement Era* 73 (Feb. 1970): 70–71.

16. Bruce McConkie, "All Are Alike Unto God," address given to Church Education System Religious Education Symposium, BYU, Aug. 18, 1978.

17. A full account of events in Brazil that may have influenced Church policies and practices is given in Mark L. Grover, "The Mormon Priesthood Revelation and the São Paulo, Brazil, Temple," *Dialogue* 23 (Spring 1990): 39–53.

18. See Lowry Nelson, "Mormons and the Negro," *The Nation*, May 24, 1952, 488; Armand Mauss, "Mormonism and Secular Attitudes toward Negroes," *Pacific Sociological Review* 9 (Spring 1966): 91–99; Stephen Taggart, *Mormonism's Negro Policy: Social and Historical Origins* (Salt Lake City: University of Utah Press, 1968); Newell G. Bringhurst, "A Servant of Servants . . . Cursed as Pertaining to the Priesthood: Mormon Attitudes toward Slavery and the Black Man, 1830–1880" (Ph.D. diss., University of California at Davis, 1975); and Naomi Woodbury, "A

Legacy of Intolerance: Nineteenth Century Pro-Slavery Propaganda and the Mormon Church Today" (master's thesis, University of California at Los Angeles, 1966). An excellent review of the literature is in Lester E. Bush Jr. and Armand L. Mauss, eds., *Neither White nor Black: Mormon Scholars Confront the Race Issue in a Universal Church* (Midvale, Utah: Signature Books, 1984).

19. Hugh B. Brown said in his memoirs that he had not seen any justification in the scriptures for denying the priesthood to blacks and that the practice was "a policy, not necessarily a doctrine." Edwin B. Firmage, ed., *An Abundant Life: The Memoirs of Hugh B. Brown* (Salt Lake City: Signature Books, 1988), 129. Brown presented a proposal to change the policy, but this was opposed by one member of the Twelve who insisted it would require a revelation (142–43). Sterling McMurrin, a professor emeritus of philosophy of the University of Utah and former commissioner of education of the United States, revealed to me that McKay had told him in the strongest terms that denial of the priesthood to blacks was a practice, not a doctrine.

# 12

# The Mormon Experience

We glory in tribulations, knowing that tribulation worketh patience;
and patience, experience; and experience, hope.
　—Romans 5:3–4

OUR FINAL HURDLE in writing and publishing a major history of the church was the one-volume history of the Mormons contracted with Knopf in 1967. Not having completed the project in the six years that had elapsed since that agreement, I wrote to the First Presidency on May 14, 1973, to say that Alfred Knopf, then eighty-one years of age, had been pleading with me to finish this much needed work. I pointed out to the First Presidency that Knopf and I had in mind a history designed primarily for non-Mormons—for secular historians, university students, and the general reading public who desired an "objective" look at Mormonism. This was to be the kind of book that would be acquired by libraries and used as a standard reference on the LDS Church. Unfortunately, as we all knew, a large number of libraries in the United States carried just four books on the church: W. A. Linn, *Story of the Mormons* (1902), a viciously anti-Mormon work; Thomas F. O'Dea, *The Mormons*, by a Roman Catholic sociologist; *The Year of Decision*, by Bernard DeVoto, which is basically sympathetic with Mormon achievements but not its doctrine; and *No Man Knows My History* by Fawn Brodie, a book repudiated by both LDS and RLDS officials and regarded as seriously flawed by most knowledgeable historians. I was sure the church was not happy to be represented exclusively by such works. As a historian I was disturbed that these were the primary references available to the general public.

On July 2, 1973, in a letter signed by all three members of the First Presidency—Harold B. Lee, N. Eldon Tanner, and Marion G. Romney—I was given permission to use the facilities of the Historical Department to complete the work. Their only expressed reservation was that I should donate one-half the royalties to the Mormon History Trust Fund to be used to support the research and writing program of the History Division. I had always intended to do so in any case.

In the months that followed, I asked Davis Bitton to collaborate with me. We agreed upon chapters and divided them equally. We also employed some help during summer months. Among those who worked on the project were Richard Daines, David Whittaker, Christine Rigby Arrington, Scott G. Kenney, Eugene England, Rebecca Foster Cornwall Bartholomew, Sharon Lee Swenson, and several of the historians on our History Division staff. I was obviously involved in many projects—the writing of the Charles C. Rich, David Eccles, and Edwin Woolley biographies, the writing of the history of the First Security banking system, *Building the City of God,* and similar ventures—and so the project lagged.

Four years later, in the summer of 1977, Davis and I had finished a preliminary draft. We gave a photocopy to our managing director, G. Homer Durham, for his review and comments. As we turned the copy over to him, I wrote in my diary: "Davis and I both feel it may be too frank for the Brethren and too mild and innocuous for the professional readers. So nobody will like it—and possibly the publisher won't publish it." Characteristically, I followed this mournful note with a light one: "Anyway, Davis and I like it. Maybe we ought to get it published under some meaningless name like Alex Zobell. Or Thankful Osnaburg."

We were relieved to learn that Durham liked it. He made suggestions that were easily incorporated; it was ready to go to the First Presidency on August 31. At the same time we sent a copy to Alfred Knopf. Then in his eighty-fifth year, Knopf was delighted, and wrote one of the most heartwarming letters I have ever received, expressing his approbation and enthusiasm. Knopf asked the respected Western historian Rodman Paul of the California Institute of Technology to read it. Paul responded within a month in very complimentary terms. The First Presidency, as I anticipated, gave it to Packer to read. By the end of October he had read it and suggested about twenty-five minor changes, which posed no problems. Formal clearance came on November 22, 1977, when Francis Gibbons, secretary to the First Presidency, sent Durham a memo advising him that the church "will interpose no objection" to the book's publication.

Durham, who had lobbied vigorously for the book, felt positive about this basic approval from such a critic and predicted that the book would have a great future, especially since it had passed such a rigorous review. I was pleased, of course, but less optimistic. I noted that Packer systematically criticized "clever expressions" and humor and expressed no direct commendation beyond the deliberately phrased and twice repeated admonition that we had "gone about as far as" we could in satisfying both the publisher and the church. He did, however, agree that the First Presidency could not object to the work.

To our satisfaction, *The Mormon Experience* continued its course to publication in 1978. Knopf returned the edited manuscript on February 16, 1978, and Davis, who was in the office when it arrived, reported "that the copyediting job was superb." The principal suggestion was to cut down on the "cheerleading," meaning give more analysis and description and less constant praise of the church. This we had intended to do, but sometimes we got carried away with saying nice things. Some sections in the narrative called for clarifications to help non-Mormon readers. By March 3, Davis and I had finished our work on the edited manuscript and made some final decisions. "The revision has improved it further," I wrote in my diary, "but while it is a better book, it is no Pulitzer Prize winner. It's more interpretive and impressionistic and less history, which means it will appeal to thoughtful and inquisitive people." It came and went once more that summer, and the editor, Ashbel Green, stopped by the office while on vacation to say that Knopf planned to print 15,000 copies and sell them for $15. They were aiming to have the book out for April conference, 1979.

At that time, the advertising department of Alfred Knopf asked Davis and me to cite the specific contributions of *The Mormon Experience*. Here is the list we made up, and this conveys some of the spirit of the book.

1. Instead of leaving the non-Mormon reader wondering why anyone could be attracted to this new religion, the book specifically analyzes the "appeals" of Mormonism as they must have appeared to converts to the faith in the past century, making it clear that there was a powerful combination that satisfied various needs.

2. Persecution of the Mormons, while not excused, is treated in the context of the American vigilante tradition, lessening the impression that there were only "good guys" and "bad guys."

3. This book provides the best existing chapter-length study of polygamy; but instead of sensationalizing it, the system of plural marriage is placed in the larger context of the Mormon family.

4. For the first time the general audience will be able to read an extended description of the Mormon concept of the eternal family and its implications for the roles of men and women. Discussions of sex role stereotyping of LDS women, which goes on in much non-Mormon literature, will hereafter be more balanced.

5. This book contains the best chapter-length study of the role of women in Mormon history. Low-key in tone, this chapter makes it clear

that Mormon women have had many opportunities for expression and growth and leadership.

6. The chapter on the Mormon ward is the first to describe the significance of the ward in Mormon culture and history.

7. The chapters on the Indians is the first systematic chapter-length summary that details the relationship of the church and Native Americans.

8. A chapter on "the temporal foundation" gives the first complete and authentic analysis of the church's relationship to business and a summary of businesses in which the church has a proprietary interest.

9. A chapter on the period following Wilford Woodruff's Manifesto gives the first succinct summary of the church's adjustment to the problems resulting from the struggle for statehood—the end of polygamy, the end of the church political party, and the end of extensive church economic planning.

10. One chapter gives for the first time a review of the church's program today, as seen through the eyes of a Mormon family.

11. For the first time in a one-volume work intended for the general reader, this book gives a good sense of the vigorous expansion of the church overseas since 1950.

In the midst of publication, however, the First Presidency announced the revelation that all worthy men would be eligible to receive the priesthood. Recognizing that this would necessitate a revision of our text, Davis and I wrote to Ashbel Green, asking for permission to delay for three weeks our shipment of the final text so we could make alterations. That was a fortunate circumstance. If the revelation had come a month later, we could not have included it and at the very time of publication the volume would have been outdated. This small delay also made it possible for us to make a few changes in the chapter on women.

By October 1, 1978, Davis and I received galleys of the entire book. We had provided photographs and maps, and spent the week before Christmas reading page proofs and preparing the index that was mailed December 28.

With the coming of the new year, I resolved not to be defensive about *The Mormon Experience,* even though some people would surely think it too impartial, too cold, too analytical to have been written by a church historian and an assistant church historian who had testimonies. Having been given First Presidency approval on the book, however, I resolved, as I wrote in my diary, "to make the best books professionally out of the manuscripts turned in for the sesquicentennial history, and not be swayed by 'expediency' or points of view that in the short run might serve our interests but would not serve the long-run interests of scholarship or the

Church. I resolve to do my best to see that our publications represent impeccable scholarship and are, at the same time, exciting to read." I further resolved "not to be discouraged professionally about the History Division, despite some of our superiors' attempts to gradually liquidate the division and put the writing of history 'on a risk-royalty basis.'" "I do believe," I wrote, "that the interests of the Church are well served by having a staff of persons who work fulltime with the documents and have a comprehensive view of the history of the Church and the problems of writing it."

In June 1979—a time when *The Mormon Experience* had sold ten thousand copies in less than three months—I negotiated with Knopf about the proposed Brigham Young biography. *The Mormon Experience* had opened the right door. The First Presidency had given me permission in May to sign such a contract "with the understanding that the manuscript be submitted to the First Presidency for review in advance of submission to the publisher." It was a distinct triumph and I rejoiced as I signed the contract in August.

Response to *The Mormon Experience* was, in fact, astonishingly positive. Durham, who had read final proofs in mid-January, reported that it was "a great book" if one could get past the first chapter with its accounts of the different versions of the First Vision.

Copies arrived for Davis and me on March 12 and we instantly pored over them, looking for mistakes. There were few. Davis was surprised to find that he had acquired the initial "C," one reference was incorrect in the chapter on women, the cartographer's credit had been omitted, the names of the paintings used had been omitted—but basically we were very pleased. "It is a handsome book—one we can be proud of," I wrote to our children, then teased, "Now for the displays, the autograph parties, the reviews and the comments of IMPORTANT PERSONS."

By the second week in January, the 400-page topical history had been selected as an alternate in the History Book Club of America, with a guaranteed distribution of about 2,500. Knopf arranged for simultaneous publication in Great Britain with Allen and Unwin. Deseret Book ordered 1,500 copies and planned autograph parties in four of its outlets; Sam Weller (Zion Book Store) displayed about thirty in the front left window with a five-by-eight poster on March 23 and ordered 500 copies. ZCMI ordered 500 and scheduled an autograph party. On May 14, a representative from Random House, owner of Knopf, reported that a paperback edition that would sell for between $5 and $7 was scheduled for the spring of 1980. This would be in the prestigious Vintage series. We were honored. A second printing of 3,500 copies was ordered on July 3 following an order from

Deseret Book for another 1,300 copies. I immediately interpreted this to mean that Deseret Book was intending to promote it—by advertising it and listing it in its book club. It also meant no contradiction by church authorities. As we learned, the volume had received an appreciative welcome from Kimball and Tanner and several members of the Twelve, who voiced their gratitude for a book that, as they stated, they could give to their well-placed non-Mormon friends.

Royalties, which went to the Mormon History Trust Fund, permitted us to make supplemental payments to Edyth Romney, who was being retired from church employment on July 23. When I mentioned something to Durham about leaving her on church service and slipping her occasional support money, I received no protest and thus felt justified in continuing a monthly check from the Mormon History Trust Fund. I also reserved about $3,000 for a research assistant on the Brigham Young biography and other expenses.

The first review of *The Mormon Experience* was a rave notice in *Publishers Weekly:* "This superb history of the Mormons is everything a religious history ought to be and seldom is" and used phrases such as "solidly based in fact," "fine research," "unfailing and admirable professional objectivity," "beautifully written," and "an outstanding and definitive study, a very model of religious-historical scholarship."[1]

Other reviews followed: *Library Journal,* the *San Francisco Chronicle,* the *Saturday Review,* the *Deseret News,* the *Salt Lake Tribune,* the *Los Angeles Times,* and the *Dallas Morning News.* However, there was no mention of it in the *New York Times Book Review.* Although different reviewers picked different aspects to criticize, there were no reviews that were less than commendatory and most glowed. The Mormon periodicals also reviewed it, but John Hart of the *Church News* wrote a review that did not pass the Correlation Committee and therefore could not be published; no reason was given. Obviously, no one on the committee had been told that the book was approved by the First Presidency or, if so, members regarded their view as final.

As friends and family members began reading the book, their reports matched the general reception and the reviews. A Public Communications representative glowingly reported to me that not only he liked it but that both his fifteen-year-old son and his father-in-law had become totally absorbed in reading it. Carmon Hardy, a professor at California State University in Fullerton, dropped in to tell me that when he had placed an order through the History Book Club, he had received a letter apologizing that the supply had been exhausted because of "a surprisingly heavy demand for this book" that would delay shipment three weeks. Durham said that he had held a copy of the book aloft in the First Council of the Seventy meeting, described the history of the project, said that it had been approved by the First Presidency in concept and execution, and specifically informed the members that "it was a splendid product and . . . the Church should be proud of it."

In many newspaper articles I had been identified as director of the History Division. Some friends asked if this meant I was no longer church historian. I replied that I had never been released as church historian, but on my own request officials had given me an additional title . . . better understood and more secular. The new title also implied that I didn't have to be a spokesman for the church in the same sense. I told friends that I was pleased with the new title and welcomed it, but that I still might be called church historian by people who remembered and revered that historic honorific title.

The role was convoluted in many ways. Officially I was the church historian but not a member of or a consultant to the Sesquicentennial Planning Committee; an acknowledged leader of Mormon history studies yet not a member of the Religious Studies Center at BYU; the approved editor of the sesquicentennial volumes, yet the First Presidency and the Twelve seemed to have no interest in getting my recommendations on manuscripts with historical material, letters with inquiries on historical matters, or talks on historic subjects. *The Mormon Experience,* although cleared by the First Presidency, could not be mentioned or cited in the *Church News, The Ensign,* or church manuals, even in footnotes, let alone reviewed or mentioned as a source. No official reasons were ever given. No general authority except for Durham (and S. Dilworth Young, who congratulated me on the Woolley biography) had ever called or written to express appreciation for any of my articles or books or to discuss historical matters, although I knew that many of them had presented copies to non-Mormon friends to acquaint them with the church. How satisfying it is today to note how frequently *The Mormon Experience* is cited in the four-volume *Encyclopedia of Mormonism.*

In an August 1979 interview of Davis and me conducted by writers for *Sunstone,* we took the opportunity to discuss the book. Among church members, a popular chapter was the last, entitled "Group Personality: The Unsponsored Sector." To understand the totality of the Mormon experience, we thought it was erroneous to assume that everything had to take place within the bounds of official church programs. We didn't know of any treatment that had started from that perspective and so we thought we did something valuable in informing the national audience, not only about the Mormon church, but about Mormon activity in a private capacity. To a question about how we decided how much or how little to include when we had unlimited access to primary documents, we pointed out that any history is a selection from a vast reservoir of possible details and facts and documents. The basis of selection is *relevance*. In determining how much space to give to various topics, we had to use good judgment and much discussion, based on our long experience with people and with historical writing. We certainly wished to present a truthful picture. We did not wish to leave out anything that would convey wrong impressions.

To a question about the relationship between faith and history, we responded that we felt no conflict between maintaining our faith and writing historical truth. The Lord, we pointed out, doesn't require us to believe anything that is untrue. What is potentially damaging to faith depends on one's expectations. Any kind of experience can be shattering to faith if the expectation is such that one is not prepared for the experience. A person can join the church with a totally unrealistic mind picture of what it means to be a Mormon or to be in a Mormon ward. To go into a real Mormon ward where there are children crying and where there are uninformed comments made in Sunday school classes can be damaging to an unprepared person's faith. The problem is not the religion; the problem is the incongruity between the expectation and the reality. Davis and I had not found any shattering incongruities in history that had been devastating to our faith. Our faith had changed and deepened, had become richer and more consistent with the complexities of human experience. Having made a long study of the facts of Mormon history, we still had strong testimonies of the gospel.[2]

In the fall of 1979, shortly after the book appeared, I taught a new class at BYU called Mormonism in American History. There were about thirty-five students, both upper division and graduate. All were expected to read *The Mormon Experience* as well as other material I suggested. The students, mostly male, were very bright and knowledgeable and intensely interested. Some were history majors, others working to become seminary and Institute teachers. Some majored in other fields and wanted to listen to and raise questions with the church historian. I gave lectures on topics in LDS history not often covered in conventional treatments and always allowed plenty of time for questions. Several of the students have since told me how much they gained from the class and how much more meaningful our history was when pursued in some depth. Recently, however, I have learned that the chairman of the Committee for Strengthening Members, always suspicious of "intellectuals," approached two registered students to spy on me and report to him weekly on what transpired in class. One of them has confessed to me that he reported twice and then gave up the assignment.

The other, however, continued to make reports throughout the semester. I was not aware of this activity, of course. I presume that the reports were not disturbing enough to warrant my being called in for "counsel" by the university president or a general authority, because nothing transpired. That spying of this nature was going on in 1979 suggests the determination of some people to build a strong case against any BYU instructor who tried to look upon Mormon history as professional historians would do.

Davis and I have heard many stories of people who have read *The Mormon Experience* and have been influenced to join the church or to return to activity. One day I received a telephone call from a man with a heavy accent. He said he was a Dane from Copenhagen in Salt Lake City on a visit. He had always been interested in religion, though not a member of any church. In the course of his reading, he ran across a mention of the Mormons. He wanted to know more, and in talking with one of his friends, learned that a book on the Mormons had been published in England by Allen and Unwin. The friend offered to buy him the book the next time he was in London. The book was *The Mormon Experience*. The caller read it with enormous interest, he said, and decided to find some Mormons to tell him more. The missionaries came to his home, and after several sessions with them he was baptized. Now, said the proud telephoner, he was bishop of the Copenhagen Ward.

### Notes

1. *Publishers Weekly,* Jan. 29, 1979.
2. "An Interview with Leonard Arrington and Davis Bitton," *Sunstone* 4 (July–Aug. 1979): 38–41.

# 13

# Brigham Young: American Moses

Life is for us, and it is for us to receive it today, and not wait for the millennium. Let us take a course to be saved today, and, when evening comes, review the act of the day, repent of our sins, if we have any to repent of, and say our prayers; then we can lie down and sleep in peace until the morning, arise with gratitude to God; commence the labors of another day, and strive to live the whole day to God and nobody else.
—Brigham Young, July 15, 1860

ANYONE MAKING A STUDY of pioneer Utah inevitably comes to an understanding of the importance of Brigham Young. He was involved in each of the hundreds of colonization projects, he was the founder of many important agricultural and business enterprises, he was the foremost speaker and preacher, and he was everybody's friend (or enemy). He generated an enormous amount of material. He wrote four diaries and dictated eleven diaries and approximately thirty thousand letters.

There are countless records of projects he was connected with, and he is mentioned, sometimes extensively, in the diaries and histories kept by many associates. He was the longest serving president of the church, from 1847 to 1877, and he was an eager participant in every important activity and policy decision.

In 1966, in a special history issue of *Dialogue* that I edited, the English historian Philip A. M. Taylor published an article entitled "The Life of Brigham Young: A Biography Which Will Not Be Written." Taylor came to this conclusion because of the enormous mass of material in the Church Archives and the unlikelihood that the church would ever open the material for study. I do not recall whether I agreed with this at the time. I had said a great deal about Brigham Young in *Great Basin Kingdom*, and I had given talks on aspects of his life and character, and I suppose I was satisfied with that window on his pioneer activity.

An attempt was made by Stanley P. Hirshson, Ph.D. graduate of Columbia University and professor of American history at the City University of New York, to write a biography, which was published by Alfred Knopf in 1969 under the title *The Lion of the Lord*. After he was granted a Guggenheim fellowship, he essentially based the book on articles published in New York newspapers during Brigham Young's life, which Hirshson seldom checked against documentary sources. Misled by an improper reliance on these biased newspaper reports, Hirshson, who had previously written a biography of Grenville Dodge, portrayed Young as a liar and a scoundrel, ignoring his genuine accomplishments as a leader.

In 1975 we proposed to our advisors the preparation of a multivolume history of Brigham Young, to be compiled in the same spirit as the acclaimed multivolume biographies of Washington, Jefferson, Lee, and other prominent Americans. Each volume would be written by a different historian. Each would cover one aspect of Young's life—colonizer, family man, businessman, church president, governor, superintendent of Indian affairs, and contributor to Mormon doctrine and practice. We had people in mind to prepare each of these volumes, and there was certainly enough material to warrant such extensive treatment. The studies would establish Brigham Young, once and for all, as one of America's great leaders.

Following the established procedure we first took up the matter with our advisor Delbert Stapley, asking him to present it to Kimball. Stapley reported on January 20, 1976, that he had discussed the project with Kimball at least twice but still had not received an answer. On June 2 the advisors finally met with the First Presidency. A one-volume biography was approved but the seven-volume work was "taken under advisement" until the authors were identified and royalty payments determined.

While the matter was being discussed, I had the opportunity of meeting with Kimball. He asked us to hold the seven volumes in abeyance; he wanted us to concentrate on a one-volume biography to be finished in his lifetime. I had proposed Jack Adamson, a professor of English at the University of Utah and biographer of Sir Walter Raleigh and other persons, as the finest LDS biographer. Adamson had written the introduction to Dean Jessee's *Brigham Young's Letters to His Sons* in 1974, and we knew he had an interest in Young. He agreed to begin as soon as his biography of Chief Joseph was completed, assuming that his name would be cleared. But he suffered a mortal heart attack on September 9, 1975, before he was ready to start. Although I proposed other names to Kimball, he pointed his finger at me and told me to do it. He had liked my biography of Edwin D. Woolley, which his wife Camilla had read to him. Camilla told me he'd chuckle every so often and marvel at how good it was. I suspect that because he liked the Woolley biography, he thought I could do justice to Brigham Young. That may be how I ended up with the assignment.

Kimball recommended finding a national publisher. He wanted the biography written in a manner that would make it imperative for libraries to place it on their shelves, and he specifically instructed me not to send it to the Correlation Committee because its members didn't know history. He advised me to consult with a variety of historians, both members and nonmembers of the church. As for Mormon historians, he emphasized that I should consult not only traditional historians but also with what he called "*Dialogue*-type historians" to get "liberal" as well as "conservative" points of view. He wanted the biography to be honest, objective, many-sided, and to make good use of the information in the previously unexamined manuscripts we had uncovered.

Kimball spoke with feeling about the lack of good LDS history books in most libraries around the country; he pointed out that most libraries had only anti-Mormon, or at least unfriendly, books. With all of the Brigham Young material previously untouched by historians, and with my national reputation for telling it straight, he said, I had a marvelous opportunity to present a clear picture of Young, in his greatness as a prophet, as a leader of his people, and as a human being. Kimball said the Lord would bless me to do the job well.

Historians are always excited when new materials are discovered or become accessible, and this was true of our History Division staff. Our volunteer elderly typist, Edyth Romney, had typed the holograph diaries of Young, the minutes of meetings during the Young period, the office journals kept by Young's secretaries, and all the thousands of letters signed by Young. Ron Esplin was interested in doing a volume on Young as president of the church; Dean Jessee endeavored to write on the Brigham Young family; and Jill Mulvay Derr wanted to do an article on Young and women. Ron Walker went through the *Journal of Discourses* to get all autobiographical and other statements by Young relating to "culture" and his attempts to elevate it among the Latter-day Saints. He and Ron Esplin published an article on Young's autobiographical references in his talks and letters.

The year 1977 was the centennial of Young's death, and my colleagues and I felt that something should be done to commemorate that event, well before a biography could be completed. When I expressed this feeling to the editor of *BYU Studies,* he agreed that I might edit a special Brigham Young issue. This edition came out in the spring of 1978, with articles by eight historians on Brigham Young's family, his "Gospel Kingdom," his relationship to women, his friendship with Heber C. Kimball, his Indian policies, the records he left, and other aspects of his life and thought. Eugene England also began writing *Brother Brigham,* which was not published until 1980. My son James Arrington did a one-man show, *Here's Brother Brigham,* that was seen by many thousands in Utah, Idaho, and even in Hawaii and Great Britain. Also in 1977, thanks to the work of Ron Esplin, a seventy-page guide to Brigham Young materials in the Church Archives was ready for use.

It was clear that a biography of Young was a major task—a task not for one person alone but for a corps of willing researchers. The Young papers, as we were discovering, constituted one of the largest collections of papers of any nineteenth-century American. Ninety-nine percent of these had never been studied by any scholar before 1972. In addition to the twenty-nine volumes of letterpress copy books, each with about one thousand letters, and the forty-eight-volume (about one thousand pages each) "Manuscript History of Brigham Young" kept by his clerks, there were the four holograph diaries; several thousand pages of minutes of meetings; several hundred sermons, many of them not previously published; diaries of several dozen persons closely associated with Brigham Young; seven telegram books with perhaps two hundred telegrams in each; nine office journals, with about three hundred pages each; the historical records of all the wards, stakes, colonies, and communities that Young supervised; and several hundred ledgers of business enterprises that he helped to start. Not to be ignored were thousands of incoming letters, diaries of those associated with him, and many other documents relating to the period— his papers as governor, his papers as superintendent of Indian affairs, the histories of the colonizing companies he dispatched, and so on. Several persons had spent five years just organizing and cataloguing the material and preparing a guide that detailed the collection properly.

Because of the inherent interest and importance of some of the documents, we gave serious consideration, particularly in 1977–78, to editing the papers at the rate of, say, one volume per year. We applied to the National Historical Publications Commission for a grant, and it gave a tentative award to help us complete the editing. But a release had to be signed by the First Presidency, and there was no prospect that we could get this release because of the extreme caution of church leaders. So we went ahead with a one-volume biography.

My effort toward a biography began in the fall of 1978 when I prepared a packet of materials illustrative of my proposed organization and approach. The packet included a projected table of contents, an extended preface, the first chapter, one of the last chapters, some samples of the documents, and a letter to the publisher. I then wrote to Kimball, on May 1, 1979, asking his permission to send the packet to Alfred Knopf in New York. I pointed out that Knopf had worked with us cooperatively in publishing *The Mor-*

*mon Experience,* that it was a good press, that it was well-respected, and that it had excellent marketing connections. Ashbel Green was friendly and knowledgeable. "I have enough confidence in myself as a biographer to believe that I can write a biography that is both scholarly to the general reader and inspiring and edifying to Latter-day Saint readers," I concluded in my diary. Kimball replied on May 11, giving me approval. With this go-ahead, I sent the packet to Ashbel Green; he was delighted with the possibility. At my request he even sent an advance to help me pay for assistance in going through the source materials. I signed the contract September 4, 1979, and began to work each Friday on the biography.

In 1980, as we shall see in chapter 14, our History Division was transferred to Brigham Young University to constitute the Joseph Fielding Smith Institute for Church History. The monumental task of writing a definitive biography became a private one. My assistants and I would continue to have access to the material, but the project was no longer under church control. With the Knopf advance I employed several assistants to work through the materials and write task papers: Linda Wilcox, Rebecca Foster Cornwall Bartholomew, Lavina Fielding Anderson, and JoAnn Jolley. Several members of our staff devoted days and weeks to the project: Ronald Esplin, Ronald Walker, Carol Madsen, Davis Bitton, William Hartley, Maureen Ursenbach Beecher, Jill Mulvay Derr, Dean Jessee, and Richard Jensen. And there were specialists who generously helped with their findings and talents: Eugene England, Jeffrey Johnson, Lawrence Coates, James B. Allen, Ronald G. Watt, and L. Dwight Israelsen.

Having accumulated and organized sufficient source material, I began writing, according to my diary, on May 23, 1981. The first draft of twenty chapters was finished on December 23, 1981. The next phase was the reading of the manuscript by my colleagues: Davis Bitton, who read every chapter as I finished it and made suggestions; and Ronald Walker, who also made recommendations. My work on the manuscript was interrupted by the death of my dear wife Grace of heart disease on March 10, 1982, and I was not in a frame of mind to resume work until that fall. I distributed many of her things to our three children, worked on a history of her life, and organized and duplicated her diaries, letters, and photograph albums. Grace was buried next to her mother, who had died in 1981, on a lot in the Logan Cemetery where I expect to be buried as well.

Grace and I had had thirty-nine years of adventurous and productive marriage. We had been happy in Logan and Salt Lake City, we had been together on many trips, we had a family we were proud of, and our marriage had been happy and harmonious.

After a brief and happy courtship, on November 19, 1983, I married

Harriet Horne, who was the eldest daughter of a well-known Salt Lake gynecologist. She had been previously married and had four grown children, all then living in Salt Lake City: Annette Rogers, a stockbroker and novelist and former manager of *Utah Holiday;* Frederick "Rick" Sorensen, a major in the Air National Guard; Heidi Swinton, a public relations specialist and writer; and Stephen Moody, a talented artist-photographer. All were married except Rick, and all except Rick had children. Harriet had lived in my father's ward in Twin Falls, Idaho, 1950–53, and had served as his Relief Society president when he was bishop. She was bright, charming, beautiful, active in the church, and keenly interested in history. We were married by Marion "Duff" Hanks in the Salt Lake Temple. Our marriage has been exciting and loving.

By the time I acquired this additional family, my son James had already married Lisa Rasmussen and lived in Orem, Utah; Carl had married Christine Rigby and lived in New York City; and Susan and Dean Madsen were living in Hyde Park, Utah.

I sent the final manuscript of the biography to Knopf on February 24, 1983. I ended up dedicating the book "To my associates in Camelot." "Camelot" was the name given by Davis Bitton to our happy period of scholarly association in the Church Office Building from 1972 to 1982.

After I received the edited manuscript in the spring of 1984, I set to work on the revisions. Ashbel Green had done a splendid job and protected me from many mistakes. Green, who had read the manuscript twice, suggested that I should cut down on the "cheerleading," repeating a term he had used when editing *The Mormon Experience* that referred to what he considered bias in favor of the subject; that I should clarify some terms that were "Mormonish"—not meaningful to non-Mormon readers; and finally that I should give more attention throughout to John Taylor, who was mentioned as having replaced Brigham Young as president of the church. Obviously Taylor was an important person, yet because he was not one of Brigham's circle of close advisors he had been hardly mentioned in my first draft. Ashbel said that I must pay attention to Taylor's doings, his relationships with Brigham, and his succession to Orson Pratt as president of the Twelve, so that a non-Mormon reader would be prepared for his accession after Brigham's death. The final revised manuscript was mailed on August 3. Galleys came in November and December 1984 and final page proof and indexing in January, February, and March 1985. I did the index myself, a task that required two weeks.

In the meantime, I had submitted the manuscript to the David Evans and Beatrice Cannon Evans Biography Award in its first year of competition. I was notified on April 23, 1984, that the manuscript had won the

$10,000 prize, awarded annually for the best biography of a person whose life had been significant to the culture or history of Mormon country. As it happened, I was on the hospital bed with a sextuple heart bypass operation at the time of the ceremony on April 27; Harriet represented me. The distinguished judges, who were unanimous in the choice, were Howard Lamar, dean of Yale College, Yale University; Merlo J. Pusey, a national biographer and writer for the *Washington Post;* and Ray B. West Jr., former professor of creative writing at Iowa State University and historian and novelist. The executive secretary of the Evans Award governing board was Bruce Clark, dean emeritus of BYU's College of Humanities. Lamar's statement about the book was similar to those of the other judges:

> In my judgment *Brigham Young: American Moses* deserves to be ranked first, for it is a personal biography rather than an official one despite the fact that Dr. Arrington is the Church Historian. It is full of new information about Young of the sort that makes him a believable human being. It manages to demythologize him as the leader of the Saints while at the same time explaining how his personality helped make him their leader. Even the critical accounts of the way Young handled some problems and issues help one to understand him. Somehow, Arrington manages to be both candid and compassionate rather than defensive or apologetic. While there are whole areas of Young's public career that are not covered, Young, the man and the religious leader, are portrayed fully. The footnotes and bibliography reveal just how thorough and masterful Arrington's research has been.[1]

The book was out in April, but the advance notice in *Publishers Weekly* came out in the March 22, 1985, issue. It declared the book "straightforward and fair-minded . . . [and] meticulously documented. The portrait that emerges is of a complex titan: a forceful if nonintellectual preacher, business genius, lusty enjoyer of the good things in life and genuine father of his people, a man whose basic kindness was never smothered by his stubbornness or tendency toward irascibility and sarcasm."

Other reviews followed shortly in most major newspapers and in the *Church News.* Beginning in the summer, reviews, most of them laudatory, appeared in many scholarly publications—*Western Historical Quarterly, American Historical Review, Journal of American History, Christian Century, Journal of the West, New York Review of Books, New York Times Book Review, New England Quarterly*—and in many state and regional historical journals. The book was adopted by the History Book Club and was nominated by the National Book Critics Circle as biography of the year. Though it did not win the top award, I felt that Brigham Young had finally come into his own. He was definitely recognized as a prominent national leader. I was especially glad when Camilla Kimball told me that President Kimball was pleased with the book and with its national reception. He had to be especially pleased that the book was placed in several thousand regional and local libraries. By 1996 the book had sold approximately 60,000 copies.

I felt, and still feel, particularly good about *Brigham Young: American Moses*. I think it is an informative and sound biography. The previous biographies and biographical articles about Young had seldom portrayed the whole man. He was a disciplinarian on the trail West, a hardheaded businessman, a practical politician, and a visionary prophet. But he was also, as my associates and I learned by reading all the sources, a kind and helpful human being—tender, understanding, and compassionate, and with a lively sense of humor.

Contemporary letters and diaries furnish abundant evidence that nineteenth-century church members regarded Young as a great man. This helps explain why the people were so willing to follow him, so willing to respond to his calls. He did not put on airs, he was a good listener, and he was quite willing to get his hands dirty to help out. He went out of his way to talk with everyone as he visited new wards or settlements; he attended their dances and participated in all their activities. He was liberal in expressing appreciation for services people rendered on behalf of the church. Sometimes when he went into a home and saw persons who were suffering from injuries or painful illnesses, he wept. When he observed families without adequate food, he instructed the local bishop to see that they were supplied from the local storehouse.

Not having access to the abundant handwritten sources, previous biographers tended to use published sources and hearsay in interpreting Young. The diaries in his own hand; the thousands of letters he dictated, to which he occasionally added postscripts in his own hand; the dictated diaries and office journals; and, above all, the day-by-day record of his activities as president, governor, Indian superintendent, counselor, businessman, head of family, and traveling sermonizer offered many new insights. He was a practical man, as other biographies had declared, but he was also deeply spiritual. He was hardheaded, as the folklore warranted, but he was also generous and compassionate and did not take himself too seriously.

It pleased me to learn that Young had often invited orphans into his home to stay with his family. (Because of the high death rate from the 1850s to the 1870s, children were often deprived of one or both of their parents while they were growing up.) Some of these stayed many years—until they were married or went away to work. By actual count, more than one hundred persons were taken into his family for short or long periods of time, and some ever after regarded him as their father. He paid the tuition for many young people to go to the University of Deseret—not only his own children and adopted orphans but also many others whose parents could not afford the fees.

The sources also helped me to show that Young had a well-balanced attitude toward life. He believed that the Lord wanted people to *enjoy* life. To provide amusement and wholesome recreation for the people, Young built the Social Hall, the old Salt Lake Theater, and other facilities for recreation. He said: "When I was young I was kept within very strict bounds. . . . I had not a chance to dance when I was young, and never heard the enchanting tones of the violin until I was eleven years of age, and then I thought I was on the highway to hell if I suffered myself to linger and listen to it. I shall not subject my little children to such a course of unnatural training, but they shall go to the dance, study music, read novels, and do anything else that will tend to expand their frames, add fire to their spirits, improve their minds, and make them feel free and untrammeled in body and mind." Let everything come in its season, he said. There is a time to dance and a time to pray, a time to work, and a time to sing. And we must always keep learning.[2]

People who wrote about Young were often puzzled by the love that people expressed for him. The assumption was that he was the Saints' prophet and their beliefs had disposed them to idolize their leader. But there was more to it. They loved him because he helped them, showed tenderness toward them, and encouraged them to seek a better life. They loved him also because he had a sense of humor and did not take things too seriously. A certain Elizabeth Green wrote to Brigham Young in 1850 asking that her name be removed from the records of the church; she had become a spiritualist. He answered: "Madam: I have this day examined the records of baptisms for the remission of sins in the Church of Jesus Christ of Latter Day Saints, and not being able to find the name of 'Elizabeth Green' recorded therein I was saved the necessity of erasing your name therefrom. You may therefor consider that your sins have not been remitted you and you may therefore enjoy the benefits therefrom."[3]

As a former resident of Cache Valley, I was delighted to notice Young's one-line letter to an early Cache Valley settler who had poured out his heart about matters that were troubling him. Young, who thought people should trust in the Lord and "not worry about the balance," wrote simply, "Brother—, don't fret your gizzard about all those problems you wrote about."[4]

Despite his capacity for joking fun, Young had a deeply spiritual nature and an appreciation of spiritual phenomena. He had spiritual gifts, was benefited by miracles and assisted in the miraculous healings of others, and had dreams and visions that so impressed him that he left a record of them. He had the spirit of prophecy, and several dozen people left accounts describing the occasion, on August 8, 1844, when the mantle of the Prophet Joseph Smith came upon him signifying the Lord's acceptance of him as leader of the church.

Nevertheless, as I was pleased to learn, Young was not a self-righteous person, not overly proud of himself. He said: "There are weaknesses in men [and women] that I am bound to forgive, because I am right there myself. I am liable to mistakes, I am liable to prejudice, and I am just as set in my feelings as any man that lives. But I am where I can see the light, and I try to keep in the light."[5] In his counseling, he was realistic enough to realize that not everybody would take his advice.

Biographers had sometimes found sarcasm and "strong doctrine" in his sermons. In checking into these incidents, I determined that this was one technique he used in motivating people to do what they should be doing. For example, in 1873 he called a group of young men from the Salt Lake Valley to go to Arizona and begin the settlement of that territory. But they became discouraged and returned without accomplishing their mission. Young was disappointed, of course, and at a private meeting held after their return, he did not mince words:

> Had we sent the sisters of the Relief Society, some of our pioneer sisters, they would have held that place and accomplished the mission. But instead we sent a passel of Squaws down there—some of our pets whom we have raised in Salt Lake City. [We have] raised them on a feather pillow with silver spoons in their mouths. Men that don't know anything about a hard day's work or a privation—and they came away because the sun shone hot and the wind blew! Can you imagine such faint hearts! They gave up their inheritances without a stroke.[6]

One would be reasonably sure that the next group of colonizers would work hard to avoid such public humiliation. In fact, successful Latter-day settlements in Arizona were made beginning in 1876.

I was delighted to discover that, contrary to the popular image, Young had a high opinion of women and their worth to the Lord's kingdom. Under his leadership, women in Latter-day Saint communities exercised an important influence in agriculture, medicine, economic and business development, literature, and politics. He pushed for the education of young women, believed that their duty was not limited to housekeeping and having babies, and thought they should be encouraged to serve as lawyers, doctors, and accountants as well as teachers and stenographers.

A favorite story of many people, first told by Artemus Ward, had been that Young encountered an unfamiliar little ragamuffin, asked him who he was, and he responded, "Sir, I am one of Brigham Young's little boys; do you know where he is?" The story was obviously fictitious, and it illustrated an image I was happy to correct, for Young had a close relationship with his children. He did not believe in corporal punishment but thought a child should be disciplined through an educational process of example and precept: "It is not by the whip or the rod that we can make obedient children, but it is by faith and by prayer, and by setting a good example before them." When children are bound too tightly and rigidly to the moral law, he said, duty will become loathsome to them, and "when they are freed by age from the rigorous training of their parents, the children are more fit for companions to devils than to be the children of such religious parents."[7]

That parental philosophy worked. Young had seventeen sons who grew to maturity. Eleven of them served "foreign" missions, one went to West Point to become an Army engineer, and one attended Annapolis to become a naval officer. Four studied architecture and engineering at Rensselaer Polytechnic Institute in New York, and one graduated from the University of Michigan School of Law in Ann Arbor. As Dean Jessee demonstrated in *Brigham Young's Letters to His Sons,* the president wrote letters to all of these while they were away, informing them of developments in Utah Territory and in the church and encouraging them to make the most of their stay away from Zion.

The oft-reiterated theme in Young's sermons and letters was his plea for the Latter-day Saints to maintain a strong sense of community. When Young joined the church in 1832, he discontinued his business operations, laid away his account books, and covenanted to spend the rest of his life promoting righteous principles and encouraging the Saints to be of one heart and mind. "I expected," he said, "we should be one family, each seeking to do his neighbor good, and all be engaged to do all the good possible."[8] He said:

> After we believed the Gospel we were baptized for the remission of our sins—and by the laying on of hands we received the Holy Spirit of Promise and felt that "we shall be one." I felt that I should no longer have need to keep a day book and ledger in which to keep my accounts, for we were about to consolidate and become one; that every man and every woman would assist by actually laboring with their hands in planting, building up and beautifying this earth to make it like the Garden of Eden. I should therefore have no farther occasion to keep accounts. I should certainly accumulate and earn more than I needed, and had not a single doubt but what my wants would be supplied. This was my experience, and this is the

feeling of every one who received the Gospel in an honest heart and con-
trite spirit.[9]

The Prophet Joseph Smith, of course, had revealed the Law of Consecration and Stewardship in 1831, and Young had witnessed its application and had been imbued with the rhetoric connected with it. He believed,
with the early Saints, that members of the church constituted a community, or church family. They must work together, just as they worshipped
together; they must share with each other; and they must work to build
up the Kingdom of God, not as individuals but as a group, not by competition but by cooperation, not by individual aggrandizement but by community development, not by profit-seeking but by working without thought
of self to build the kingdom.[10]

In Nauvoo, where Young was the business manager of the church, in-
migration of skilled workers and capitalists was encouraged, local facto-
ries and shops were erected, and extensive public works projects provided infrastructure and employment. Highly committed to "the Lord's law,"
the Saints consecrated their time, talent, and material resources to realizing the goal of building the kingdom. Impressed with Nauvoo emerging
Phoenix-like out of a swamp on the edge of the Mississippi, D. H. Lawrence
remarked, "It is probable that the Mormons are the forerunners of the
coming real America."[11]

Shortly after he succeeded Joseph Smith as president of the church in
1847, Young received a revelation in Winter Quarters showing the organization of the kingdom of God as one great family. Although this revelation has not been incorporated in the Doctrine and Covenants, it was precious for him and he often referred to it in sermons. After the Saints reached
Utah, under Young's direction, various attempts were made to apply parts
or all of the Law of Consecration. In 1854–56, for example, more than
half of the seven thousand families in the territory deeded all of their property to the church in a gesture of good will, as we showed in *Building the
City of God*. None of the property was ever taken over by the church, but
one can hardly deny that during most of the 1850s and 1860s Mormons
came close to giving all their surplus in the form of tithing and other donations, and that in responding to Young's admonitions on colonizing and
establishing new industries they treated their property as a stewardship.
They approached the goal of living as a united community of Saints. Harmony and unity were achieved through improved organization—priesthood quorums, relief societies, village cooperatives, and ward united orders. People would get their pay in what they produced, and a fund would
be accumulated to purchase machinery and supplies from the those in the

States. To accomplish spiritual as well as temporal union, each village drew
up a list of rules according to which each person should live. No lying,
backbiting, or quarreling; all were to live like good Christians ought to live.
They were to pray daily, not use liquor or tobacco, and obey their leaders. Everyone would be frugal and industrious and cultivate "the simple
grandeur of manners that belong to the pure in heart." To emphasize the
spiritual side of it, each person was rebaptized and made new covenants.
In St. George and some other communities, the people promised the following: "We agree to be energetic, industrious, and faithful in the management of all business entrusted to us; and to abstain from all selfish
motives and actions, as much as lies in our power. We desire to seek the
interest and welfare of each other; and to promote the special good of the
Order and the general welfare of all mankind."[12]

Despite the eventual discontinuance of the formally organized United
Orders, the "divine" law remained a remembrance of the "oneness in mind
and heart" that God had prescribed for his people, a goal toward which
to aspire, a forecast of a better future.

Speaking to the first settlers of Cache and Weber Valleys in 1860, Young
admonished:

> Keep your valley pure, keep your towns pure, keep your hearts pure, and
> labor as hard as you can without injuring yourselves. . . . Build cities, adorn
> your habitations, make gardens, orchards, and vineyards, and render the
> earth so pleasant that when you look upon your labors you may do so with
> pleasure, and that angels may delight to come and visit your beautiful
> locations. . . . Your work is to beautify the face of the earth, until it shall
> become like the Garden of Eden.[13]

Such was the vision of Brigham Young for his people's future.

### Notes

1. Statements of the judges, *Brigham Young: American Moses* files, Leonard J.
Arrington Collection, Special Collections and Archives, Utah State University Libraries, Logan.

2. Brigham Young, sermon, Feb. 6, 1853, in *Journal of Discourses*, 26 vols.
(Liverpool: F. D. and S. W. Richards, 1854–86), 2:94, ellipses mine. See also Leon-
ard J. Arrington, "Brother Brigham: The Human Side," *This People* 11 (Spring
1990): 26–32. A year following the appearance of *Brigham Young: American
Moses,* my friend Newell G. Bringhurst published *Brigham Young and the Expand-
ing American Frontier* for the Library of American Biography edited by Oscar
Handlin (Boston: Little, Brown and Company, 1986). Based also on the Brigham
Young papers in the Church Archives, this is a scholarly, well-written work.

3. Brigham Young to Elizabeth Green, Dec. 18, 1851, Brigham Young secretary drafts, Arrington Collection.

4. Arrington, "Brother Brigham," 31.

5. Manuscript history of Brigham Young, Apr. 30, 1860, copy of excerpt in Arrington Collection.

6. Biographical record of Martha Cox, typescript, 266, copy in Arrington Collection.

7. Young, Feb. 6, 1853 sermon.

8. Brigham Young, sermon, Feb. 20, 1853, in *Journal of Discourses*, 1:314.

9. Brigham Young, sermon, Oct. 8, 1876, in *Journal of Discourses*, 18:260.

10. See Pearl of Great Price, Moses 7:18–19, and *The Evening and the Morning Star* (Independence, Mo.), July 1832, 1.

11. D. H. Lawrence quoted in *Studies in Classic American Literature* (New York: Viking Press, 1961), 94.

12. Leonard J. Arrington, Feramorz Y. Fox, and Dean L. May, *Building the City of God: Community and Cooperation among the Mormons* (Salt Lake City: Deseret Book, 1976), 390–91.

13. Brigham Young, sermon, June 10, 1860, in *Journal of Discourses*, 1:345; Brigham Young, sermon, June 12, 1860, in *Journal of Discourses*, 8:80–83.

# 14

# Our Move to BYU

Know thou, my son, that all these things shall give thee experience, and
shall be for thy good.
  —Doctrine and Covenants 122:7

## 1980: The Sesquicentennial Year

Although we had many assurances that we in the History Division were
doing something commendable, there was a cloud on the horizon. At first
no bigger than a man's hand, the shadow became larger and seemed to
become permanent. Seldom experiencing the exuberance of our initial
period of production and expansion, our historians were frequently reminded by our managing director that contraction was the byword.
Durham expressed the belief that professional historians should function
in a university atmosphere. It was inevitable, he thought, that some church
leaders would not support the "secular" (as they would regard it) writing
of church history. He believed historical research should be done independently. We watched the departure of more than one-third of our staff—
Bruce Blumell went to law school in Calgary, Alberta, and Jill Mulvay Derr
left to devote more time to her family and to work with the Relief Society
on the history of LDS women. Jim Allen went to BYU to chair the department of history; Glen Leonard became the director of the Museum of
History and Art then being built; Dean May went to the University of Utah;
Gene Sessions left for Weber State College. We were not permitted to make
replacements. The community of LDS historians was aware of what was
going on; knowing glances and the shaking of heads greeted us on all sides.
Morale fluctuated between pessimism and resignation.

Yet the cloud did not fill the whole sky; sunshine broke through from
time to time. We were still producing scholarly works. The most important publication of 1979 was *The Mormon Experience;* its reception was
a happy, even exhilarating, surprise. Through it and the resulting reviews,
talks, and interviews, we recognized that we had written an improved

brand of history, straightforward yet positive. Another large clientele was well served through the series of articles I wrote on Mormons in Nevada, which was separately published as a book by the *Las Vegas Sun*. Our division continued to write vignettes for each issue of the *Church News*. *The Ensign* carried several articles by our people during the course of the year, as did professional journals. Although our proposal to prepare a much-needed biographical encyclopedia was turned down, the Brigham Young history project was enthusiastically approved.

We made contributions to understanding the church's administrative history with the completion of *Sisters and Little Saints,* a history of the Primary Association by Jill Mulvay Derr, Carol Madsen, and Susan Oman; Bill Hartley's studies of deacons, teachers, and Seventies; Dale Beecher's study of bishops; and Richard Jensen's history of the Relief Society, 1847–67. Jim Allen had essentially completed a history of the Genealogical Society, which was finally published by *BYU Studies* in 1995 with Jessie Embry and Kahlile Mehr as coauthors, and a surprisingly positive reception was given to Ron Esplin's dissertation on Brigham Young and the Twelve and to Scott Kenney's unpublished history of the Mutual Improvement Associations. We did not consider ourselves self-appointed educators, but we hoped a climate of receptivity could be fostered.

Our departmental retreat in the summer of 1979 at Carol Madsen's cabin near Oakley, Utah, provided therapy as well as some good laughs and deepened our personal relationships. We braced ourselves for a further diminishing of our numbers—by transfers to other divisions and other attrition—that would leave only a nucleus in the History Division but also the hope that there would always be a willingness to use dedicated talent. We did have friends that would help in this delicate readjustment: Glen Leonard in Arts and Sites and Ron Watt in the Archives Division. We hoped a spirit of good will would continue.

My efforts were directed toward doing everything humanly possible to keep momentum, to function within the guidelines while taking advantage of every element of flexibility. I did not allow myself to become filled with doom and gloom. I tried to provide protection and give assurances that would enable each member of the dwindling staff to function and produce, even to speak out in public with an optimistic voice.

The year 1980 was expected to be especially busy, with the church celebrating its sesquicentennial anniversary. Many wards, stakes, and auxiliaries were holding historical meetings. We were called upon to give historical lectures, write historical articles for local and regional newspapers and magazines, and, of course, to publish the five sesquicentennial histories already in hand—those by Richard Bushman, Lanier Britsch, Milton

Backman, Richard Cowan, and Thomas Alexander. Other manuscripts in the final review process were the history of the Welfare Program by Bruce Blumell, Dean Jessee's editing of Joseph Smith holographs, and Jim Allen's history of the Genealogical Society.

The principal event of the year, April general conference in 1980, carried out the sesquicentennial theme. Instead of the usual sessions broadcast from the tabernacle in Salt Lake City, some sessions were held in Fayette, New York, where the church had been organized 150 years earlier. The log home of Peter Whitmer had been restored and Kimball gave his inspiring address and prophetic blessing from the original pulpit in that setting. Modern technology conveyed the scene to a national audience via satellite transmission with no technical problems. Viewers saw wonderful scenes of the interior and exterior of the restored Whitmer home and Fayette Branch chapel. Tastefully and authentically decorated and furnished, the Whitmer home evoked memories of April 6, 1830, when fifty or more men and women signified approval of Joseph Smith's proposal to organize the church.

The church further acknowledged the occasion and sentiment by having as honored guests a great-granddaughter of Joseph Smith and great-grandsons of Hyrum Smith and Samuel Smith: Lorena Normandeau, Patriarch Eldred G. Smith, and Melvin T. Smith. The conference addresses were moving, particularly those of Kimball, who, at eighty-five, spoke slowly and had some trouble following his text; Howard W. Hunter's "God Will Have a Tried People"; and Boyd K. Packer's "A Tribute to the Rank and File of the Church." Perhaps because of the rapid spread of the church in Mexico and South America, I overheard many Spanish-speaking Mormons in the congregation. I thought it would have been helpful to have had two or three women speakers and that it would have been more equitable to have invited to the conference some Relief Society presidents along with bishops and stake presidents.

My schedule was demanding. I presented addresses over radio and television stations; gave an interview to *Century,* a student magazine at BYU; wrote with Davis Bitton nine articles on phases of church history for the *Church News;* spoke at many symposia, firesides, sacrament meetings, and High Priest classes; and, of course, continued to teach a semi-weekly class at BYU. Early in the year I spoke on Joseph Smith for a symposium at the LDS Institute in Logan; delivered "The Spirit of Mormon History" to an assembly of the student body of Ricks College in Rexburg, Idaho; spoke to a sesquicentennial fireside at BYU on Mormonism's spirit; and addressed BYU's economics honor society with "Five Pillars of Utah's Pioneer Economy." During April, I spoke to a Rocky Mountain farm conference in Sun Valley on the future of the family farm; to an "ethnic dinner" at Los Angeles Stake on church history; at Idaho State University in Pocatello on Mormons in the southeastern part of the state; to the LDS Institute of Religion in Tucson, Arizona, on Mormon colonization of the area; to the Jenson Living Historical Farm in Logan on Cache Valley agriculture; and to the Wilmette, Illinois, women's day program on Latter-day Saint women in history.

In May the Mormon History Association (MHA) held its annual conference at Canandaigua, New York, near Fayette and Palmyra, on the theme "Early Mormonism and American Culture." Prior to the conference Richard Bushman, Jan Shipps, and I spoke to a group at Cornell University on Mormon history from contemporary approaches. The MHA had sessions at the Sacred Grove, near Palmyra, the site of Joseph Smith's First Vision. At one session my son James dressed as farm boy Joseph Smith and gave a moving reading adapted from Joseph Smith's account of the First Vision. We sang "Oh How Lovely Was the Morning," adapted from Kabalevsky's war requiem; heard "Thoughts on the Mission of the Prophet Joseph Smith" by Richard Bushman and Alma Blair; and were inspired by "Prologue and Prophecy" by Crawford Gates, a sesquicentennial hymn commissioned by the Mormon History Association, rendered by a chorus, brass quintet, timpanist, and Roy Samuelson, Metropolitan Opera baritone. We also went to Aurora, New York, where Brigham Young had once lived; the John Young residence and farm; the Tomlinson Inn, where the Book of Mormon was left by Samuel Smith and circulated among the Young family; Brigham Young's mill; and the Fisher Museum, which contained many Brigham Young artifacts.

At the conference I delivered "The New York Beginnings of Mormonism," which was later published in *New York History*. At the end of the conference, I offered a brief history of Mormonism to a group of LDS students in the New York City area, to a ward in Morristown, New Jersey, and to ward firesides and dinners in Raleigh, Hickory, and Asheville, North Carolina.

Other events in May required talks: two sacrament meetings in Salt Lake Valley, the Sons of the American Revolution meeting, a conference on agriculture in the Southwest at Texas A&M University, and the World Conference on Records in the Salt Palace in Salt Lake City. June featured meetings of the Institute of Pacific Studies at Laie, Hawaii; the Haight family reunion in Oakley, Idaho; several firesides in Salt Lake City, Provo, and Logan; and a reunion of my graduating high school class in Twin Falls, Idaho.

For all of these and other presentations I delivered original papers, often written with the help of my research assistant, Richard Jensen. We employed Richard in 1972 at the completion of his master's degree at Ohio State University. Originally from Logan, where his father was a professor of plant science at Utah State University, Richard lived in our Logan Tenth Ward. His father was a member of our stake high council; his mother served for several years as our ward Relief Society president. Richard graduated in history from Utah State University and during at least two summers served as my research assistant in Logan. He served a mission in Denmark and became adept in Danish. A dedicated and resourceful scholar, Richard worked with me on several projects—biographies, professional papers, and addresses. In addition, he conducted his own research and published articles in professional journals, chapters in books, and articles in church magazines. He was a thoughtful and marvelously productive research assistant.

During the early months of 1980, Davis Bitton and I were also in the process of preparing a book that treated the human, rather than the institutional, side of Mormon history. Through short biographies of seventeen Latter-day Saints, we sketched Mormonism from its earliest beginnings to modern times. These were Saints presented not as objects of veneration but as human beings who, like the rest of us, struggled to be worthy of the title Latter-day Saints. The book was published by Signature Books in 1981 as *Saints without Halos: The Human Side of Mormon History.*

Two of the seventeen, Lyman Wight and George F. Richards, were apostles. Wight was an enthusiastic supporter and friend of Joseph Smith who eventually left the main body of the church to lead his own band to Texas. Richards was a link in the chain of a renowned family whose positions in the leading councils of the church spanned virtually the entire history of Mormonism.

Except for Thomas L. Kane, a colorful non-Mormon advocate, the other fifteen individuals were "ordinary" Latter-day Saints—faithful members who helped realize the vision of their prophetic leaders. Joseph Knight was a personal friend of Joseph Smith; Jonathan Hale, a New England missionary; Lucy White Flake, an Arizona pioneer; Helen Sekaquaptewa, a Hopi convert; Jean Baker, a British convert-immigrant; Margrit Lohner, a Swiss convert-immigrant; Edwin Woolley, a pioneer Salt Lake businessman and bishop for twenty-six years; Charles L. Walker, a pioneer poet and mason in St. George; Ephraim and Edna Ericksen, Utah's leading philosopher-politician duo; Edward Bunker, founding bishop of a communal living arrangement in southern Nevada; T. Edgar Lyon, a missionary, educator, and historian; and Chauncey West, a teenage pioneer. Based primarily on diaries, the book focused on the rich diversity of Mormonism as well as its unity of purpose.

## The Transfer to BYU

When first Durham proposed that our History Division be disbanded, he decided that Jim Allen, Davis Bitton, and I would return full-time to Brigham Young University or the University of Utah; Dean Jessee and Gordon Irving would shift to the Library or Archives Division; Maureen Ursenbach Beecher and Carol Madsen would return to their homes to look after their families; and the remainder of the staff would be released to seek other employment.

Instead, Durham worked out an alternative plan with Gordon B. Hinckley, one of the Historical Department advisors. They moved our trimmed-down division to Brigham Young University, where we would be less tied to the church and the Archives and still be in a position to write sound history. Although I had been warned of this possibility as early as 1978, this action was taken without consulting me.

On June 26, 1980, Durham called me to a meeting with Jeffrey Holland, church commissioner of education and president-designate of Brigham Young University. The meeting was in Holland's office in the Church Office Building. After casting about for some way to honor Joseph Fielding Smith—having already a Joseph Smith Building and a Joseph F. Smith Building—the Board of Education, the First Presidency, and the Twelve had decided to create the Joseph Fielding Smith Institute for Church History at BYU. To the newly created institute they had transferred the History Division of the Historical Department, with myself as director and with all present staff (nine persons) as staff members. We would remain physically housed in the Historical Department until August 31, 1982, at which time we would be moved to the Knight Magnum Building at BYU. The History Division budget, beginning September 1, 1980, would be operated through BYU, and my responsibilities would be under the direction of Martin Hickman, dean of the College of Family, Home, and Social Sciences at BYU. Certain functions would remain permanently a part of the Historical Department, which, beginning September 1, would consist only of Administration, Library-Archives, and Arts and Sites Divisions. Those few functions would be attached to the Administration Division, including the James Moyle Oral History Trust Fund and its two regular staff members, Gordon Irving and Cindy Mark. Davis Bitton would presumably return to the University of Utah in the fall of 1982, and Debbie Liljenquist Biggs would continue to serve as our typist but would be under the direction of the administration. Dean Jessee would be attached to the Church Archives, and Ron Walker would be placed with the LDS Institute in Salt Lake City in the fall of 1981. The Mormon History Trust Fund would be transferred to BYU and we would have no limitations on the amount solicited for it.

This major restructuring, desired by the general authorities of the church and BYU, was orchestrated by Durham and Hinckley to place the History Division under a university rubric. I was later informed that a prime consideration was timing. Kimball was in failing health and not expected to live long, and these arrangers wanted to keep our work alive by shifting us to BYU before Benson assumed control as president and eliminated our division and discontinued our functions. Durham and Hinckley were, as they believed, doing a favor to us, to BYU, and to the church. An added factor was an apparent agreement that access to archival material be more carefully restricted. "Safeguarding the records" meant limiting their use. Since we were allowed to request documents from the archives relating to the Brigham Young project, however, we interpreted this broadly enough to enable us to see nearly every document we needed for our approved projects.

For a day or two I seriously considered resigning and going to the University of Utah or to Utah State University. But I decided to remain with the staff. The hallowed experience in the UNC library in 1950–51 was still compelling. After all, we would now be placed in an academic atmosphere that would help to preserve our professionalism and the professional respect for our work. We would be responsible to academic administrators rather than ecclesiastical officials who seemed to be more intent on protecting records than in writing documented history.

The principal disappointment was the prospect of working without my close associate and friend, Davis Bitton, whose affiliation with us would cease in 1982. However, as it turned out, I was able to persuade BYU to appoint him as a consultant to our newly created Joseph Fielding Smith Institute, with an honorarium of $1,000 per year, although after two years BYU terminated this arrangement. The positive aspects of the move were that we would be allowed to remain at our Salt Lake posts for two years; at BYU we would be responsible to Martin Hickman, a friend and supporter; there would be less hassle with any authorities who were not sympathetic with our goals; and we would be freer to pursue our research unhampered. The church would no longer have to assume responsibility for what we researched, wrote, and published. If awkward facts were presented and questions raised, they could be ignored or repudiated or reinterpreted.

There was a final advantage. As I reassured myself in a letter to my children:

The people with whom I work are intelligent, good-willed, well-trained, loyal, and pleasant. To have the opportunity of working with these wonderful people is not only a blessing—it is a blessing every day, every hour. Despite occasional administrative and financial frustrations, my professional life, like my family life, is one of recurring pleasure and happiness. I thank the Lord for my appointment and for my work.

While I regard some of the decisions that are made respecting us and other departments as being ill-advised, a product of ignorance or misplaced zeal, I have experienced or observed nothing that would cause me to be less than enthusiastic about the Church, the gospel, the Kingdom. Neither cynical nor discouraged, I am, I hope, a valiant and thoughtful member of the Lord's Church.

Durham and Holland had asked me to keep the news of the departmental restructuring quiet until July 1, when they would meet with the staff and make a formal announcement. Durham, who conducted that meeting, started out with two quotations: "There is hope smiling brightly before us," from "Come, Come, Ye Saints" by William Clayton, and "Theirs not to reason why, Theirs but to do and die," from Alfred Lord Tennyson's "Charge of the Light Brigade." Durham pointed out that the transferred History Division staff members would be given professorial rank at BYU based on their qualifications, that all would get a salary raise because BYU salaries were higher than those paid by the church, and that BYU had agreed to maintain, not to lower, our budget.

Durham then said he'd like to editorialize a bit. This is a great thing for BYU, he said, and it would preserve the writing and research and quality developed in the History Division by our staff. Although everything that comes out of church headquarters is subject to criticism, this will not be true at the university. Of course, each writer must take responsibility for his or her writing and research, but the university is a more appropriate umbrella.

Holland began by confessing that he was anxious to do something more with church history at BYU. He believed that the field of history has its legitimate function at the church's university. He felt it to be a providential development, a marvelous thing for BYU. It would not only draw attention to the accomplishments of the university but would also provide us with opportunities we did not have while directly under the eye of the church. He was glad that he had two years to review the business of appropriate academic assignments and teaching positions. He wanted to be open and warm in discussing and developing the Joseph Fielding Smith Institute.

The news release distributed that afternoon emphasized the creation of the institute, not the demise of the History Division. A sesquicentennial angle was also integrated into the release. Kimball was quoted as saying, "This transfer . . . is a forward step. The stature, objectivity, and effectiveness of our fine professional historians will be enhanced by association with the church's university, where they can perform their scholarly tasks in a university atmosphere with increased interchange with professional colleagues and the teaching process."[1]

I resolved to minimize the effects of the move on our staff members and their continuing research as much as possible during the next two years, a tactic that was met by the implacable resistance of Durham and Earl Olson, who did their best to disassociate themselves from us—a policy that one friend regarded as paranoia about our physical and psychic presence. I tried to get those in the Church Archives to set aside a small room or work area for our use while we researched archival materials after our departure. They refused. They wanted us to be gone for good by 1982.

In an attempt to demonstrate his cordiality, and I think with sincerity, Durham wrote me two effusive letters. The first was in celebration of my sixty-third birthday, which had come one day after the public announcement of the move.

> You have writ your name large in the annals of Utah, the West, and America. You have generated many projects of great and unusual significance, more than a dozen other men ordinarily achieve in a lifetime. You have been blessed with enormous vitality, health, strength, and a most affable, pleasant disposition. You have been further enlarged and ennobled by the companionship with your wonderful wife, Grace, and your devoted family.
>
> What more can be said as you arrive at another anniversary of your birth! Perhaps only to say, that with the recent changes in administration for the work, including the establishment of the new Joseph Fielding Smith Institute of Church History, that your life and efforts may possibly be enlarged as you move into the next decades.
>
> Richard L. Evans, on his fiftieth birthday, remarked that it was sobering to think that more of mortality had now passed, than remained; but that he was grateful for what lay beyond, eternity.
>
> May much more lie ahead for you both in mortality and in eternity! Congratulations and best wishes for a Happy Birthday.

The second letter, equally expansive, was hung on the peg of my article in the August *Ensign* on Brigham Young's family, of which his wife Eudora was a member:

> I thought your piece in the August *Ensign* on Brigham Young's parents, brothers and sisters, was excellent and will be exceptionally well received in the field and at headquarters.

I am personally proud of your achievements and all you have accomplished. I am grateful for the decision of the Presidency and Twelve to shift the work of the division to the new Institute. In my opinion, that will guarantee permanence and continuation of the enterprise you launched under President Lee in 1972. The University auspices are highly appropriate for research and writing such as was your original "charter." When that charter was modified, it may have become possible for the work to have been phased out so far as headquarters are concerned, in my opinion. Accordingly, the new situation and the physical move to BYU by August 1982 will assure many, many fine things that will come over the years ahead. They will advance the Kingdom and provide substantial basis for new scholarly interpretations of the Restoration in the world of scholarship, which has been limited and localized, despite the efforts of many, many people going back over a century. I know the dream of my father in the field of the musical arts, based on his sacrifice to gain five years of study at the New England Conservatory of Music; and the earlier dreams of Dr. John A. Widtsoe and the little group that went to Harvard a few months after the Manifesto. The dream has continually taken on shape, size and substance.

He concluded this letter with a reference to a recent communication from Elmer J. Culp, a life-long sugar technologist and economist with the American Sugar Refining Company in New York City, with whom Durham and Eudora had stayed in July 1980. The Durhams had given them a copy of *The Mormon Experience*. Culp replied:

I purposely delayed writing this letter until I had read enough of the book to comment about my reaction to it. I can now say without doubt that it is a very remarkable publication. Having read many other books about Mormonism—both pro and con—it is a relief to find one that is both scholarly and objective in its treatment of the subject. *The Mormon Experience* surely meets the need for that kind of writing. Incidentally, the fact that the church condoned its publication shows how much progress your people have made in facing up to the real world of the present and its historical underpinnings.

The same month as the announcement of our move, I gave "Across the Plains with the Pioneers in 1848," the devotional address at BYU. It was my first invitation to speak at that institution since the BYU centennial in 1975. The invitation had, of course, been extended while the change in our department was in the making and may have been made deliberately to give an official stamp of approval to the new assignment. At this rare devotional without a general authority, I gave a speech that has been replayed on radio station KBYU several times. I rushed away immediately after delivering it to speak to the Salt Lake Rotary Club about July 24 in Utah history.

On July 30 Grace and I flew to Hawaii, where we met with friends, went sight-seeing, had dinner with university officials, and made two presentations at the Mormon Pacific History Conference.

Upon our return I gathered the staff for our first Joseph Fielding Smith Institute for Church History dinner with spouses, to continue our traditional summer gatherings. In the weekly letter to my children I wrote:

> We sang some early Church songs, accompanied by Davis Bitton on the piano and led by Carol Madsen. Each person read or told some interesting item he or she had found in his/her research. One item from Sister Edyth Romney: "President Young sent four of the brethren to break the road over the second mountain, to feed them well, and to give them a bottle to cheer their spirits through the snow." Another: "George A. Smith injured his lungs in offering morning prayer." Another: "Brother Ray preached to a travelling congregation, then we sang a hymn for dismissal, when Heber C. Kimball got up to make a remark and pray—and preached for 1 1/2 hours!" We had good food and good get-together.[2]

I had many other speaking appointments in 1980, but I turned my primary attention to the Brigham Young biography, for which I had iron-clad approval from Kimball. Just prior to Grace's death, on January 25, 1982, I received a personal letter from the First Presidency informing me that I had been released as church historian and as director of the History Division. They were unrestrained in expressing praise for the work we had done during our ten-year incumbency.

## The Hofmann Crimes

On April 18, 1980, just twelve days after the celebration of the church's 150th anniversary, when I was at an agricultural history symposium at Utah State University to speak on Mormons, agriculture, and economics in the West, I was approached by A. J. "Jeff" Simmonds, a former student of mine who was special collections librarian at Utah State. Jeff asked if he might have a private meeting with me at the conclusion of the symposium. We went to his office, where he told me that the previous day, Mark Hofmann, a USU pre-med student who collected coins and currency, had brought him a 1668 Cambridge edition of the King James Bible to examine. Hofmann had bought it the previous month at an estate sale, he told Simmonds, because it contained the signature of Samuel Smith and had reportedly belonged to Catherine Smith Salisbury, sister of Joseph Smith.

Hofmann said he thought it might have been the Bible of the Smith Family of Topsfield, Massachusetts. Upon examining the Bible, Hofmann confided, he had found a folded sheet of paper placed between pages of the Book of Proverbs that were partially stuck together by glue. Hofmann asked Simmonds how to open the pages without damaging the Bible. After Simmonds separated the pages he saw that the note between the pages was the document the prophet had made for Martin Harris to take to Professor Anthon, of Columbia University, in 1828—the earliest known holograph writing of Joseph Smith. A miraculous find for the sesquicentennial year! There were vertical columns of Egyptian hieroglyphs supposedly copied by the prophet from the gold plates and Smith's handwritten instructions to Martin Harris to show them to learned professors in New York who might verify the authenticity of the hieroglyphs as ancient writing. The paper appeared to be the Anthon Transcript of 1828, a document long supposed to have disappeared. Excitedly, Hofmann took the document to Dan Bachman, a historian at the LDS Institute of Religion in Logan. Bachman drove Hofmann to Salt Lake City to show the document to Dean Jessee, the handwriting expert in our History Division. Jessee asked for a weekend to examine the document more carefully.

When I resumed work the following Monday morning, Dean showed me the document and cautiously said it might be genuine. I reported this to Durham when he returned Tuesday morning. Durham arranged for Hofmann to show it to church officials that afternoon, and the "discovery" was announced at a press conference. The Anthon Transcript had been found, it was announced, and, in return for coins, currency, and rare books given to Hofmann, had been turned over to the church for further authorization. None of us had any reason to doubt the document's authenticity. We had no way of suspecting that Hofmann had bought the Bible when he was a missionary in England, had quietly and cleverly forged the document, and, in his misleadingly shy and self-effacing manner, had set us up for this "miraculous" discovery.

Mark Hofmann, a son of German convert-immigrants, had grown up in Salt Lake City, fulfilled an LDS mission to Bristol, England, had married, and he and his wife eventually had four children. He had been active in his ward and stake and had been a diligent student at USU. He had also been an eager history buff. In 1979, investigators later learned, while he was a student, Mark had written his mother about doubts and uncertainties about Mormonism. He told his mother of doing research in the Church Archives. He was concerned that the church should be honest in its history. He told her of a visit to me, of an article he had written that required access to the Journal History of the Church, and that I had told him I could not give permission, that "my hands were tied." As we learned later, Hofmann had made up this story to persuade his mother that the church was guilty of institutional hypocrisy. The facts are that I did not control access to the Church Archives, that I was not visited by Hofmann in 1979 or any time before April 1980, and that if he had wanted to see the Journal History of the Church he could have seen it, or virtually all of it, on microfilm at the USU Library, to which the church had given a copy in 1977. Hofmann was already fabricating history to serve his own purposes.

The fame that descended on Hofmann for the "discovery" of the Anthon Transcript caused him to abandon his pre-med studies, and he gave full attention to dealing in rare books and manuscripts. To all appearances he had unusually good luck in his searches and sold some for substantial sums. Here is a sample of important documents he eventually "found" and sold:

1. In March 1981 he sold to the LDS Church a blessing on the head of Joseph Smith's son, Joseph Smith III, bestowing on him the right of succession as president and prophet of the church. Knowing of the particular interest of the RLDS Church in the document, the LDS Church presented it to that church, which had the blessing on display until it was pronounced a forgery.

2. Shortly thereafter, he presented to the LDS Church a letter from Thomas Bullock to Brigham Young, dated January 27, 1865, accusing the president of destroying evidence of the same Joseph Smith III blessing. The church did not publicly acknowledge receipt of this letter until 1985.

3. In July 1982 he introduced a letter of Lucy Mack Smith, mother of Joseph Smith, dated January 23, 1829, discussing the translating work of Joseph Smith.

4. In January 1983 he sold to the church a letter from Joseph Smith to Josiah Stowell, dated June 18, 1825, which portrayed Joseph Smith as an experienced treasure hunter.

5. In January 1984 he sold a letter from Martin Harris to W. W. Phelps, dated October 23, 1830, with a strange account of the coming forth of the Book of Mormon that featured enchantments and mythical tricksters. Not the Angel Moroni but a white salamander had figured in the delivery of the gold plates, and for that reason it is usually referred to as the Salamander Letter.

6. To support his introduction of the Salamander Letter, Hofmann publicly claimed in 1985 that he had seen a "secret" handwritten history that Oliver Cowdery had written that had a nontraditional account of the gold plates and the Book of Mormon. The book, which he described rather precisely, as if he had seen it, was, he claimed, in the vault of the First Pres-

idency; the church had suppressed it because the account was not traditional. Although none of our historians had access to the vault, the church officially announced that it had no "Cowdery history." Dean Jessee later learned that the described history was in the handwriting of James Mulholland, Joseph Smith's secretary; that it was the first draft of the official history of the church later published in seven volumes under the editorship of B. H. Roberts; and that the account *is* the traditional account. Hofmann, who had not had access to the vault of the First Presidency as he had claimed, had made up the whole story to support the authenticity of the Martin Harris letter.

7. The Solomon Spalding [Spaulding]–Sidney Rigdon Land Deed, introduced in July 1985. Dated 1822, the purported deed linked Sidney Rigdon with Spaulding, who, according to anti-Mormon accounts of the 1830s, actually wrote part of or all of the Book of Mormon.

I had little to do with the examination or purchase of any of these documents; they involved transactions with Gordon B. Hinckley or Donald Schmidt, our Historical Department librarian. I was asked to make a public comment on the Salamander Letter, which I did, acknowledging that Joseph Smith had once been involved in treasure hunting, that Martin Harris was an untrustworthy reporter during part of his life, and that faithful members could rely upon Joseph Smith's own account of the Book of Mormon because it had been verified by many other contemporary accounts. I had no reason to deny that the Martin Harris letter might be genuine, and I admitted that those in the First Presidency had never given me access to their private historical vault and had no personal knowledge of what the vault contained. We had consulted forgery experts in New York, who had tested the paper, the ink, the postmarks; even the FBI had been called in, in the case of the Martin Harris letter, and had declared it genuine. There was almost unanimous agreement that many of the documents were genuine.

By the summer of 1983, three years after the Anthon Transcript presentation, my colleagues and I had concluded that at least some of the documents sold or announced by Hofmann were fraudulent. These included the documents containing the signatures of Sidney Rigdon and Solomon Spaulding, the announced history of Oliver Cowdery purportedly located in the vault of the First Presidency, some of the "Mormon" currency Hofmann was peddling, and the confrontive Thomas Bullock letter to Brigham Young which I had never believed existed. By August 1985 there were serious questions about the authenticity of all the Hofmann "finds."

On October 15, 1985, Steve Christensen and Kathy Sheets were murdered by pipe bombs; three days later, Hofmann himself was seriously injured by a bomb that exploded as he opened the door of his car. After weeks of investigation, the county attorney's office determined that Hofmann had murdered Christensen and Sheets and injured himself with a bomb intended for another person, probably Brent Ashworth. Document professionals soon demonstrated that Hofmann had cleverly manufactured all of the documents he had marketed. The documents, it was clear, were intended by Hofmann, a closet nonbeliever from his teenage years, to rewrite Mormon history. In a subsequent plea bargain to escape the electric chair, Hofmann admitted to and explained forgeries of the above and many other documents. He was sentenced to a lifetime in the Utah State Prison. According to Kenneth Rendell, a leading rare and historical documents dealer in Boston, Mark Hofmann was one of the most skillful forgers in modern history.[3]

Thirteen years have passed since those cold-blooded murders and the public knowledge of unsettling forgeries. Because I was church historian when the earliest Hofmann "discoveries" were brought to light, I would like to say that during that time, I developed enormous confidence in the honesty, integrity, and faithfulness of LDS historians. Unlike certain other interests, LDS historians did not sensationalize, did not jump into new interpretations, and did not alter their balanced, honest, and faithful approaches to LDS history. They were cautious and careful and continued to do serious research. Our principal plea was for honesty and openness to verified evidences.

Fortunately, Latter-day Saint history is rich in source material. We have not had to depend upon one or two or even a dozen documents. A new document that comes to light is still just one of the many evidences, and its principal usefulness is that it causes us to look again at *all* the evidence and reconsider what we have previously concluded. The principal impact of the Hofmann forgeries was to force our historians to examine more carefully the many sources we already had and to see if there were any that we might have overlooked or misinterpreted. We set out to study more fully the newspapers, diaries, letters, and recollections generated in the period the alleged new document related to.

Historical accounts do not change as rapidly as books in the sciences, but the discovery of new evidence, its assimilation into previous knowledge, and the checking and counterchecking to achieve complete authenticity is the essence of research—in every field, including history. Every history, though written as truthfully as possible, is always subject to future corrections and amplifications. That is the nature of our craft, just as in economics, sociology, anthropology, and other social sciences. We learn something, or think we learn something, and then we get new evidence and we have to revise our thinking. Then we discover that our new evidence was flawed and we have to rethink again. Our restless reexamination forces us to work out new understandings that are consistent with the known facts. This precise study, honest and sincere as it is, adds to our appreciation for our past. I can speak for most of my associates when I say that evidences continue to accumulate that deepen and strengthen our attachment to our faith.

Hofmann's inventions and his attempts to create new historical evidence put me in mind of Mark Twain's praise of the duckbilled platypus. He was so versatile an animal, wrote Twain, that "if he wanted eggs he laid 'em."

## Achievements of Our History Division

During the ten years our History Division was affiliated with the Historical Department, 1972–82, we dedicated ourselves to writing books and articles on many aspects of church history. In addition to hundreds of talks in sacrament meetings, firesides, historical occasions, professional societies, and study groups, members of the staff published twenty books; completed eight book-length manuscripts, most of which have since been published; submitted 364 articles for publication in church magazines, professional journals, and other periodicals; and wrote about 300 other papers, most of which were later published. No one questions that this was a prodigious output of scholarly work. The prizes awarded for some of these publications indicate the high quality of the work. Surely, President Tanner's commission that we research and write our history in a professional way was met during this era.[4]

In the process, our History Division proudly made contributions to the Mormon History Trust Fund. In addition to other projects, we supported Edyth Romney, who transcribed thousands of letters signed by Brigham Young and the diaries of Willard Richards and other church officials, producing one of the most remarkable legacies of our stay in the Historical Department—thousands and thousands of pages of typed transcripts.

In evaluating our experience in working those ten years in the Historical Department, I freely employ the well-known historical device of hindsight by offering four comments.

First, I can plainly see that, after the death of Dyer in 1973, we would have done well to have published a regular newsletter or circular to inform general authorities of the work we were doing. Dyer had carried this responsibility for us. This would have given authorities more information about our efforts and provided a sound basis for decisions about our activities in the years that followed.

Second, we performed an immense benefit to the church by agreeing to serve as a resource for the newspapers and media on the many historical controversies that arose during the decade we were at church headquarters. Church leaders seemed to have a rule that they rarely gave interviews. Public Communications would furnish material on various questions but had no expertise on history. We therefore gave accurate written and oral responses to the many questions that were posed. In doing so I had the approval of our managing directors. There were interviews with newspaper columnists, magazine writers, television reporters, and even filmmakers. They included representatives of the BBC, CBS, ABC, NBC, PBS, *Time*, *Newsweek*, the *Christian Science Monitor* (one of the fairest of all), the *New York Times*, the *Atlanta Constitution*, the *Los Angeles Times*, the *Philadelphia Enquirer*, the *Chicago Tribune*, the *Chicago Sun-Times*, the *San Francisco Chronicle*, and various local radio and television stations. All of the questioners were interested in some "dirt," but they had respect for my scholarship and usually were honest though selective in using quotations. I was able to protect the church's and historians' images in most instances, but not in all. Predictably, a few of the reporters were unfairly adversarial. In some instances, where the truth was complex, I asked a reporter to check back with me when he or she had written the story, to be sure it was correct. Despite earnest promises, they never did. To this day, newspaper and television reporters and document editors come to me for help on Western and Mormon history. Apparently, persons in Church Communications still give out my name when asked for an independent source on some historical question or controversy.

Third, in all fairness, the move to BYU had some real benefits. For one thing, the church was embarrassed about the salaries we were being paid. Even though we received less than we would have earned as university professors, we were, in fact, among the highest paid employees. This did not bother Tanner, who believed in paying people what they were worth, but it was a concern to some who believed that the church should pay modestly—less-than-competitive wages and salaries. I personally never urged the issue of satisfactory pay; but for some of my associates who were buying homes and raising young families, the issue was important. From this standpoint it was logical for the church to transfer us to BYU, where administrators immediately raised our salaries. This, of course, pleased the wives and husbands of the research and teaching professors in the Joseph Fielding Smith Institute.

Fourth, our experience demonstrated conclusively that the enormous mass of material in the Church Archives was constructive and faith promoting, revealing positive and inspiring glimpses of the church and its officers. As to the few items in the archives that have been viewed as damaging to the church, copies were made by unfriendly people long before we began our work; the appearance of these documents is not traceable to our policy of openness but to theft or permissions wrongly given well before our research. Although some urged us to spend our time answering the unfavorable accounts that appeared, we were counseled by our advisors to proceed with our task of writing the church's history. This is what we did.

Through the Joseph Fielding Smith Institute and other Latter-day Saint scholars at BYU and elsewhere, splendid books and articles have been and will continue to be produced; and I have faith that this work will continue to have the blessing of the Lord. Our loyal historians, now located in many parts of the world, are pursuing Mormon history with a vigor and realism that equals, perhaps exceeds, what we had initiated during our years together in the Historical Department. Our History Division experience was a little like the Zion's Camp episode of the 1830s: It did not succeed in its ostensible objective, but it may have identified a corps of leaders and provided valuable experience out of which great things developed.

## Notes

1. "New BYU Institute to Take History Role," *Deseret News,* July 2, 1980.

2. See my letter to my children, Aug. 8, 1980, copy in Leonard J. Arrington Collection, Special Collections and Archives, Utah State University Libraries, Logan.

3. Kenneth W. Rendell, *Forging History: The Detection of Fake Letters and Documents* (Norman: University of Oklahoma Press, 1994), 124–40. Histories of the Hofmann forgeries and murders include Linda Sillitoe and Allen D. Roberts, *Salamander: The Story of the Mormon Forgery Murders* (Salt Lake City: Signature Books, 1988); Robert Lindsey, *A Gathering of Saints: A True Story of Money, Murder, and Deceit* (New York: Simon and Schuster, 1988); Steven Naifeh and Gregory White Smith, *The Mormon Murders: A True Story of Greed, Forgery, Deceit, and Death* (New York: Weidenfeld and Nicholson, 1988); and Richard E. Turley Jr., *Victims: The LDS Church and the Mark Hofmann Case* (Urbana: University of Illinois Press, 1992). A splendid appraisal of Hofmann literature is David J. Whittaker, "The Hofmann Maze: A Book Review Essay," *BYU Studies* 29 (Winter 1989): 67–124. There were allegations that I and other historians, believing at first that Hofmann was innocent, refused to cooperate with investigating officials. I cannot recall having placed any obstacles in the way of such officials at any time during the months following the murders. And, of course, I had not been church historian since 1980, having been replaced shortly after the Anthon Transcript episode.

4. The best account is Davis Bitton, "Ten Years in Camelot: A Personal Memoir," *Dialogue* 16 (Autumn 1983): 9–33.

# 15

# The Ongoing Process of Writing
# Mormon and Western History

Thy time shall be given to writing and to learning.
—Doctrine and Covenants 25:8

AFTER THE TRANSFER of our historians to Brigham Young University in the summer of 1982, I remained in our home in Salt Lake City and commuted to BYU frequently. Knowing I would be unable to make most of our Tuesday noon Rotary meetings in Salt Lake City, I resigned. I felt group members had asked me to join in 1972 because I had been appointed church historian, and I could no longer claim association as an officer of a business, professional, or religious organization. I had enjoyed my association with Club 24 very much, had served as secretary, had been named chairman of the Fellowships and Education Committee, and had written a history of the club that is still in print. In addition to the Tuesday meetings and the writing of (I hope) entertaining minutes, Grace and I enjoyed the opportunity of playing host to two visiting women students. For the academic year 1975–76, we entertained in our home Masako Yahata, from Japan, who took classes at the University of Utah. In 1981 we were hosts for four months to Marion Newmarch, a high school senior from Australia. These were pleasurable experiences for us and, we hope, for Masako and Marion. We also often entertained for dinner other Rotary exchange students.

At BYU I continued to teach a class in aspects of Mormon history each spring and fall semester; directed master's theses and doctoral dissertations; gave addresses to student groups, townspeople, and professional and church groups; and continued a program of research and writing. In addition to the Brigham Young biography, I continued to work on other projects in which I was interested. I collaborated with Richard Jensen in writing the economic life of Chesterfield, Idaho; published "New Deal Programs and Southwestern Agriculture" in *Southwestern Agriculture: Pre-*

*Columbian to Modern;* and gave five lectures at Utah State University on Mormon and Utah history. In 1983 I spoke at Idaho State University in Pocatello on Mormon literature; to an Idaho Falls civic group on the history of that city; and gave the Dello Dayton Memorial Lecture at Weber State College, which I entitled "Utah, the New Deal, and the Depression of the 1930s." Rebecca Foster Cornwall Bartholomew and I did an article for *BYU Studies*—"Mormon Danites in Five Western Novels"—and I gave the presidential address to the American Historical Association, Pacific Coast Branch, "The Sagebrush Resurrection: New Deal Expenditures in the Western States, 1933–1939."

In the spring of 1984 I underwent a sextuple heart bypass operation by Dr. Russell Nelson, renowned Utah cardiologist and heart surgeon. He agreed to perform the operation on April 24 even though he was sustained as a member of the Twelve and was ordained an apostle on April 12. He told me afterwards that the operation was historic (the first by an apostle and the last of his career). He joked that he was especially delighted it was performed on a historian. Dr. Nelson conferred upon me the "Order of the Split Sternum." Dear Harriet tenderly nursed me back to health.

Later in 1984, with the help of John Alley Jr., I wrote *Tracy-Collins Bank and Trust Company: A Record of Responsibility, 1884–1984,* and, with my daughter Susan Madsen, *Sunbonnet Sisters: True Stories of Mormon Women and Frontier Life.* Other articles on aspects of Mormon history were published in 1984–85 in *Agricultural History, Dialogue, Sunstone, Utah Holiday,* and the *Church News.*

While *Brigham Young: American Moses* was being published in 1985, I also worked on essays on Joseph Smith, Brigham Young, and Harold B. Lee for the new edition of *Presidents of the Church,* of which I was editor. With my stepdaughter Heidi, I wrote a history of the Hotel Utah, at the time owned primarily by the church, for its seventy-fifth anniversary in 1986. The church later closed the hotel, remodeled it, and it functions now as the Joseph Smith Memorial Building, which is a church office building with two restaurants on the roof. Thanks to Heidi's expertise and Stephen Moody's photography, it was a classy book, complete with artwork, color photos, and all. The next year, Heidi and I collaborated on a history of the Utah Governor's Mansion, published under the title *In the Utah Tradition.* This, again, was a beautiful coffee-table book suitable as a gift to Utah's distinguished visitors. Also in 1987 my daughter Susan and I wrote *Mothers of the Prophets,* published by Deseret Book Company, with biographical essays on the mothers of each of the presidents of the church. Other 1986–87 articles appeared in *Utah Historical Quarterly, Idaho Yesterdays, Journal of Mormon History, BYU Studies,* and *Religious Studies and Theology* (a Canadian publication). In addition I gave addresses to groups at Brigham Young University, the Western History Association, Utah State University, Nottingham University in England, Whitman College in Washington, and Northern Nevada Community College.

Under the sponsorship of the Mormon History Association, Harriet and I made a two-week trip to England in 1986 to speak to stakes and wards and general audiences on the Mormon experience in England, in preparation for the British Mission sesquicentennial in 1987. We gave lectures on Mormon English history in Reading, St. Albans, Leicester, Nottingham (to two university classes as well as the general public), Chester, Birmingham, Staffordshire, and Hyde Park Stake in London. At each location, we were entertained by the stake president and his wife, who usually took us to interesting sites in their bailiwick. Lecture titles included "Mormon Women in Nineteenth Century Britain," "Brigham Young's 1840 Mission to Great Britain," "The Lighter Side of Mormon History" (for young people), and still others on Joseph Smith and Brigham Young. There were good audiences at each location. We visited the British Museum, Liverpool, many cathedrals, historical museums, and universities. We ate Yorkshire pudding, saw a thatched roof home, and visited the Wedgwood display center. In London we saw *Les Misérables* and visited Westminster Cathedral and Abbey, St. Paul's Cathedral, Sunday Market, and Windsor Castle. At Amersham we saw Milton's home and William Penn's burial site. The entire experience was unforgettable and inspirational. We followed it by flying over the Alps to Rome, where we spent four days visiting places of interest that I was well acquainted with and that I wanted to show to Harriet.

While we were gone, I was notified that I had been elected a member of the Society of American Historians—the first Utahan and first Mormon to be so elected. Now I am pleased to say that Richard Bushman and Laurel Ulrich are both members of this elite society.

In 1987 the Mormon History Association held its annual meeting at Oxford, England, and Harriet and I were present for that. We took a week's tour of Wales before the conference and a week's tour of Scotland at the end. We were also in Canada to celebrate the centennial of Mormon settlement in 1987 and to meet with the Canadian Mormon Studies Association.

On July 2, 1987, I reached seventy years of age, and BYU administrators decided I should be terminated. The Lemuel Redd Chair of Western History went to James B. Allen, and I had earlier relinquished the Charles Redd Center directorship to Tom Alexander. New director of the Joseph Fielding Smith Institute for Church History was Ron Esplin. I was allowed to keep my office, but shared it with Jill Mulvay Derr, and I was allowed to continue to use the services of our institute secretary, Marilyn Rish Parks.

I was invited to address the graduates in the College of Family, Home, and Social Sciences at their 1987 commencement, and I also addressed the centennial of Utah State University in Logan.

Since my termination from Brigham Young University in July 1987, I have continued to work at the desk in my study in our Salt Lake City home. Occasionally, I have sent articles and professional papers to Marilyn to put on the computer. My wife Harriet has typed some things, and I have typed some of them myself. I have continued to present papers at professional conventions, to carry on correspondence with historians, friends, and relatives; and to respond to questions that I receive once or twice a week from persons who think I am still church historian or, having once been, can help with some historical problem. Since 1987 I have written or co-written six books, three pamphlets, and some seventy or eighty articles and chapters in books. Some of the articles have appeared in encyclopedias, others in LDS publications, and still others in professional publications and university periodicals. For the benefit of my children, grandchildren, brothers and sisters, and friends, I have also done a series of desktop histories of my personal life and experiences, amounting in all to eight publications, each less than one hundred pages in length. I have also written a history of my parents and grandparents.

Harriet has published a brief biography of her grandmother, Alice Merrill Horne, which was preliminary to a full biography I am helping her with. Entitled "Alice Merrill Horne, Cultural Entrepreneur," the paper was given by us at the annual Women's Conference at Brigham Young University and later published in *A Heritage of Faith* by Deseret Book in 1988. Harriet's essay entitled "Alice Merrill Horne: Art Promoter and Early Utah Legislator" was published in *Utah Historical Quarterly* and later as a chapter in *Worth Their Salt: Notable but Often Unnoted Women of Utah.*

For the volume *Teachers Who Touch Lives,* I wrote a biography of my former teacher at the LDS Institute of Religion in Moscow, Idaho, George S. Tanner. I also wrote "Joseph Smith, Builder of Ideal Communities" for *The Prophet Joseph: Essays on the Life and Mission of Joseph Smith,* and "Brigham Young and the Great Basin Economy" for *Lion of the Lord: Essays on the Life and Service of Brigham Young.* I gave the annual lecture of the Nevada Humanities Council in 1988, which I entitled "The Mormon Utopia." Having been stricken with the Spanish influenza in 1919 when I was a baby, I did research articles on the influenza epidemic of 1918–19 in Idaho for *Idaho Yesterdays* and on the influenza epidemic in Utah for the *Utah Historical Quarterly.* I also produced articles on Latter-day Saint women for the *John Whitmer Historical Association Journal,*

*BYU Studies,* and the *Journal of Mormon History.* For the *Encyclopedia of American Business History and Biography: Banking and Finance, 1913–1989,* published in 1990, I prepared essays on Marriner and George Eccles. I also wrote the text for the pamphlet that was distributed by Congress on the occasion of the acceptance and dedication of the statue of Philo T. Farnsworth, presented by the State of Utah for the rotunda of the National Capitol in 1991. I gave the Juanita Brooks Lecture at Dixie College in 1993, entitled "St. George Tabernacle and Temple: The Builders." I wrote essays on several Utahans for the *Dictionary of American Biography* and on aspects of Mormon history for the *Encyclopedia of Mormonism,* published in five volumes by Macmillan in 1992.

In 1988, the University of Utah Press published *Mormons and Their Historians,* a book of essays on Mormon historians that Davis Bitton and I had worked on for several years. In the book are chapters or sections on Willard Richards, George A. Smith, Edward W. Tullidge, Andrew Jenson, Orson F. Whitney, B. H. Roberts, Andrew Love Neff, Ephraim Edward Ericksen, Bernard DeVoto, Fawn Brodie, Dale Morgan, Juanita Brooks, and a more recent generation of historians, beginning with 1972.

Also in 1988 the president of Steiner Corporation, in preparation for the corporation's centennial the next year, asked me to write a history of the company. I worked on the project for several months and completed a 235-page manuscript, duly approved by the officers of the company, that we submitted to the University of Utah Press for publication in a Utah business history series. The press kept the book for a year and finally replied that it was not going to undertake such a series and would not publish the volume. The company then decided to serve as its own publisher, and the printing was done by Publishers Press in Salt Lake City. A volume was finally issued at the end of 1991.

In one century, the company had grown from a foot-traffic operation delivering clean towels and aprons in Lincoln, Nebraska, to a multinational miniconglomerate servicing businesses around the world. Originally the company was named American Linen Supply Company, then renamed Steiner-American in 1959; in 1976 the name was changed to Steiner Corporation. A $500 million privately held corporation, Steiner has directed its far-flung empire from its home in Salt Lake City since 1895. The book was published under the title *From Small Beginnings: A History of the American Linen Supply Company, Its Successors and Affiliates.*

As that project was being wound up, I was approached by Barnard Silver to write a biography of his father, Harold Silver, a Salt Lake City–born inventor and businessman who had spent most of his life in Denver, Colorado. The 250-page volume was printed by the Utah State University Press and appeared in the summer of 1992. Born into a family of mechanical engineers, craftsmen in iron and steel, Harold Silver had an unequaled role in creating the machinery that received and processed sugar beets and extracted sugar from them, dramatically reducing labor needs and increasing production capabilities. Having revolutionized the sugar beet business, he then created a new way of obtaining sugar from its other main source, sugar cane. His influence on coal mining was perhaps even more important, earning him a place among America's greatest inventors. Silver's continuous coal miner, a teethed monster of a machine, tore out coal by the wall, moved it from the mining face, and loaded it for transport to the surface. It replaced back-breaking hand labor by miners, integrated the various tasks of several less-efficient machines, and made coal mining safer, less expensive, and more productive.

His leadership of the Colorado business community, especially during World War II, his important benefactions, and personal tragedies in his family made for a compelling story of joy and public accomplishment.

In 1993 the Silvers asked me to prepare a biography of their mother, Madelyn Cannon Stewart Silver—a Salt Lake–born poet, teacher, clubwoman, and philanthropist who lived thirty years in Denver. I worked on the project with available time in 1994 and 1995 and in 1996 completed a draft, typed by Harriet, of a 400-page biography that is now being reviewed by a university press. I enjoyed the research and writing and believe I have written a superior biography.

This was my first full biography of a woman. In preparation for writing it, I read twenty or thirty books about women, all of which, not surprisingly, avowed that men could not write about women. (Women, of course, could write successful biographies of men). With an unmistakable talent for short story writing and poetry, and yet brought up in a culture that emphasized domesticity—supporting husband, bearing children, and an unending round of entertaining—Madelyn found a substitute for creative activity in teaching literature and in using her poetry and short stories to illustrate her class presentations, lectures, and religious talks. Inevitably, her life was accompanied by a tension between the desire to create through literature and the desire to create through a fulfilling domesticity.

A fourth project, commissioned by Hardy Redd, oldest son of Charlie Redd, a Utah cattleman and sheep grower who spent most of his years in southeastern Utah, appeared in 1995. As the first occupant of the Lemuel Redd Chair of Western History at Brigham Young University, which Charlie established in honor of his father, and as the first director of the Charles Redd Center for Western Studies at BYU, also established by Charlie, I enjoyed working on Charlie's life. The 282-page book was published by the Redd Center and the Utah State University Press.

I had known Charlie for several years in the 1960s, and until his death in 1975, liked his sense of humor, his knowledge of and interest in Mormon history and culture, and his support of *Dialogue* and other public discussion activities. In 1964 I had received the first of Charlie's biennial $1,500 awards, given through the Utah Academy of Sciences, Arts, and Letters, for a significant contribution for the betterment of humankind in the previous five years in the field of the humanities and social sciences. Rancher, state legislator, entrepreneur, humanist, and philanthropist, Charlie built up one of Utah and western Colorado's largest livestock operations. The heir of Mormon "Hole-in-the-Rock" pioneers, he remained firmly rooted in the red-rock canyons and pine-crested mountains of southeastern Utah. Committed to traditional agrarian ideals of stewardship and to the value of the intellect, he employed both in striving to improve the conditions of cattle, sheep, people, and the land. He was an extraordinary rancher.

A major assignment was the centennial history of Idaho. In 1990 the Idaho legislature passed a measure approved by Governor Cecil Andrus commissioning me to write a full history of the state. Harriet and I visited nearly every town and city, from Franklin on the southeast to the Montana border, and from the Duck Valley Indian Reservation on the southwest to the Canadian border north of Bonners Ferry. We spent much time in the Idaho State Historical Society Library and Archives and some time in the libraries of each of Idaho's colleges and universities and in the public libraries of most cities in the state. I completed a 1,000-page history within eighteen months, and the manuscript was delivered to Judith Austin, editor of the Idaho State Historical Society, in November 1991. Harriet helped speed the work by entering my manually typewritten drafts onto the computer, thus providing up-to-date working chapters at each stage of the preparation of the final manuscript.

In many ways, Idaho is four states. The northern section is part of the Inland Empire centered on Spokane, Washington, only sixteen miles from the Idaho border. Southwestern Idaho, focused on Boise, the capital, includes an agricultural and industrial area reaching into eastern Oregon. Southeastern Idaho is usually regarded as part of the Mormon culture region centered in Salt Lake City, one hundred miles south of the border with Idaho. South-central Idaho, where I grew up, owes no particular allegiance to any of the other three or to any outside cultural center; its residents are independent farmers and business people who help hold the state together and strengthen its unity. I faced a challenge in bringing unity to the story of Idaho. Many who have read the completed work have congratulated me on achieving this goal.

I truly enjoyed writing this history of my native state; I don't know of a project I have undertaken in recent years that gave me so much pleasure—and income. The two-volume work, which has won several awards, appeared in elegant slipcases in 1994.

During the winter of 1996–97, I wrote a biography of W. W. Clyde, leading Utah contractor, who had built thousands of miles of Utah highway and who had jointly built the high-rise Church Office Building and the ZCMI Center in downtown Salt Lake City. The family hopes to publish the book in 1998. A former bishop, Boy Scout executive, mayor of Springville, and president of the Associated General Contractors of Utah, Clyde has also made important benefactions to the University of Utah and Brigham Young University.

I have helped Harriet work on a biography of her grandmother Alice Merrill Horne. Zorah Horne Jeppson, Alice's daughter, and Joseph Jeppson Jr. and Mary Alice Jeppson Clark, children of Zorah, have provided us with copies of Alice Merrill Horne's diaries, letters, scrapbooks, clippings, personal histories, and other papers that are extensive and will enable us, if we do it right, to write a prize-winning biography. We hope to have it completed by 1998. I also have material to write a history of the activities in Utah of New Deal economic agencies during the 1930s.

I have had many opportunities to write and give lectures since retirement, and I am grateful for continued good health and productivity. Our work has made it possible for Harriet and me to do considerable traveling. We joined others in attending the Mormon History Association meetings in Kingston, Ontario, in 1995 and spent an extra week visiting Quebec City, Montreal, and Toronto. We made two trips to Hawaii to attend conventions and spent another two weeks in 1994 as guests of Brigham Young University's campus there, where I delivered five lectures on faith and intellect. We visited Honolulu and Maui. We have attended Mormon History Association conventions in Lamoni, Iowa; Independence, Missouri; Nauvoo, Illinois; and Logan, Ogden, Salt Lake City, and St. George, Utah. In connection with speaking assignments, we have also been to Toronto, Canada; Boston, Massachusetts; Washington, D.C.; Portland, Oregon; Seattle, Washington; Billings, Montana; Boise, Idaho; and various places in Utah. We attended the World's Fair at Vancouver, British Columbia, in 1986. Harriet and I have enjoyed taking friends out to dinner and having friends and relatives in our home for dinners and parties and celebrations. Harriet has been an inventive and gracious hostess and has warmly welcomed friends, visiting historians, and students into our home. Among other things, we held a reception for Davis and JoAn Bitton when they married in 1984. We have also held Christmas dinner parties for the Joseph Fielding Smith Institute staff and spouses and friends of Mormon history most of the years since our marriage.

# 16

# Writing Latter-day Saint History:
# Philosophy and Testimony

All the minds and spirits that God ever sent into the world are susceptible of enlargement.
—Joseph Smith, April 7, 1844, King Follett Sermon,
*History of the Church* 6:311

WHETHER ONE IS A Roman Catholic, Buddhist, Muslim, Jew, or Mormon, there are many challenges in writing religious history. On the one hand the historian must convey the facts of history in an honest and straightforward manner. The historian must strive against the conscious or unconscious distortion of events to fit the demands of current fashions; he or she must renounce wishful thinking. On the other hand, many religious historians wish also to bear testimony of the reality of spiritual experience. We all know by now that the pretense of "objectivity" can be a hypocritical dodge to cover up unspoken, perhaps even incorrect, assumptions.

Speaking for myself and, I think, for most of the historians who have worked with me, some tension between our professional training and our religious commitments seems inevitable. Our testimonies tell us that the Lord is in this work, and for this we see abundant supporting evidence. But our historical training warns us that the accurate perception of spiritual phenomena is elusive—not subject to unquestionable verification. We are tempted to wonder if our religious beliefs are intruding beyond their proper limits. Our faith tells us that there is moral meaning and spiritual significance in historical events. But we cannot be completely confident that any particular judgment or meaning or significance is unambiguously clear. If God's will cannot be wholly divorced from the actual course of history, neither can it be positively identified with it. Although we see evidence that God's love and power have frequently broken in upon the ordinary course of human affairs, our caution in declaring this is reinforced by our justifiable disapproval of chroniclers who take the easy way out and use divine miracles as a short-circuit of a causal explanation that is obviously, or at least defensibly, naturalistic. We must not use history as a storehouse from which deceptively simple moral lessons may be drawn at random.

I hope that LDS historians will be known for the sense of reverence and responsibility with which they approach their assignments. There should exist a certain fidelity toward and respect for the documents and a certain feeling for human tragedy and triumph. LDS history is the history of the Latter-day Saints, in their worship and prayer, in their mutual relationships, in their conflicts and contacts, in their social dealings, in their solitude and estrangement, in their high aspirations, and in their fumbling weaknesses and failures. We must be responsive to the whole amplitude of human concerns—to human life in all its rich variety and diversity, in all its misery and grandeur, in all its ambiguity and contradictions.

Undeniably, part of that human life is its religious dimension. Latter-day Saint historians will not do their subject justice, will not adequately understand the people they are writing about, if they leave out the power of testimony as a motivating factor in their lives. In his "Second Century Address" at Brigham Young University in 1976, Spencer Kimball gave wise counsel. "As LDS scholars," he said, "you must speak with authority and excellence to your professional colleagues in the language of scholarship, and you must also be literate in the language of spiritual things."[1] The great histories of our people, a few of which have been written, must reflect both the rigor of competent scholarship and the sensitivity to recognize, as the New Testament records, that "the wind bloweth where it listeth" (John 3:8).

I firmly believe that a person may be a converted Latter-day Saint *and* a competent and honest historian of the religion. That others support us in this calling, even while criticizing some products of our labors, is suggested by the remark of Harold B. Lee to me before his sudden death. "Our history is our history, Brother Arrington, and we don't need to tamper with it or be ashamed of it." Paraphrasing a remark of Pope John XXIII, Bruce McConkie said to our executives: "The best defense of the church is the true and impartial account of our history."

I have tried in this memoir to bear witness to the loyalty of my colleagues and associates to the Latter-day Saint ideals of professional competence, sincere truth-seeking, and unquestioned integrity, trustworthiness, and dedication. Our historical scholarship was accompanied by firm convictions of the truth of Mormonism. If we did not measure up, we can at least say that we sincerely tried.

May Latter-day Saint historians lengthen their stride as they strive to develop capacities that will enable them to write histories worthy of the marvelous work and the wonder that is their heritage.

*Note*

1. Spencer W. Kimball, "Second Century Address," *BYU Studies* 16 (Summer 1976): 446.

# SOURCES

The principal sources for this book are my diaries, letters, and other personal papers, which are housed in the newly created Leonard J. Arrington Collection, part of the Special Collections and Archives Division at the Utah State University Libraries. In 1977 I made my diaries and letters available to Rebecca Foster Cornwall Bartholomew to write an unpublished history entitled "From Chicken Farm to History: The Life of Leonard Arrington, 1917–1977." Her well-written 359-page text covered the years to 1972, and I added a short chapter on the years from 1972 to 1977. The biography was intended only for my children and close friends. Because she read all of the daily letters I wrote when I was a soldier in North Africa and Italy in the 1940s, and all of my diary entries from the 1950s and 1960s, this history is far more detailed for those years than the present volume.

In 1982, when I was released as church historian, I asked Lavina Fielding Anderson to use my diaries and letters for the period 1972 to 1982 to write "Doves and Serpents: The Activities of Leonard Arrington as Church Historian, 1972–1982," a 243-page work that I duplicated for my children and close associates but which has not been submitted for publication. Anderson has given me permission to use portions of her history in the present work. Because of the exemplary work of these talented friends, I have dedicated this volume, in part, to them. It is a way of publicly thanking them for their interest, discretion, understanding, and writing skill.

My family background is traced in a book that Rebecca and I wrote in 1976 and that has been distributed to the family under the title "Tar Heels, Hoosiers, and Idahoans: A History of the Noah and Edna Arrington Family to 1933." This was followed in 1992 by the publication of *Magic Valley Pioneers: A Photographic Record of N. W. and Edna Corn Arrington* (Salt Lake City: Historian's Press, 1991), an illustrated history that I wrote as a device to share my photos and those that others loaned to me with my brothers and sisters and their children and grandchildren. The book also contains introductory essays on N. W. and Edna.

The life of my first wife was told by her to Rebecca and distributed to family and friends in 1977 under the title "I'm Glad My House Burned Down: The Personal Story of Grace Fort Arrington." After her death in 1982 Rebecca prepared a complementary volume, "The Grace of Our Lord Was with Her: Grace Fort Arrington, 1943 to 1946 and 1977 to 1982."

A biographical sketch of myself is found in each edition of *Who's Who in America,* 1973–98, and in Allan Kent Powell, ed., *Utah History Encyclopedia* (Salt Lake City: University of Utah Press, 1994), 24.

Other sources of this history include some biographical, historical, and autobiographical articles that I and others have prepared for oral delivery and for publication in professional and semiprofessional magazines and journals. Among these are the following, listed chronologically by date of presentation or publication.

### Autobiographical and Historical Papers and Articles by Leonard J. Arrington

"Cassandra in Pursuit of Clio; or, Why Economists Become Historians," typescript, duplicated by Department of Economics, Utah State University, Logan, Utah. Luncheon address to the Pacific Coast Branch, American Historical Association, Los Angeles, California, Aug. 27, 1964.

"Scholarly Studies of Mormonism in the Twentieth Century," *Dialogue* 1 (Spring 1966): 15–28.

"The Search for Truth and Meaning in Mormon History," *Dialogue* 3 (Summer 1968): 56–66.

"Church History and the Achievement of Identity," *Commissioner's Lecture Series* (Salt Lake City: Church Education System, 1972).

"The Many Uses of Humor," Last Lecture at Brigham Young University, Jan. 17, 1974.

"History Is Then and Now: A Conversation with Leonard J. Arrington, Church Historian," *Ensign* 5 (July 1975): 8–13.

"Historian as Entrepreneur: A Personal Essay," *BYU Studies* 17 (Winter 1977): 193–209.

"'Clothe These Bones': The Reconciliation of Faith and History," address delivered at History Division retreat, Ensign Peak, Salt Lake Valley, June 23, 1978.

"Learning about Ourselves through Church History," *Ensign* 9 (Sept. 1979): 6–8.

"The Prayer for a Miracle," in *Turning Points* (Salt Lake City: Bookcraft, 1981), 53–55.

"The Writing of Latter-day Saint History: Problems, Accomplishments, and Admonitions," *Dialogue* 14 (Autumn 1981): 119–29.

"Recalling a Twin Falls Childhood," *Idaho Yesterdays* 25 (Winter 1982): 31–40.

"Reflections on the Founding and Purpose of the Mormon History Association, 1965–1983," *Journal of Mormon History* 10 (1983): 91–103.

"Personal Reflections on Mormon History," *Sunstone* 8 (July–Aug. 1983): 41–45.

"Why I Am a Believer," in *A Thoughtful Faith: Essays on Belief by Mormon Scholars,* ed. Philip L. Barlow (Centerville, Utah: Canon Press, 1986), 225–33.

"Christmas Eve in Front of the Open Oven Door," in *A Celebration of Christmas* (Salt Lake City: Deseret Book, 1988), 41–44.

"In Praise of Amateurs," *Journal of Mormon History* 17 (1991): 35–42.

"Great Basin Kingdom Revisited," *Dialogue* 26 (Summer 1993): 173–83.

*A Soldier in North Africa and Italy, 1943–1946: A Pictorial History* (Salt Lake City: Historian's Press, 1995).

*Growing Up in Twin Falls County, Idaho* (Hyde Park, Utah: Historian's Press, 1996).

*Farm Boy at the University of Idaho, 1935–39* (Hyde Park, Utah: Historian's Press, 1996).

*In the Land of the Tar Heels: "Jimmie" in Raleigh and Chapel Hill, North Carolina, 1939–43, 1949–50, 1952* (Hyde Park, Utah: Historian's Press, 1996).

*Years of Achievement and Pleasure in Logan, 1958–72* (Hyde Park, Utah: Historian's Press, 1996).

*Life in Happy Valley: Early Years in Logan and Our First Sabbatical, 1946–58* (Hyde Park, Utah: Historian's Press, 1996).

### Articles and Book Chapters about Leonard J. Arrington by Others

David J. Whittaker, "Leonard James Arrington: His Life and Work," *Dialogue* 11 (Winter 1978): 23–47.

"An Interview with Leonard Arrington and Davis Bitton," *Sunstone* 4 (July–Aug. 1979): 38–41.

JoAnn Jolley, "Leonard J. Arrington: Mormon History's Leading Man," *This People* 1 (Sesquicentennial Issue 1980): 14–19.

"Western History Association Prize Recipient, 1984: Leonard J. Arrington," *Western Historical Quarterly* 16 (Jan. 1985): 17–26.

Maureen Ursenbach Beecher, "Entre Nous: An Intimate History of MHA," *Journal of Mormon History* 12 (1985): 43–52.

Heidi Swinton, "Leonard Arrington: And That's the Way It Was," *This People* 7 (Nov. 1986): 30–39.

Davis Bitton, "Introduction," in *New Views of Mormon History: A Collection of Essays in Honor of Leonard J. Arrington*, ed. Davis Bitton and Maureen Ursenbach Beecher (Salt Lake City: University of Utah Press, 1987), vii–xvii.

Stanford Cazier, "Honoring Leonard Arrington," *Dialogue* 22 (Winter 1989): 55–60.

"Coming to Terms with Mormon History: An Interview with Leonard Arrington," *Dialogue* 22 (Winter 1989): 39–54.

### Other Relevant Publications

Thoughtful books by others on the experiences of Mormon historians include Jan Shipps, *Mormonism: The Story of a New Religious Tradition* (Urbana: University of Illinois Press, 1985); Richard D. Poll, *History and Faith: Reflections of a Mormon Historian* (Salt Lake City: Signature Books, 1989); D. Michael Quinn, ed., *The New Mormon History: Revisionist Essays on the Past* (Salt Lake City: Signature Books, 1992); and George D. Smith, ed., *Faithful History: Essays on Writing Mormon History* (Salt Lake City: Signature Books, 1992).

Helpful articles and book chapters include Richard L. Bushman, "Faithful History," *Dialogue* 4 (Winter 1969): 11–25; William Mulder, "Mormon Angles of Historical Vision: Some Maverick Reflections," *Journal of Mormon History* 3 (1976): 13–22; Robert B. Flanders, "Some Reflections on the New Mormon History," *Dialogue* 9 (Spring 1974): 34–41; Rodman W. Paul, "The Mormons as a Theme in Western Historical Writing," *Journal of American History* 54 (Dec. 1967):

511–23; Philip L. Barlow, "Since Brodie: The Writing of the Mormon Past, 1945–1981," typescript copy in my possession; C. Robert Mesle, "History: Faith and Myth," *Sunstone* 7 (Nov.–Dec. 1982): 10–13; Thomas G. Alexander, "Toward the New Mormon History: An Examination of the Literature on the Latter-day Saints in the Far West," in *Historiography of the American West,* ed. Michael T. Malone (Lincoln: University of Nebraska Press, 1983), 344–68; Davis Bitton, "Ten Years in Camelot: A Personal Memoir," *Dialogue* 16 (Autumn 1983): 9–33; Robert Gottlieb and Peter Wiley, "The New Renaissance," *America's Saints: The Rise of Mormon Power* (New York: G. P. Putnam's Sons, 1984), 235–45; David B. Honey and Daniel C. Peterson, "Advocacy and Inquiry in the Writing of Latter-day Saint History," *BYU Studies* 31 (Spring 1991): 139–79; entries under "Historians, Church" and "History" in Daniel H. Ludlow, ed., *Encyclopedia of Mormonism,* 4 vols. (New York: Macmillan, 1992), 2:589–92, 595–648; William Mulder, "Telling It Slant: Aiming for Truth in Contemporary Mormon Literature," *Dialogue* 26 (Summer 1993): 155–69; Clara V. Dobay, "Intellect and Faith: The Controversy over Revisionist Mormon History," *Dialogue* 27 (Spring 1994): 91–105; and Marvin S. Hill, "Positivism or Subjectivism? Some Reflections on a Mormon Historical Dilemma," *Journal of Mormon History* 20 (Spring 1994): 1–23.

I have also made obvious use of the books described in this memoir: Dean C. Jessee, *Brigham Young's Letters to His Sons* (Salt Lake City: Deseret Book, 1974); James B. Allen and Thomas G. Alexander, *Manchester Mormons: The Journal of William Clayton, 1840–1842* (Layton, Utah: Peregrine Press, 1974); Davis Bitton, *Wit and Whimsy in Mormon History* (Salt Lake City: Deseret Book, 1974); Leonard J. Arrington, *Charles C. Rich: Mormon General and Western Frontiersman* (Provo, Utah: Brigham Young University Press, 1974); Leonard J. Arrington, *David Eccles: Pioneer Western Industrialist* (Logan: Utah State University Press, 1974); Gene A. Sessions, *Latter-day Patriots: Nine Mormon Families and Their Revolutionary War Heritage* (Salt Lake City: Deseret Book and LDS Historical Department, 1975); Leonard J. Arrington, *From Quaker to Latter-day Saint: Bishop Edwin D. Woolley* (Salt Lake City: Deseret Book, 1976); James B. Allen and Glen M. Leonard, *Story of the Latter-day Saints* (Salt Lake City: Deseret Book, 1976); Leonard J. Arrington, Feramorz Y. Fox, and Dean L. May, *Building the City of God: Community and Cooperation among the Mormons* (Salt Lake City: Deseret Book, 1976); Leonard J. Arrington and Davis Bitton, *The Mormon Experience: A History of the Latter-day Saints* (New York: Alfred A. Knopf, 1979); Leonard J. Arrington, ed., *Voices from the Past: Diaries, Journals, and Autobiographies* (Provo: BYU Campus Education Week Program, 1980); Leonard J. Arrington and Davis Bitton, *Saints without Halos: The Human Side of Mormon History* (Salt Lake City: Signature Books, 1981); and Leonard J. Arrington, *Brigham Young: American Moses* (New York: Alfred A. Knopf, 1986).

More recent books I have written or edited with Mormon themes include *The Presidents of the Church* (Salt Lake City: Deseret Book, 1986); *Mothers of the Prophets,* with Susan Arrington Madsen (Salt Lake City: Deseret Book, 1987); *Mormons and Their Historians,* with Davis Bitton (Salt Lake City: University of Utah Press, 1988); *Harold F. Silver: Western Inventor, Businessman, and Civic Leader,* with John R. Alley Jr. (Logan: Utah State University Press, 1992); *History of Idaho,* 2 vols. (Moscow: University of Idaho Press and the Idaho State Historical Society, 1994); *An Illustrated History of the History Division of the LDS*

*Church, 1972–82* (Salt Lake City: Historian's Press, 1994); *Utah's Audacious Stockman: Charlie Redd* (Logan: Utah State University Press and the Charles Redd Center for Western Studies, 1995); and several articles in Daniel H. Ludlow, ed., *Encyclopedia of Mormonism*, 4 vols. (New York: Macmillan, 1992).

Books that deal with the challenges of writing religious history include Van A. Harvey, *The Historian and the Believer: The Morality of Historical Knowledge and Religious Belief* (New York: Macmillan, 1966); C. T. McIntire, ed., *God, History, and Historians: An Anthology of Modern Christian Views of History* (New York: Oxford University Press, 1977); Robert N. Bellah, *Beyond Belief: Essays on Religion in a Post-Traditional World* (New York: Harper and Row, 1970); George Santayana, *The Life of Reason: Reason in Religion* (New York: Charles Scribner's Sons, 1936); Herbert Butterfield, *Christianity and History* (New York: Scribner's, 1950); E. Harris Harbison, *Christianity and History* (Princeton: Princeton University Press, 1964); Arnold Toynbee, *An Historian's Approach to Religion* (New York: Oxford University Press, 1956); William Zinsser, ed., *Spiritual Quests: The Art and Craft of Religious Writing* (Boston: Houghton Mifflin, 1988); and Davis Bitton and Leonard J. Arrington, *Mormons and Their Historians* (Salt Lake City: University of Utah Press, 1988).

# INDEX

Adamson, Jack H., 116, 196
Alexander, Thomas G., 59, 122, 167, 229
Allen, James B.: work with Church Historian's Office, 76–77; appointed assistant church historian, 81–85; member of historical reading committee, 99, 167; assigned a research assistant, 109–10; coauthor of *Manchester Mormons,* 122; coauthor of *Story of the Latter-day Saints,* 140–50; transferred to BYU, 161, 209; Lemuel Redd Chair at BYU, 229
Alley, John, Jr., 228
Allied Commission for Italy, 2, 27
Anderson, Joseph: appointed managing director of Historical Department, 97; approves Historical Department programs, 100, 102, 112, 120; released as managing director, 158–62, 165
Anderson, Kathleen Hardy, 87
Anderson, Lavina Fielding, 5
Arrington, Carl Wayne (son), 5, 28, 32, 38–39, 88–89, 200
Arrington, Edna Corn (mother), 6, 21
Arrington, Grace Fort (wife), 32, 39–40, 54, 78–79, 88–89, 104, 107–8, 199–200
Arrington, Harriet Horne (wife), 5, 199–200, 228, 230, 234
Arrington, James Wesley (son), 5, 28, 32, 38–39, 88–89, 198, 200

Arrington, Lee Roy (grandfather), 6
Arrington, Noah Wesley (father), 6, 21
Ashton, Marvin J., 148
Ashton, Wendell, 162–63

Backman, Milton V., Jr., 167, 173nn.3 and 4
Bair, JoAnn Woodruff, 151
Bancroft, Hubert Howe, 67–68
Bartholomew, Rebecca Foster Cornwall, 86, 134–35, 228
Beecher, Maureen Ursenbach, 85, 94, 99, 109–10, 126, 129, 167
*Beet Sugar in the West* (Arrington), 37
Bennion, Lowell, 21, 62
Benson, Ezra Taft, 128, 144, 165, 215
Bentley, Harold, 18
Bible, 6–7, 11, 23, 80, 158, 186
Bitton, Davis: officer of Mormon History Association, 59; work with Church Historian's Office, 76–78; appointed assistant church historian, 81-85, 87; author of *Mormon Diaries,* 93; member of historical reading committee, 99, 167; assigned a research assistant, 109–10; author of *Wit and Whimsy in Mormon History,* 123; coauthor of *The Mormon Experience,* 187–90, 194; reads draft of *Brigham Young: American Moses,* 199; writes about Historical Department as "Camelot," 200; coauthor of *Saints without Halos,* 213; returns to Universi-